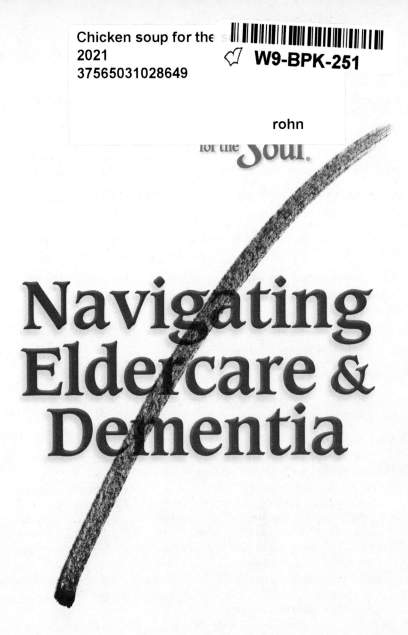

for the Soul.

Navigating Eldercare & Dementia

Chicken Soup for the Soul: Navigating Eldercare & Dementia
101 Stories for Family Caregivers
Amy Newmark

Published by Chicken Soup for the Soul, LLC www.chickensoup.com
Copyright ©2021 by Chicken Soup for the Soul, LLC. All Rights Reserved.

Front cover photo courtesy of iStockphoto.com/RelaxFoto.de (©RelaxFoto.de)
Back cover and interior photo courtesy of iStockphoto.com/Lisay
(©Lisay)
Photo of Amy Newmark courtesy of Susan Morrow at SwickPix

Cover and Interior by Daniel Zaccari

Distributed to the booktrade by Simon & Schuster. SAN: 200-2442

Publisher's Cataloging-In-Publication Data
(Prepared by The Donohue Group, Inc.)

Names: Newmark, Amy, compiler.
Title: Chicken soup for the soul : navigating eldercare & dementia : 101 stories for
    family caregivers / [compiled by] Amy Newmark.
Other Titles: Navigating eldercare & dementia : 101 stories for family caregivers |
    Navigating eldercare and dementia : 101 stories for family caregivers
Description: [Cos Cob, Connecticut] : Chicken Soup for the Soul, LLC, [2021]
Identifiers: ISBN 9781611590821 (paperback) | ISBN 9781611593228 (ebook)
Subjects: LCSH: Older people--Care--Literary collections. | Older people--Care--
    Anecdotes. | Adult children of aging parents--Family relationships--Literary
    collections. | Adult children of aging parents--Family relationships--Anecdotes.
    | Dementia--Patients--Care--Literary collections. | Dementia--Patients--Care--
    Anecdotes. | LCGFT: Anecdotes.
Classification: LCC HV1451 .C45 2021 (print) | LCC HV1451 (ebook) |
    DDC 362.6/02--dc23

Library of Congress Control Number: 2021934475

PRINTED IN THE UNITED STATES OF AMERICA
on acid∞free paper

25 24 23 22 21   01 02 03 04 05 06 07 08 09 10 11

Navigating Eldercare & Dementia

101 Stories for Family Caregivers

Amy Newmark

Chicken Soup for the Soul, LLC
Cos Cob, CT

Chicken Soup for the Soul

Changing your world one story at a time®
www.chickensoup.com

Table of Contents

❶
~Accepting a New Reality~

❷
~Perseverance~

❸
~Next Steps and Tough Choices~

❹
~Strategies and Tips for Coping~

❺
~Blessings & Gratitude~

❻

~The Lighter Side~

❼

~Lessons Learned~

❽

~Self-Care~

❾

~All You Need Is Love… and Patience~

⑩

~It Takes a Village~

Accepting a New Reality

Mother Nature...
Mother Nurture

The leaves of memory seemed to make
A mournful rustling in the dark.
~Henry Wadsworth Longfellow

I am losing my mother in pieces. She is like an autumn tree: beautiful, colorful, and dying. The breeze of Alzheimer's whispers through the branches while her memory drops off with the leaves.

One day, when her tree is finally bare, I will hold a memory of her blooming strength. She weathered the storms and provided me with shelter. I will be strong and remain hopeful because of her. For now, I will hope for spring to come, so together we may see the blossoms and green growth of love.

On a September drive through the Oregon wine country, Mom asked me, "What will we see once the leaves have all fallen?" She answered her own question. "Skeleton trees."

I gather what is falling: her stories, her looks, her insights, and her love. Nature's beauty is my rake. I rake these moments we share, embracing them as simple gifts.

Another day, she smiles and says, "Oh, the little fast birds are here." I look out the window to the hanging fuchsia and see the swift messengers of love and joy. Hummingbirds never seem to stop, never glide. I will them to linger. I will life to linger, to be savored, so that we can slow down and drink the nectar. Hummingbirds symbolize immortality, bravery, joy, and perseverance. I wish their flight of infinity could journey into our house and allow me to have my mom a little longer. These tiny creatures delight her with their fleeting visits and provide me with a sense of peace, knowing that I will never stop savoring the nectar of my mom's sweetness.

We rest on her bed with eyes wide and focused outward on the sky. The clouds drift. Mom comments that the sun is warm and melting the clouds. She asks what I see. I say, "I see a cloud passing as a caterpillar."

"No," she says. "It is God reaching out to us."

We are quiet as the view changes. She pities the person without imagination. On the sky's stage, an ensemble of characters parades. Herds of wild animals stampede across the horizon; musical instruments silently blow to the west; stout kings float east, followed by soaring, chubby cherubs.

"The clouds are heavy," she remarks. "It will rain, and they will be lighter."

I feel her love and the slow motion of the moment. The clouds are dark and threatening. Mom dozes while I keep my eye on the clouds, waiting for one to pass and offer me a silver lining. I will be patient.

"How many sunsets have we watched together?" Mom asks me. Before I can respond, she muses, "The sky is a Monet painting, only more beautiful." She holds my hand while we wait and watch colors transform the sky into impressionistic images. It is sunset, a day's end, bringing breathtaking moments of change, entwined with nature.

The sun is setting on my mother. The hues and tones of her life dim quietly as the dusk of the disease settles on her memories. I cling to the colors of our time now. I embrace the brush strokes of the afterglow and realize that twilight approaches. Then, darkness will come.

Magically, the clouds part for the moon. The fuzziness of the veiled moon has cleared, and a bright glow streams down upon us as our nightlight. We watch the moon rise while the stars decorate the sky. We talk as if we are young girls on a sleepover.

Mom wonders if Ireland has a moon. She never saw it when we were last there. I assure her Ireland has a moon, and it is the same one we are viewing this night. We tease about shooting for the moon and that, if we miss, we will hit a star. Together, we count, wish and wonder.

One day, I will look at the world for both of us: capturing the beauty; wishing on the giggling stars; watching the sun playing "sneak and peek." My heart is broken as I lose my mother in pieces and watch the woman who was my mom disappear leaf by leaf. I smile, stirring up memories of the joys we share over seeing the birds, sunsets and night skies together, embracing Mother Nature. I smile for the many joys we have had together.

Grief changes us forever. There is never "normal" again. But my sorrowful and changed spirit will remember that I carry within me the beauty of my mother. She will be with me always, and the ordinary and extraordinary moments we shared with nature will heal me. My mom will always nurture me. The moon will trade places with the sun. In my darkness, I know morning will come.

I recall Carl Sandburg's line, "The moon is a friend for the lonesome to talk to." My mother's moon and I will be having many conversations.

— Lizzy Carney —

Rally with Reality

If you keep your heart open through everything,
your pain can become your greatest ally in life's
search for love and wisdom.
~Rumi

My husband won the game show. "Hodler!" he shouted triumphantly, waving his arms. He was the only contestant who knew the name of the nineteenth-century Swiss painter, Ferdinand Hodler.

I was by his side during his moment of glory—a dream that floated away when his unintelligible shout and waving right arm woke us up.

Perplexing moments like this aren't unusual for someone with Parkinson's disease, a diagnosis typically associated with older adults. It's as if my husband is living with the geriatric versions of himself (with glitchy neural connections) camouflaged inside his mid-fifties body. If anyone saw us on the tennis court, they would be surprised to learn he is experiencing young-onset Parkinson's disease, a diagnosis that accounts for 2–10 percent of the 1 million people with Parkinson's in the U.S.

The two of us are hiding in plain sight. The COVID-19 quarantine gave us privacy and time to pivot from grief and fear to learning to cope before we tell colleagues, friends and family about his incurable, degenerative disease.

We used to enjoy sharing our once-funny anecdote about the time, a decade ago, when he gave up drinking coffee to try to improve his sleep. He became, in my view, intolerably foggy. I told him in jest that if he didn't begin drinking coffee again or see a doctor to get checked out, I would begin divorce proceedings.

To our surprise, his neuropsychologist's detailed assessment offered just one recommendation: drink a single cup of coffee every morning. Our story is less amusing in retrospect because that assessment omitted important diagnostic clues. My husband, a full professor at an elite university in Boston, a biologist, could no longer do routine math in his head. He was finding it more challenging to follow conversations, review scientific papers and manage his research lab.

For the next ten years, our fulfilling life together rolled forward as the parts of his brain that generate and receive dopamine invisibly deteriorated. Our children made their way through high school and college — freeing us to devote more time to work and to enjoy renewed friendships, museums, music and travel. On days warmer than forty-five degrees, we ducked out midweek to play tennis at a park near our home. Snowstorms were our chance to disappear for quick ski getaways.

As my husband changed in unexpected ways, I adjusted with an open heart. He could no longer smell when his bath towel needed to be replaced, so I hung clean replacements. Travel became stressful, so I anticipated and planned every detail in advance.

Then one day during a meeting three years ago, he noticed his left foot had a slight tremor. He immediately suspected Parkinson's, as his grandfather had died with this disease soon after we were married.

After my husband received a definitive diagnosis a year later (with a brain scan and genetic test), his doctor reacted with an expletive. Our social worker wept at our first meeting. I am challenged to accept this future for the person I will always love, whom I've loved since I was nineteen, whose kindness, integrity, quick wit, steadiness, creativity and wisdom have been the joy of my life.

During the first year after diagnosis, we spent countless hours secretly battening down the hatches for the storm ahead — assessing our finances, disability, life and long-term-care insurance coverage, and updating our wills and related end-of-life documents. We met with therapists, connected with support groups, and enrolled him in a clinical trial.

Having Parkinson's is like a part-time job with a complex regimen of daily exercises for body, voice and mind. He must somehow fit in hours of cardio every week — the only intervention that slows the progression of this disease.

Tennis is our favorite therapeutic, a source of joy. A few months before the coronavirus quarantine began, his forehand vanished. Despite his best efforts, his racket would stop mid-swing. Then, the risk of exposure to COVID-19 deterred us from playing tennis for many months. After that long stretch of inactivity, a tremor emerged in his hands. Finally, we felt safe to play tennis wearing masks. He worked steadily to reclaim a solid forehand, to recover endurance and agility; and now he hopes to regain the toss for his serve. The tremor remains, leading to many fragmented nights of sleep.

The pandemic opened new, more convenient virtual ways to access medical care, support and connection. We joined online support groups for people with Parkinson's and their caregivers, an onboarding class for the newly diagnosed, and a mindfulness cognitive therapy clinical trial to help us prepare for our challenging future.

Someday soon, to try to relieve some Parkinson's motor symptoms, he may turn to medications, but these come with vexing side effects. Other than exercise, there is no clinical treatment available for the imperceptible non-motor symptoms that matter most to the two of us — his uncharacteristic apathy and poor focus.

Last summer, amid the isolation and stress of the 2020 quarantine, I invented my own therapeutic practice: "Scotch mindfulness." This involved sitting barefoot on a chair in our back yard, with my toes in the grass, sipping a shot of Scotch diluted with ice, weeping as I listen to a guided mindfulness meditation. Accepting my grief seems to help it dissipate.

We are inching toward sharing our news, feeling steadier, more ready to absorb and cope with the grief and questions that will come our way. Sharing our reality with friends and family may mean greater emotional support for us, a chance to glean wisdom from our four parents who are in remarkably good health in their eighties and nineties — a phase of our marriage we may never reach.

Together, we are cobbling together the courage to move forward. My husband practices swinging his arms when he walks and smiles in the mirror to fend off a frozen gait and masked expression. He skips and jumps rope for bursts of cardio and maintains a steady routine to maintain his current version of optimal wellbeing.

Thirty years into our marriage, I understand love as a verb. Love is what we do with and for each other as we adjust to our new reality. I am learning how to help him as I know he would help me if the tables were turned. I don't know how or where I will find the courage to endure what lies ahead. For now, I will nurture my soul when my body is worn out. And I will tend to my body when my soul despairs.

I will focus on each day because, for us, today is as good as it will ever be.

— Margaret Bloch —

Home

The ache for home lives in all of us, the safe place
where we can go as we are and not be questioned.
~Maya Angelou

When Mama slipped into the sundowning phase of her Alzheimer's journey, every day near sunset she'd suddenly announce to me, "I'm ready to go home." Then she'd gather her coat or sweater, grab the well-worn handles of her fake leather pocketbook, and head for the front door.

In 1969, she and Daddy cut every possible corner to build their Jim Walter kit house on the two acres of land they'd bought from a family friend on Graveyard Road. They had been forced to buy the land and build the house after having to give up sharecropping because the eleventh of their thirteen children (me), like the rest of my older siblings, had wasted no time in leaving home after graduating from George Washington Carver High School. I'd accepted the invitation from my Korean War vet first cousin, William Bryant, and his wife Eunice, to move to Fullerton, California, and babysit their three-year-old son, known as Junebug, and his brother Danny, in exchange for room and board and the possibility of attending the junior college down the street.

By mid-June 1965, only my younger siblings Phillip and Janice, a high-school sophomore and freshman, were left at home. At the height of the Civil Rights movement, Janice had decided to opt out of Carver High and integrate Temple High instead. That summer, she and Phillip convinced nine other Temple Black kids to join them. Two others joined them later during the first semester. In keeping with the growing militancy of the day, they tagged themselves The Temple Eleven.

Although I had given Dad no reason to believe that I would stay in Temple a minute longer than I had to, he went ahead and planted a full fifty acres of cotton. His remaining family members and church friends, all well into middle age, pitched in and helped them get the crop in that fall. They made Dad promise that he was done with sharecropping. When Dad broke the news to the prominent white man who owned those fifty acres that our family had worked for almost nothing for more than ten years and rarely did better than break even, he asked the old man to sell him the house and two or three acres around the house. The old tightwad not only turned Dad down but added insult to injury by saying, "We don't want no niggers on this road." Dad was crushed to think all those years of being a "good negro" had not been good enough to entitle him to buy the place that his labor and that of his wife and children had paid for ten times over.

In 2000, more than thirty years away, I relocated to Temple to become caregiver to Mom. She was showing serious signs of Alzheimer's and was unable to continue living on her own. Dad had passed away in May 1999. With her declining memory, Mom could only imagine one explanation for Dad's sustained absence: "The 'shaff' got him locked up in jail." Once when she asked about him, I made the mistake of showing her his death certificate, only to watch her have a major meltdown.

"When was the funeral? I'm his wife. Why didn't you take me to his funeral?" she yelled at me, as if I could do something so cruel.

Then her eyes filled with tears as her fair-skinned face turned red with rage and confusion. She sobbed into one of Dad's old pocket handkerchiefs. Soon the entire episode was over and forgotten, and she lay down in the bedroom that she and Dad shared for the last thirty years of their sixty-seven-year marriage.

Having crossed over into my seventh decade on Planet Earth, knowing Alzheimer's is in my family tree and having witnessed my mom's once brilliant mind being reduced to incompetency, a few years ago I began to contemplate what genetic hand I've been dealt. I hope that I got the longevity genes without the Alzheimer's.

A few years ago when I reported to my primary care doctor my concern about short-term memory lapses, she referred me to a neurologist. During the first visit, while reassuring me that I did not have dementia, he wrote me a prescription for Donepezil. The drug's only approved use is for dementia. I took the first pill and was immediately struck with very strong bouts of vomiting and diarrhea that lasted two days. I didn't take another one of those pills. I asked my doctor for another neurologist referral.

While waiting for the second referral, I've begun to collect my memories in my iPhone. I'm still amazed at the staying power of Mom's oldest memories. Even after she entered her nineties, Mom could still recite long poems that she had learned as a child. When she passed away in 2008, I deduced that the *home* that she had wanted to go to was a place in time where her fondest and strongest memories had been formed — before her mother died leaving her ten-year old baby daughter (my mother) an orphan in the care of her older siblings. Their father, and an older sister and her husband, had died in the 1918 flu epidemic. I tried driving Mom around to places where she had previously lived. But clearly none were the *home* she was seeking.

Now at age seventy-three, and standing on the precipice of time, I am looking death and dying in the face every day. And every few days, I experience a new foreshadowing of the fading light that has allowed me to create and explore worlds beyond the tangible. I am writing this as a gift to my siblings in remembrance of our parents. In case of a dementia diagnosis, the note below is for my caregiver:

> *To My Future Caregivers,*
>
> *If I start saying I'm ready to go home at the end of each day, I am probably longing to go back in time to my childhood, to see my parents and my brothers and sisters again when all of us were young, beautiful, happy and healthy — and nothing too bad had happened to any of us yet.*
>
> *My favorite memories are of our wonderful Christmases. Remind me to tell you about the year Myra and Daisy decorated*

our tree with pink angel hair that got into the eye of the first grand baby, Phyllis, causing it to swell up as big as a peach. Dad was not amused. And how Mom and the oldest girls would bake a half-dozen Christmas cakes two weeks before Christmas. And the year they baked chocolate cupcakes each topped with a peppermint candy cane. And how Mom did not discover, until Christmas Day, that we kids breached the cake safe and licked off all the stripes.

If I behave like I don't know who you are, just remember that I don't need to remember who you are because you remember who I am. And that's good enough.

— Carolyn Gray —

You Are Here

I am going into an unknown future, but I'm still all
here, and still while there's life, there's hope.
~John Lennon

Aah... A wave of pure peace and calm washed over me as I unfolded the precious map in my lap. It was like a drug. My heartrate slowed, I breathed easier, and I relaxed.

I have always loved maps and globes. I have early memories of taking out the maps in my father's *National Geographic* magazines and poring over them. I remember turning the outdated globe in our family den for hours, playing "Where will I be in ten years?" I have my own outdated globe now, and a huge, beautifully detailed topographical map of the world hangs in my study. My glove compartment is filled with state maps I pick up at welcome stations. I adore my maps!

The summer before her senior year of high school, my daughter, along with my husband and me, took a trip through the South to visit colleges. As the perpetual navigator of the family, I had the route mapped out, a plan for where we would stop for the night, and an idea of how long it would take to get to each destination. I had that glove compartment full of maps, and we had the GPS.

Going north on I-65 toward our first stop, Nashville, I opened the glove compartment to get out the map. There was no map! We had taken my husband's car and there were no maps in his glove compartment! I calmed down, reasoning that I knew where we were generally going, and the GPS could get us to a specific location. It would be fine.

Heading east out of Nashville, I plugged in the next college destination on the GPS. Yikes! It said we were twelve hours away. This could not be right; I had mapped it all out before we left. I decided to trust my prior research and ignore the stupid GPS. If only I had a map! Well, I reasoned, I could do this without a map. It would be fine.

As we closed in on the North Carolina border and its welcome station, however, I knew I had to get a map. I could not stand it. A supplier was just around the corner. I could feed the hole in my soul, fill up the void, and make the anxiety go away with a simple map. I didn't really *need* the map; I just wanted it for the moment. I was doing fine without it.

We stopped at the North Carolina welcome station and got a map. That's when the wave of relief washed over me. Aah…

Why did I want that map so badly? Why could I not trust my instincts to get us where we were going? I needed to see the big picture and where we fit in. I needed to see the small details of roads and towns and mileages. Does it say something about me that I need to know where I am, where I've been, and where I'm going? How would my life be different if I just rode the road before me, trusting that I would get to where I was supposed to be?

And then it hit me. This Alzheimer's World my husband and I had entered did not come with a map. The neuropsychologist didn't diagnose my husband, tell him he should not work anymore, and then hand us a guidebook that outlined exactly where we were going. I asked, "What is my husband's likely course? Where will he be in five years?" I got, "Every person is different. We cannot say."

We were plopped down in the middle of Alzheimer's World without a map, and we have to navigate the way. I would rather have a map of the future; I want to know where we are and where we are going. I want to see the big picture. I want to know what we will see along the way and know how long it will take us to get there.

Maybe I am developing a map of sorts for my husband and me. I research. I read. I look ahead, tentatively, at what the future may hold. I ask myself questions like, "How will I know when he should not drive?" Then I work out possible answers. I know I won't be able to anticipate everything, but it calms me to think ahead and plan, creating a map for myself.

And what are my guideposts? How will I know we are on the right road and didn't take a wrong turn? I'll have to rely on my instincts for that and how my husband responds. I will trust wise friends to point me in a different direction if we are veering off — if they see that one or both of us is not coping well. I will continue to take care of myself in all the ways I have in the past and look for new ways along the way.

Our map may not be the detailed thing of beauty that hangs in my study, but it will be one we create together and is uniquely ours. I may not have a guidebook, but I have my heart, faith, trust, and grace.

— Renée Brown Harmon —

The Black Wall Phone

Memories warm you up from the inside.
But they also tear you apart.
~Haruki Murakami, Kafka on the Shore

"Hello, I'd like to disconnect a phone line," I said. "No, it's not mine. It's my parents' number. Dad died, Mom has Alzheimer's, and I have her power of attorney."

I'd memorized the number fifty years earlier when we moved to be nearer to Dad's job. Back then, the black rotary phone hung on the kitchen wall. A few years later, Dad added a longer cord that reached the table. It wasn't until I was in high school that Mom ordered a newer tan model with buttons rather than a rotary dial.

Though the phone I held was cordless, I didn't move from the kitchen as I spoke to the customer-service representative. "Yes, the number is Adams 44058." There was silence on the other end of the line. "Sorry, that's the way we said phone numbers back in the 1960s when I learned it. The first two letters correspond to the first two numbers." There was another pause as I imagined the customer-service agent's furrowed brow. "Never mind, it's 234-4058."

When we moved into the new house, I was fourteen and excited to learn about our new town. That summer, my brother and I explored the streets on our yellow banana-seat bicycles. Times were different back then. Parents allowed their children more freedom.

We pedaled downtown and found the movie theater alongside Joe's Pizza. Then we ate lunch at the Kresge counter, where busy downtown merchants hurried through their lunch. Next, I remember the Ben Franklin store wasn't air-conditioned as we roamed the aisles. Patrons rushed in and out of the newspaper office where I'd later pay my paper-route bill. We passed the hospital on our way home, and then the junior high that we'd attend.

Those businesses have closed, as did the factory where my father worked. They even demolished the old junior high. After my father died, I spent weeks going through my parents' belongings. I tossed most of the memorabilia of my childhood. I found many worthless items that had value only to my mother. Of the things my brothers and I had brought home from school, we kept only a few. But I still use the napkin holder I made in eighth-grade shop class. I pondered the longest over the greeting cards. I didn't know that Mom had saved them. She didn't seem the sentimental type, so I couldn't throw them away. I returned them to the senders. Bonus, I found a twenty-dollar bill my father gave Mom on her birthday.

With the house almost empty, I called the phone company. When I hung up the receiver, I paused and looked at the floor. A chapter in my life had just ended, and I felt the finality. I could never call home again. So many milestones came to mind.

"Hey, Mom, can I stay over at Rod's house tonight? His mom said it's okay."

"Dad, I've got a flat tire on my bike. Can you come and get me?"

"Mom, we're home from the school trip. Will you pick us up?"

"Dad, I found a car I want to buy. Will you come to look at it?"

"Mom, thanks for the housewarming gift. We love it."

"Dad, I need help wiring a ceiling fan. Can you come?"

"Mom, the baby is here. It's a girl."

"Dad, I've got a new job. We'll be moving away."

"Mom, when we retire, we'll visit more often."

"Dad, how'd the doctor visit go? Can they do anything for Mom's dementia?"

"Dad, how are you doing? Do you think you should get someone to come in a few days a week to help?"

In later years, I conversed longer, but only with my father. Mom couldn't hold normal conversations, and Dad was lonely. I wish we'd spoken more often.

After hanging up the phone and staring at the floor, I looked up at my mother. She was gawking at me with a blank expression because Alzheimer's had erased her memory. She was like the phone line to our home — disconnected. I couldn't reach her, though I had questions. Why didn't I ask her more when she could remember?

"What was Grandpa like?"

"When did you learn to drive?"

"What was your dinner-roll recipe?"

"Where's the key to the safe-deposit box?"

How did she find the ability to make her last phone call? Mom dialed my brother to say she couldn't wake Dad. Dan rushed over and found Dad dead. But she doesn't remember the events of that day. Sometimes, Mom asks if Dad went to work. I reply, "Yes," and she's satisfied.

Before leaving the house for good, I wandered the rooms where my parents had raised four boys, and I reminisced. I visualized the Christmas tree in the living room surrounded by presents. My oldest brother passed out the gifts. Now he, like Dad, had died. I glanced into the dining room where we celebrated Thanksgiving. In my youth, Mom hosted various family members like aunts and uncles. In the later years, it overflowed with her children and grandchildren.

I passed the bedrooms. We boys had left the nest one by one, but the bedrooms remained much the same until we emptied them for the new owners. It felt surreal as I returned to the kitchen and picked up the wall phone. The line was now dead.

I escorted Mom from the house and helped her into the car. She didn't know it was her last day there. We made the trip to Florida by train.

Now, five years later, she lives with me. Her destructive disease progresses at a crawl. She spends most of her time asleep in bed or sitting in her chair. We don't even turn on the television anymore. She's unaware.

Yesterday, a physician's assistant examined Mom, and she whispered to the nurse, "She's skin and bones. She can't last much longer." Her comment didn't surprise me because Alzheimer's disease took my mother years ago. I'm just waiting for her body to leave. Meanwhile, I care for her as she cared for me when I was a child.

One day in the not-too-distant future, I'll make the inevitable call to my brothers. They won't pick up a house phone. They'll pull a smartphone from their pocket and listen to my voice breeze across the airwaves. I'll say, "Mom's gone."

Others who have traveled this journey before me say there will be a feeling of relief when it's over, but I know I'll experience sorrow, too. It will be the last step down the long, winding staircase of her disease. When that day comes, maybe I'll wish I could call home again and hear Mom answer the old black phone on the kitchen wall. How wonderful it would be to say, "Hi, Mom. How's Dad?"

— Ronald Milburn —

Mother and Daughter

My mother is the bones of my spine,
keeping me straight and true. She is my blood,
making sure it runs rich and strong.
~Kristin Hannah

I look up from my magazine. Somehow, even with all the beeps and buzzes, hallway noises, and the loud, one-sided cellphone conversation from another visitor just outside the door, my mom has managed to fall asleep. Her snoring has the rhythm I grew up with. Her silver hair looks like a fluffy halo around her head. Her glasses are still on, and the book she was reading is lying on her lap in her slack hands.

The thought crosses my mind: *How did we get to this moment?* In the next instant, I berate myself, *I know exactly how we got here.* It was a pathway of thousands of moments, rolled together like a quilt intertwining both our lives.

Had I known then what I know now, I would like to think that I would have hugged you more often. I would have been more grateful for the hundreds of dinners you fed me night after night after night. I would have realized and expressed sincere appreciation for the sacrifice you made to come to every one of the five performances of the play I was in at high school. I would have known that you wanted me to call you every Saturday from college because you missed me, not to check up on me. I could have been more caring when I returned home after being overseas for eighteen months and you said that you would never let me go again. It wasn't because you were trying to run my life; it was because I was your life.

Five and a half years after you bought me a beautiful birthstone opal ring for my fiftieth birthday, it broke something in me when you admired its beauty with absolutely no recollection that you had given it to me. I chose not to say, "Why, you bought it for me, Mom. Don't you remember?" Instead, I said (truthfully), "It's the nicest ring I own." You lost interest and wandered out to the kitchen to fold up brown grocery bags to add to your collection. That gave me a chance to wipe my moist eyes without you seeing.

I worried then. How am I going to do your taxes for you? You were always the smart one with money. How did I end up being your power of attorney in charge of your finances? Have I got all the details ready for your funeral? What have I forgotten to do?

The nurse comes in and checks all the connections. You rouse yourself, and I can see it takes a moment for you to realize where you are, and even who I am. I smile as big as I can and say, "Good morning, Mom!" even though it is evening.

A glimmer of recognition starts to glow in your eyes.

"Hello, sweetie," you say to me, like a thousand times before. "How long have you been here?"

"Not very long, Mom." I smile back.

— Michelle L. Jones —

Plan B

Being optimistic is like a muscle that gets stronger with
use. Makes it easier when the tough times arrive.
You have to change the way you think in order
to change the way you feel.
~Robin Roberts

I f you ask me how my mom is doing, I will probably be honest and say, "Not so good." She's failing fast, not eating, not drinking any liquid, refusing medication. She's huddled like a shivering bunny under three hospital blankets with only stiff strands of silvery hair poking out above her tightly closed eyes.

I'd like to close my own eyes to this.

Mom's name is Sherri. I refer to her as Sherri these days, although I say "Mommy" to her face because it makes her happy. Once, I called her "she" while talking to someone else. Mom yelled at me to never refer to her as "she" again. I guess it really struck a nerve.

Sherri is dying, but that's an ugly word, so we say she's passing on, leaving us, going to be with her parents. After all, we are going to fly her body from Minnesota to California so she can be stored in the mausoleum with her mom and dad. It's like being a library book in the stacks, except you never come off the shelf.

In the five-minute stretches when she is awake, Sherri attempts speech. But the words just sound like *aaaaaa* or *uuuuuuu*, so we only ask questions with yes or no answers. She can still nod and shake her head.

If you ask me how my mom is doing, I might ask if I can share a story or two about her life — how she taught Japanese flower arranging, or how she was the popular girl in high school who eloped at nineteen, married the nice Jewish doctor (what a catch), got pregnant immediately, and had four kids. She wanted six.

She was the best of moms; she was the worst of moms. Aren't we all?

When I see old photos of my mother, I am in awe of her creamy, clear complexion, and then surprised by the gray hair that appeared in her early forties. I don't recall her being so overweight when I was a teenager. Now she is seventy-nine and has a crumpled, ninety-five-pound body that is shutting down, but her skin is still good. Go figure.

If you ask me how my mom is doing, I might wonder why you don't ask how I'm doing. Is that selfish? I mean, she's being taken care of, and she's got good drugs. I sit home worrying. I don't want to die, but I wouldn't mind having some of those drugs.

I might share that my mother is delusional, hallucinating about my dad. He divorced her thirty-five years ago. She never got over the blatant rejection, but now she believes he's back in her life. He comes into her bed at night and has put $3 billion into her USAA account. And his second wife? Oh, she's there, too — one of Mom's best friends now.

I really do want some of those drugs.

If you ask me how my mom is doing, I might say she's scaring the shit out of me. We have the same genetic makeup, and I inherited the mutated gene for Parkinson's disease. That's what she's dying from. I don't like to hear the details.

I never can watch the side effects of her Parkinson's, the times when she's frozen and looks paralyzed and petrified, or the dyskinesia that manifests like a bicycle tire blowing out: kick, snap, fly. I'm surprised she never got whiplash.

If you ask me how my mom is doing, I might tell you about the article, complete with four full-color photos, that the *Los Angeles Times* published about her in 2011. They highlighted Sherri taking charge of the greenhouse at her assisted-living facility. The writer opened his story with Mom's motto, one that I heard at least a hundred times more than I needed to: "Life is all about how you handle Plan B."

I'll tell you she might have two days or two weeks remaining. The body shuts down at its own pace. As long as she is comfortable, it's all good.

If you ask me how my mom is doing, I might change the subject and ask how your mom is doing. I hope you can share a good story with me.

Or I might share some favorite lines of poetry from Lesléa Newman:

May she go light,
May her burdens release,
May she grieve nothing,
May she know peace.

If you ask me how my mom is doing, I might just say, "She's okay. Thanks for asking."

— Pamela Lear —

Excerpt from "Vigil" ©2015 by Lesléa Newman from *I Carry My Mother* (Headmistress Press, Sequim, WA). Used by permission of the author.

Reflection Ralph

In a mirror is where we find a reflection of our
appearances, but in a heart is where we
find a reflection of our soul.
~Author Unknown

Lying on our bed, I sank into the memory foam and took a deep breath, the deepest of the entire day. I exhaled all of it, trying to rid myself of the horror. Eyes closed, arms overhead, I commanded each muscle to relax independently while Peter showered. I basked in a few quiet moments until I would be called upon again to turn off the shower, hold the pajama pants open for his step, and help him brush his teeth.

I listened to the water hit the bathtub floor and heard my bald husband empty out yet another bottle of my coveted curly-hair conditioner into his palm. I knew it was running through his fingers. I took another deep inhale to remind myself it's just stuff, just conditioner.

The shower curtain slid open, the rings screaming across the metal bar. It was followed by the usual blather. "Where is she? Hello? I don't have anything!" Peter's voice continued to grow louder until he realized he was not alone, and I listened intently to a new muffled conversation. Curious, I snuck a peek through the door to see who he was talking to.

The conversation was real to Peter as he bantered with the new person in the mirror. When he saw me, he jolted. "We were just talking about school."

"Okay, let's get you dressed." I was not sure how to respond.

Peter no longer recognizes the reflection as himself. That memory, since he sees himself as twenty-something now, is gone. The man in the mirror is much older than Peter.

To watch, to immerse in this fantasy with Peter, has been gut-punching and heart-wrenching, yet comical at times. We've named our new friend Reflection Ralph — Ralph, for short — and sometimes Peter calls him "Raft." Peter doesn't know who he is or why he's visiting, but Ralph is everywhere, in every reflection — mirrors, appliances, dark windows, whether we're home, in the car, or out somewhere. Ralph is always with us.

When Ralph first appeared, Peter would sneak into the bathroom to speak to him privately. I'd ask, "Who are you talking to?" trying to understand this new phenomenon.

Then one day, it happened. Grinning and whispering, tiptoeing quietly and motioning wildly for me to follow, Peter summoned me to the bathroom for the formal introduction.

The blood rushed up through my face, and I tried to remain calm. After all, Peter was watching my every expression for any reaction, for confirmation. I assured him, "It's you!" It was not at all what I was supposed to say because one should never, never, never argue with a demented person. Alzheimer's 101.

Immediately, I backpedaled and told Ralph how nice it was to meet him. I suggested the two men get together sometime. Peter was perplexed when Ralph didn't answer my invitation, so I suggested that perhaps Ralph was shy and just needed some time. Peter agreed.

Peter is often anxious, and we have learned coping skills to quiet his mind or distract him. Months ago, I constructed a basket of things, memories for Peter to find and riffle through at his leisure. It's a marvelous way of finding forgotten treasures. He hasn't paid much attention to the basket over the past season, but occasionally he will move it from one special spot to another, as he feels its value is great.

One day, when he was looking for a golf ball, he started searching in the basket. He spent almost three hours with the special things, wondering, searching, looking, fiddling, and questioning. One of the items is a small photo album I made for him ten or twelve years ago. It contains photos of our adventures. On the opposite pages, I wrote things I love about Peter. It was chucked aside after it was received, but who knew it would be so monumental now?

Peter brought it to me and said, "I need your help." He was struggling to read the captions. I sobbed as I read, so I decided that one page was enough for the day. He settled for a long while on a picture of us on our wedding day. In the photo, Peter cradles me high in his arms on a beach in Turks and Caicos. The day is a glorious memory for me but new for Peter. I told him about our day in as much detail as he could handle, and he wept. And then he wept some more.

We held each other tightly and Peter said, "This sucks." It was a moment of clarity, as if he understood what was happening but knew he couldn't stop it. Then he disappeared, and after an appropriate amount of worrying time, I went to look for him. I found him in the bathroom, once again talking to Reflection Ralph in the mirror. He was sharing that wedding photo with his new friend. Tears streamed down his cheeks as he held the photo up to his reflection and talked through his tears about our magnificent day.

I didn't care about what was right or wrong or how to properly handle the situation. I just ran to him with my heart bursting with an abundance of pride, grief and love. I fell into his arms, sobbing out loud, shoulders shaking, melting into his chest. Peter cried with me and held me tightly.

As he rubbed my back, he promised, "Everything will be okay."

Ralph is in every reflection, and he is met with Peter's delight each time he visits. Peter does not recognize his image in photos, videos or just-taken selfies, and my heart aches when I witness this behavior. Other times, I'm thankful. Ralph keeps Peter busy for long periods of time while I'm busy. This unlikely pair has the best time together!

One evening, Peter went upstairs and was absent longer than I liked, so again I tiptoed up to see what he was doing. As I approached our bathroom, I heard loud giggling. I snuck ever so quietly around the corner and slowly moved my head so I could just barely see what Peter was laughing at without being caught.

He was standing in front of the big bathroom mirror, doubled over belly laughing, with a grin sewn on ear-to-ear and the water running furiously from the faucet. Peter was taking hands full of water and throwing them at Ralph. The mirror and sink were soaking wet, and I slowly rolled around out of view, not knowing whether I should laugh or cry.

My husband, my child, my love.

—L.B. Marshall—

9

Wisdom Served with a Cup of Tea

*Your story is the greatest legacy that you will leave
to your friends. It's the longest-lasting legacy you
will leave to your heirs.*
~Steve Saint

Last fall, my great-grandma celebrated her 101st birthday. With the arrival of my cousin's baby boy three days later, she also welcomed the beginning of her fifth generation. Following a light giggle at the news, she bowed her head in prayers of thanksgiving, voicing hope for what he will see and do over his lifetime. Over and over, she has proven to me that she is still a dreamer full of optimism, with many yet-to-be-uttered prayers, which is why she believes she has lived this long.

"Miss Martha," as she has become known at her senior home, has developed a reputation for being a storyteller, especially when knitting. I always enjoy listening because she is full of caring wisdom and wit, willing to share her life experiences with unexpected twists and turns. Now that she is nearly blind and her hands are gnarled, her life stories are like her latest knitting projects, interwoven with some do-over mistakes and a few knots, but her tenacity and attitude create a remarkable testimony. She still finds deep joy in presenting wheelchair wraps for veterans and baby blankets she has produced over the years, including the latest — sent to the Army base where her first great-great grandson was born. She couldn't be any prouder of her grandson's service to our country or her growing family.

Her hands that knit by memory also guide her around her studio apartment, which is dotted with family photos, bags of colorful yarn, an American flag, and mementos from her golden birthday party, which was the same weekend as my Eagle Scout ceremony. That was when I gave her the only gift she ever asked of me: an Eagle's grandparent pin. Her attendant told me about Miss Martha's tireless search for the misplaced pin last summer so she could wear it on her collar to supper on the Fourth of July, my sixteenth birthday.

My youth-led business provides care for rare breed rabbits and rescues, preparing them on Peacebunny Island as therapy animals. Whenever I come to visit with my "comfort bunnies" in a wagon, she lights up and starts telling childhood stories that relate to the animals. During our last trip, after the COVID-19 quarantine lifted, I moved her yarn project aside as requested and then placed Oreo Peacebunny, a spotted Mini Rex rabbit, onto a lap blanket. My great-grandma began gently cooing and then singing, bending low to whisper in the bunny's ears, stroking its velvety fur in time with the lullaby.

She leaned in very close to see my face as she said, "Caleb, you must be healthy and stay alive to reach your goals and enjoy them. So, take care of your body and spirit, and protect your heart, or you'll never reach your biggest dreams." She knows a thing or two about goals: She still aims to keep playing the piano for the weekly senior home singalong and to have "five more years" — which she has been saying since she was eighty. Even though her delivery of life lessons sometimes includes a harsh tone, her heart is a gem, highly motivated to help others avoid the pitfalls she has seen. Her drive is to help us realize what is important and to hold onto those things she finds slipping.

The dining-room staff at her senior home has learned that her loud demands are the result of hearing loss and a fear that she is becoming invisible, which she dispels by requesting more hot water for her resting teabag.

"Being genteel is not my aim at this stage in life," she quipped as she leaned in and clanked the spoon on the cup, signaling that she was still waiting. "Sometimes, the only things to look forward to are the simple things, like a good hot cup of tea with a visit from family, and I'm not ready to give up having them both at the same time."

As the staff arrived with the mini teapot, she babbled on about playing organized basketball in the early 1930s on one of the first female teams in the country. This 5'2" trailblazer tried out for the team because she thought it would be fun to try something new, a sport she had never even watched! Her eyes sparkled as she described being presented her varsity letter, even though they did not make letter jackets for girls yet. "Those two years of basketball gave me confidence to shoot for higher goals and, as you know, things in motion stay in motion."

Miss Martha never went to the Olympics, attended college, owned a business, wrote a book, or was nominated for any big awards. Her dreams were simple and sincere: to have enough food to share and still not be hungry, to be healthy and safe from war, to survive challenges, and to thrive in an ever-changing world.

She lived through both World Wars, the Great Depression, and the polio epidemic. She watched the assassinations of JFK and MLK, the Challenger disaster, September 11th, and the latest pandemic. But she quickly redirected the conversation to witnessing the Berlin Wall coming down, discovery of the polio vaccine, the first and 50th anniversary of the 1969 walk on the moon, Title IX, and Dr. King's speech as he spoke the words, "I have a dream."

As she leaned back from the table and started knitting again, she boasted about her family living out their dreams. "You know, members of our family are reaching their goals, and that's enough for me."

Great-grandma rattled off a list of family members' accomplishments. After fifteen years of countless post-polio surgeries and therapy sessions, her daughter could live on her own, raise a family, and play piano for church into her seventies. Other family members went to the Olympics, graduated college, owned their own businesses, wrote a book, and wore a varsity letter jacket. Yet my great-grandma is most proud of seeing her family serve others, try to make a positive difference, and live out their faith.

Over the years, she has repeatedly challenged me to choose joy, to work on it like a personal discipline. She firmly believes that intentional optimism has kept her "from drowning during the deluge of personal tears and from giving up on daily goals like breathing" when her world felt like it was falling apart, like when her husband was killed by a drunk driver or she buried her eighty-year-old son.

"Altogether, sweetie, those moments have led me to appreciate each day," she said with a warm kiss on my cheek. "Keep chasing those crazy dreams of yours, keep lovin' those bunnies, and don't forget to keep journaling so your grandkids will know how God has blessed you, too."

— Caleb Smith —

10

Belvedere

Love is having the courage of your tenderness.
~D. H. Lawrence

"Today, I threw the Christians to the lions, but I got away just in time," my mother announces as I pull into the parking lot at Applebee's. Later, I learn that she watched *Ben-Hur* at adult daycare, but today I don't know that. I respond carefully, focusing on her lifelong love of grilled salmon. "I'm so glad you got away," I say, "because I'm treating you to grilled salmon for supper. Would you like that?"

"Oh, yes," she says. "I've never had it before!" As I help her out of the car, I marvel at her resilience and enduring beauty. She is ninety-six. Together, we have navigated the treacherous labyrinth of Alzheimer's disease since her diagnosis eleven years earlier. Tonight, we are navigating the risk of an evening out.

Applebee's has been our favorite spot since we moved to Garner five years ago. We dine there often, and our bill has been paid on occasion by patrons both identified and mysterious. Beautiful, gregarious and kind, my mother has charmed and been charmed by nearly all the waiters and waitresses. But we haven't been there for a while, and BJ, our favorite waiter, is not working today. Yesterday's heat wave has been replaced by today's cold front, and the air in Applebee's is chilly.

I don't recognize our waiter, who smiles broadly and then dashes off for menus we don't need. I order our usual: grilled orange salmon, no potatoes, double order of vegetables (no butter), strawberry lemonade for her, unsweetened iced tea for me, and a piece of caramel apple pie to split for dessert, with coffee.

Our waiter hesitates for a moment before divulging that grilled salmon and caramel apple pie are no longer on Applebee's menu. "How could they?" I protest. While the waiter and I commiserate over the uninformed decisions of distant management, my mother draws into herself as if being dragged by a malevolent force. The strange, growing absence in her eyes unnerves me. Grudgingly, she chooses crunchy Asian salad, but her confusion and litany of complaints notch up. She is cold; the seat is hard; the salad tastes funny; the fork is too heavy; there aren't enough napkins; she doesn't like this place.

She's licking hot fudge from a spoon when suddenly her face contorts with horror and she cries out, looking over my shoulder, "Those men are killing each other!" I turn around in my seat and see that a television at the bar is previewing a violent crime drama. I chastise myself: *Why didn't I think about the televisions at the bar? Why didn't I insist on our usual window seat?* I reach across the table and grasp her hand. "It's alright, sweetie," I say soothingly. "It's just a television program. You know I won't let anything bad happen to you. Eat your dessert, and we'll go home. Everything is alright."

"I don't want to sit here and be killed!" she snaps.

Other patrons stare. I am stunned, embarrassed, sad, and angry — with the disease, with myself, with her. I have sacrificed every-thing — financial security, social freedom, community involvement, a sense of future. But I chose this road, and I would do it again. My mother will die someday, but I go right on loving her, fiercely wanting, despite all logic, to keep her forever. Love holds us to high standards, the most transcendentally difficult of which is letting go.

Today I am frustrated and fed up. I help my mother to the car, reflecting on the cruel, diabolical force that is Alzheimer's disease. She is trapped in a strange world she can neither describe nor escape. I don't know what to do.

We drive across the shopping center and park outside of PetSmart. Dogs and their owners come and go, and I point out this Poodle, that Lab, those Cocker Spaniels. My mother brightens just a little with each wagging tail, and then sinks inward again. I am about to give up when a woman cradling a Dachshund puppy emerges from a truck close by. I have learned to rely on the kindness of strangers, and I get out of my car. "Ma'am," I say, testing the waters with my warmest smile, "that is the cutest thing I have ever seen!"

She beams and introduces me to Belvedere, who wriggles with delight and licks my hands. I explain how things are, and we walk to my car and place Belvedere gently on my mother's lap. She absorbs the puppy into herself, pressing its soft warmth to her breast. Closing her eyes, holding her head down close, she murmurs softly. Belvedere squirms contentedly and relaxes. I think they have both gone to sleep when my mother suddenly raises her head and looks squarely into my eyes. She releases a dazzling smile, her eyes sparkling like emeralds.

"I love you," I say. "I love you more than Orville Redenbacher, Johnny Walker, Russell Stover or any of those guys." Sometimes, I add a long string of names to this mantra, but in this moment, I can recall only three.

"I love you too!" she says heartily. Belvedere wriggles and licks her cheek. His owner smiles. Our eyes meet, and for a moment the four of us are embraced in grace, redemption, healing and love.

As we drive home, my mother chatters happily and non-stop about everything. Nothing she says makes sense, but when we are almost to our turn, she announces, "I want some dessert! I haven't had any dessert." I don't remind her of the dessert she just devoured. I check my vanishing funds. "Well, alright, let's do it!" I say. We laugh all the way to McDonald's.

— Margaret Toman —

11

Too Many Goodbyes

*When life gives you a hundred reasons to cry, show life
that you have a thousand reasons to smile.*
~Author Unknown

I am the daughter who lives too many states away and has come for her third visit within a year. Each time I've come home, the progression of Mom's dementia alarms and saddens me.

On this particular visit, I decided to take Mom on a day trip to visit two of my sisters who live seventy miles away. Driving with my mother at this stage of her disease is emotionally exhausting. The constant repetition of the same subject for an hour and a half has tried my patience.

Once I get to our destination and am in the presence of my sisters, everything brightens. We have learned the art of tag-teaming Mom without speaking, taking turns caring for her needs as we enjoy the coffee and conversations of the day.

Dreading the ride home, I buckle my mother in her seat, and we start the trip back. I am emotionally and physically drained at this point and decide not to even try to engage in conversation. Hoping my mom will just fall asleep but knowing she won't because she never naps, I endure the long trek home. With ten minutes left of the journey, we pass a semi-truck with pictures of people on the long trailer. One of them has his hand up in a friendly gesture. Suddenly, Mom starts waving enthusiastically at the truck — first with one hand and then the other, wildly engaging both arms.

"Mom, what are you doing?" I ask, bewildered.

"I don't know who that is waving at me, but I am just waving back!"

In her mind, I realize, someone is being friendly, and she is simply returning the courtesy.

"You should wave, too," she states. As I look at her expectant face, I concede and start to wave as well. But my tears quickly well up, and I look out the opposite window to hide them from her. I realize we are waving at completely different things. She thinks she is waving at a person; I am waving goodbye to a life, because my mom has a disease that is one long goodbye. I wave farewell to someone I could bake with, someone who remembers my birthday, someone who called me weekly and sent care packages. I am getting very weary of this long farewell.

But as I watch my mother, I remember that part of what made her so charming was her friendliness. I am thankful that, even in her dementia, she has not lost that. I decide to just enjoy the moment and laugh and wave with her. Somehow, I find myself able to laugh and cry at the same time.

— Sheri Cragin —

Perseverance

12

The Promise

It's not the load that breaks you down;
it's the way you carry it.
~Lena Horne

My dad was dying. His cancer had gotten worse. I moved back home to help, but my mother was determined to do everything herself. She woke up early every morning to read a passage from the Bible to my father. He would stroke her arm lovingly as she lay beside him reciting scripture from Psalms or Proverbs, his two favorites. She always made him a special breakfast that included cheese grits. Sometimes, when the pain increased, she would need to feed him.

My mother lived to care for him. But then one day, there was nothing more she could do. My father had to go to hospice. He told my mom that not being able to have her homemade greens and cornbread anymore is what would kill him. They laughed, trying to find a humorous moment in what was happening to their forty-five-year friendship, their marriage, and a love that made even their siblings and friends a little jealous.

As tragic as it seemed, my dad stayed optimistic to the end. He talked about driving to Erie from Pittsburgh to go fishing. He said my mom would make a basket for the trip filled with fried chicken and potato salad. My mom, on the other hand, was sinking into a dark place. She felt lost without him long before he closed his eyes for the last time.

The night before my father died, he took my hand and asked me to look after my mother — as if he had to ask. I promised, and he smiled with a look of contentment on his face. The next day, he took his last breath.

After the funeral, my mom went into her room and shut the door. When I checked on her later, I found her sitting on the bed with the lights out and curtains drawn. That's where she stayed for the next two months. I had never seen my mom so sad, so listless. A vibrant woman who believed in serving others and making a difference in the community, she was depressed. I started to worry about keeping the promise I had made.

I didn't know how to help her until I rode past my Aunt Ruby's house in the Hill District on the way home from work one day. I stopped by just to check in and see if she was alright. Aunt Ruby was the family matriarch, the sister of my father's mom.

I walked to the door and knocked. A ninety-two-year-old lady with eyes like mine peeked out. "Who's there?"

"It's me, Aunt Ruby. It's Debbie."

"I need you," she said feebly. "Bob left and didn't come back."

Bob was her personal caregiver. For years, she had someone living in her home to look after her, but she was alone this particular day. Turned out, Bob had gotten sick, and Aunt Ruby was trying to take care of herself. I went in the house and cooked a meal for Aunt Ruby, got her ready for bed and locked up.

As I drove home, I thought about my mom and how she always made time for anyone in need and how much she and my dad loved Aunt Ruby. I talked to my mom through the bedroom door after delivering her dinner.

"Mom," I said. "Did you know that Aunt Ruby has been over there all by herself? Bob hasn't been there for weeks." My mother, who had only murmured a thank you to me for her meals for weeks, made a familiar sound. "Umm umm umm," she said. I was heartened by it. I knew she was listening and wanted to help. She cracked the door and asked me question after question about Aunt Ruby.

"Is she feeling well?"

"Did she say she needed someone?"

"Yes, and yes," I answered. That's how it all started.

Mom turned on the lights and opened the curtains the next morning. She asked me if I would mind dropping her off at Aunt Ruby's house.

"Not at all," I said.

I couldn't wait to get her out of the house. Aunt Ruby welcomed my mother with open arms. They sat around like old friends while my mother cooked meals, helped Aunt Ruby shower, combed her long, gray hair and twisted it into a bun. They were enjoying their special time together.

My mom, Aunt Ruby and I took several trips from Pittsburgh to Wilmington, Delaware, to see Aunt Gracie, who was in a nursing home recovering from a stroke. She was Aunt Ruby's little sister. We took the train, and Aunt Ruby and my mom would sing, "This train don't carry no loafers, this train." Aunt Ruby used to sing that song as we rode along Route 376. She moved her head from side-to-side and clapped wildly when she reached the chorus. My mother would join in as we rode along.

Mom was feeling alive again. She smiled more. It was good.

From the first time I dropped my mother off until the day that Aunt Ruby died, there was a spirit of sharing and love between them. I thought that maybe loneliness gave them a bond, but the combination of caring and service made the difference. We all long for someone to talk to, communicate with and love. It gives us a reason for living. My father would be pleased.

— Deborah Starling —

13

A New Mother

Forgiveness says you are given another chance
to make a new beginning.
~Desmond Tutu

Effie Johnson spent the last eight years of her life in a nursing home in Jackson, Mississippi. Because I live two hundred miles away in Memphis, I spent many hours, traveling to and from Jackson for bi-weekly or monthly visits before my mother's death from Alzheimer's disease in 2016. She was eighty-eight. During those eight years, I wrote over sixty blog posts about long-distance caregiving for this woman who had been verbally and emotionally abusive to me all my life. Some of those posts were humorous. Others were heart-wrenching. All were snapshots of the milestones in our journey together as mother and daughter.

I wrote about her grief at losing her purse, which was an icon of her independence. Her confusion about "the people in the box" when we tried to watch television together. The loss of her dignity when she had to wear a diaper. The time she forgot how to chew her M&M'S, putting them in her mouth and saying to me, "They're not moving around in there." The first time she didn't remember who her grandchildren were, much less two of her great-grandchildren who were brought to the nursing home to meet their Great-Granny Effie and pose for pictures of four generations of our family.

And then there were the brighter moments, like the first time I cut her hair; she was pleased with the result. As the tangles and plaques took over her brain cells, she moved into a make-believe world that seemed to be a better place than the limbo she had been suffering through since the onset of dementia. She bragged about the flowerbeds surrounding the patio at the nursing home, telling me how she had planted them all. And even when she no longer understood who I was, her face would still light up when I arrived for a visit and one of the aides announced: "Look, Miss Effie! Your daughter is here to see you!"

Just before she died in 2016, I gathered sixty of those blog posts into a collection and found a publisher who liked the book. *Tangles and Plaques: A Mother and Daughter Face Alzheimer's* was published in January 2017, only eight months after her death. One of the posts — which became a chapter in the book — is titled, "The Upside of Alzheimer's: New Mother." The title came from my six-word memoir, which was published in Smith's *Six-Word Memoirs*. Here's the story that inspired those six words.

I grew up as the daughter of a handsome "golden boy" father who loved me unconditionally and a beautiful mother I could never please. From childhood into my teens, my mother criticized everything I did and, more significantly, my appearance. She transferred her own obsession with weight onto me at a young age, resulting in my life-long battle with eating disorders, including bulimia beginning in junior high. My hair was never right, and everything I wore made me look fat in her eyes. I countered the abuse with efforts to be perfect, performing in academics, music, art, theater, journalism, and cheerleading. My successes were met with minimal praise, leaving me craving her love and approval even more.

My mother's years of heavy drinking only exacerbated the problem. It would be decades before I understood what drove her to drink, as I came to grips with the childhood sexual abuse I had suffered from my grandfather. Although Mother never talked about it, I was sure that she had also been a victim of her father's assaults. He died when I was five, and my memories of him molesting me surfaced many years later. I began to forgive my mother in light of this new understanding, but it would take Alzheimer's to repair our relationship completely.

Yes, as strange it may sound, Alzheimer's gave me a new mother.

On one of my many visits in 2009, she greeted me with words I had never heard from her: "Oh, I love your hair! Did you just get it cut?" I looked over my shoulder to see who she was talking to, only to confirm that she was, indeed, offering me a compliment. I was on unfamiliar ground, but I smiled, holding back tears, and thanked her.

Then I got out the gifts I had brought that day — a coloring book filled with flowers and a set of brand-new Crayola crayons. Mother had been very artistic in her younger days, and she was a star in her garden club. "Would you like to color some flowers with me, Mother?" She stared at the crayons, not seeming to know what to do with them. I handed her a purple one — her favorite color. I chose a green one and began coloring the stems and leaves on the page. She joined in slowly, bringing the iris to life with her purple strokes. We worked quietly, and when the picture was complete, I taped it on the outside of her wardrobe where she could see it. Suddenly, she looked at the picture and then at me and exclaimed, "You did such a good job! I'm so proud of you!" My kindergarten self, the one who didn't receive praise fifty years earlier, burst into tears. We colored a few more pages, and then it was time for me to leave.

"I've got to drive home to Memphis now, Mother," I said. "A storm is coming, and I don't want to be driving in the pouring rain."

She reached out for my hand, held it tightly, closed her eyes and began to pray: "Oh, Lord, we ask you to protect Susan as she drives. Take care of her and keep her safe...." She went on for several sentences, speaking with a clarity she hadn't shown in months, or even years. As I listened to her words, I realized that I didn't have any memories of my mother praying with me as a child. When she finished, she opened her eyes, smiled, kissed me on the lips, and said, "I love you." All the years of abuse seemed to melt away. Forgiveness gushed from my soul as I hugged her. "I love you, too, Mom."

And there it was — the most unexpected gift in the midst of a terrible disease. Alzheimer's had given me a new mother. And God gave me the grace to forgive.

— Susan Cushman —

14

Uncle Nelson

*Technology is nothing. What's important is that you
have a faith in people… if you give them tools,
they'll do wonderful things with them.*
~Steve Jobs

My dad and his older brother, Nelson, were close as kids. They played countless hours of catch in the yard and shared a love of cars. But once they were married and had children, they hardly saw each other. Every few years, though, my dad would track down Uncle Nelson and call him.

One year, Dad heard that Nelson's wife had died, and he was living in a care facility at age seventy-five. A care facility? That didn't fit his image of his brother, so Dad decided to visit Nelson. He walked into the two-story care home and was shocked by what he found. Nelson was in a recliner, nearly unresponsive verbally, feeble and wobbly when he walked, hardly able to go up and down the narrow stairs to his bedroom.

After seeing him, Dad e-mailed Nelson's daughter and asked, "Marsha, why don't you move him close to me so I can check in on him?" Soon thereafter, Nelson was placed in a nursing facility about twenty minutes from my dad's home. The nurses there were told that he was in the early stages of dementia. The first time Dad went to visit Nelson at the new place, he was confined to his bed, not getting up for meals or even to use the restroom. Each question Dad asked him was answered with a "Yeah" or "No." Even though there was a TV on the wall and activities to attend, Nelson just sat and stared at the wall.

Their mother had suffered from dementia during her final years, and the pain of not being able to communicate came back to Dad. He began visiting Nelson every Wednesday morning, but after a few more visits, Dad said, "I can't do this. I will not watch my brother waste away and stare at the wall."

Then Dad made a decision — one that changed everything: "I am going to get Nelson an iPad."

That's where I come into the story. I had an old iPad that I was not using, and when I heard of my dad's plan, I sent it to him. The first day that Dad took it to Uncle Nelson, he said, "Here, try this," and showed him how to connect to the Internet and e-mail him.

That doesn't sound like much, but every week when Dad visited Nelson, he picked up the iPad and showed him how to search for new things.

On one of his visits, Dad said, "Remember your first car? Wasn't it a '54 Oldsmobile?"

Then an amazing thing happened: Nelson perked up. He even started to talk! Nelson said, "Yeah…yeah, I think it was."

So Dad brought up a picture of one on the iPad.

That was the beginning. Nelson started to open up and talk to Dad. They looked up pictures of the shoe factory where Nelson had worked. Dad showed him how to e-mail his son and daughter. Dad showed him pictures of his own family and his home-improvement projects. On one visit, Dad showed Nelson how to text him, and he practiced right there in the room!

That week, Dad started getting texts from Nelson like clockwork, every morning at 9:00. The texts would say things like, "Good morning, brother! How are you doing on this sunny Tuesday morning? The weather today is going to be sunny with a high of 75 and a low of 48. The Pirates are playing the Cardinals tonight at 7."

Uncle Nelson was finding his voice.

After about a month of this, the nurses began commenting on the vast change they saw in Nelson and how much he had improved. He was communicating with them like he was with my dad. After some encouragement from Dad, Nelson decided to get out of bed and use the restroom! The nurses saw this and arranged for him to start physical therapy using a walker. In therapy, he practiced showering and brushing his teeth. After catching a glimpse of himself in the bathroom mirror, he decided that he wanted a shave and haircut, something he had not had for years.

Nelson texted Dad a picture of himself, and Dad could not believe the difference. Nelson looked like a new man. He began walking without the aid of a walker and soon was taking walks three times a day to the elevator and the nurses' station. When invited to join the other residents on outings to a local baseball game or to the lake for a day of fishing, Nelson agreed.

Uncle Nelson e-mailed his daughter and stepchildren and began to get visits from them. Dad took him on outings — to his hunting camp in the mountains, and to the town where he used to live and work.

To this day, the nurses tell Dad that they share "Nelson's story," as they call it, with everyone.

They rarely see transformations like his.

Dad has updated Nelson's iPad several times over the past five years. Nelson has learned how to use FaceTime and YouTube to find videos about fixing shoe-factory sewing machines, which was his job for many years. He rediscovered his love for the music of Cher and the Carpenters, and Julia Roberts movies… all of which he can access from his iPad. His conversations with Dad are lively now, and he even texts Dad pictures of the snacks that he would like him to bring on his weekly visit.

Nelson is a new man, or rather, he is the man that my dad remembers. He does not have dementia. Embracing new technology in the form of an iPad has changed his life. My dad has his brother back, and even though they can't throw baseballs in the yard anymore, they are closer than ever.

— Christina Peters —

15

Mama Was a Rich Woman

*The art of life lies in a constant readjustment
to our surroundings.*
~Kakuzō Okakura, The Book of Tea

Mama was a rich woman. Not necessarily in personal finances, although she had a comfortable retirement. Not rich in investments, either, for she and my dad had put money into a $500 life-insurance policy in 1956 with a company that no longer exists and left no forwarding address. Not even rich in family, at least not near the end of her life, as all her surviving relatives (except me, her only child) had passed away before Mama's ninetieth birthday. No, she was rich in a currency rarely recognized in the world today: Bingo Bucks.

During my first sixty-two years of life, I don't recall her ever mentioning any interest in Bingo. But that was before my mom discovered the untold wealth that could be had by yelling "Bingo!" at the proper time.

It all began when we moved Mama into an assisted-living facility. Since my dad had died the previous year, she lost all interest in the things that had once brought them joy. Even the TV went silent, with Mama preferring to sit and stare into the darkness. Her depression and dementia were undoubtedly progressing. After a crippling fall in her house, it was mutually agreed that it was time to move her. Although my mom had been fully open to this in the beginning, she began to get cold feet. As the options were limited when she was released from the hospital (she didn't want in-home care), she grudgingly agreed to give it at least a month, after which we would revisit the situation.

On moving day, Mama wasn't happy, even asking to stay in the hospital rather than be moved to the assisted-living facility. When we wheeled her into the lobby of the upscale facility, she refused any comment as the staff gathered around to greet her. One question after another was ignored by her with a blank stare. At that point, I suspected her dementia had suddenly become worse. But then the activities director spoke what seemed to be the magic words: "We have Bingo." My mother raised her head, looked straight at the director, and firmly replied, "I love Bingo!" It was then that a new Bingo hustler was born.

From then on, it seemed like she was involved in a group Bingo game almost every time we visited. Although most of these were officially sanctioned by the activities director, I've no doubt that others were pickup games organized by Mama and her Bingo cronies. At all the games, big bucks exchanged hands — $5, $10, $20, $50, $100, and even $1,000 bills — all with the words BINGO BUCKS in block letters across their multicolored paper surfaces. Although such currency may be ridiculed by those not in the know, I later learned that it was the accepted currency among those living at her residence.

About six months after she moved to the facility, I noticed her eating a candy bar. Since I didn't remember that particular brand of "chocolate nutty goodness in a caramel nougat" being part of the weekly goody bag my wife and I usually brought her, we were curious about where it came from and asked her.

"I bought it," Mama said. "I bought these, too." With a hint of pride of someone who has figured out the system, she opened the drawer of her bedside table and revealed a virtual treasure chest of senior-living swag. Inside the drawer was a horde to rival any commissary. Not only was there a large selection of candy and snacks, but there were also hair barrettes, puzzle books, Halloween and Christmas knickknacks, a small ceramic angel, numerous ballpoint pens, a cheap plastic flashlight, strands of Mardi Gras beads, and more.

"Take this," she told us as she pulled out an unopened package of #2 pencils and handed them to me. "I'll buy more."

As there were no official cash transactions among residents, I became more curious about where the hoard came from. Then I remembered the Bingo games. It turned out that Bingo Bucks could be traded for merchandise with the activities director, including candy and snacks for those who could eat them, and other things for those who could not. Mama, who had become a sort of in-house Bingo high roller, chose both.

From then on, she was always proudly showing us her latest winnings and recent purchases. There were black hair combs and red bows. There were plastic magnifying glasses. There was even a "Hello Kitty" decal. Even though Mama had no idea who "Hello Kitty" was, she got it because I liked cats, and she wanted to give it to me. I gently suggested that, with such an abundance of "stuff" — some of which was edible and had actual expiration dates — maybe she should back away from the games for a while or, at the very least, bank some of her winnings. She held a finger to her lips in the sign of "shhh" and looked around to make sure she wasn't being watched by anyone. Then she reached deep into her bedside table and pulled out a substantial roll of red, green, purple, and blue Bingo Bucks. Although I didn't bother to count the wad, I am sure it totaled in the hundreds of thousands. Mama just grinned and ate her candy bar.

I still don't know how my mother learned the game of Bingo so proficiently in just the time she had been there, or why she decided she loved a game before she ever even played it, but learn it and love it she did. And although I cannot for the life of me understand how anyone could be a Bingo shark or Bingo hustler, somehow Mama seemed to have become both.

The months turned into two years. Her dementia grew worse, and it became obvious that Mama's gaming days were just about over. Then came COVID-19. Just two weeks later, the care facility was under full quarantine. My wife, daughter and I were allowed what we thought might be our last visit with her. Although Mom failed to understand why we wouldn't visit her during the lockdown, she did understand that this might be our last time together.

But there was one more visit. After an urgent call from her nurse a couple of weeks later, we arrived to find my mom in a near-comatose state, unresponsive and looking as small and frail as I'd ever seen. Her ninety-two years had caught up with her, and we all said our goodbyes to her, hoping that she could hear them.

As to her vast Bingo Bucks fortune? It was turned in and recycled into other Bingo games that she would never be a part of. But remembering how the word "Bingo" had brightened her face when she first came here was worth every penny. Or Bingo Buck.

— Butch Holcombe —

16

A Challenge Every Day

There's always a new challenge to keep you motivated.
~Sean Connery

My mother was born in an English village in 1931, long before television, beehive hairstyles and distressed jeans. She grew up to witness the Jet Age, man's walk on the moon and pet rocks, but she had no idea how science and technology would one day help her handle the challenges and pains of advancing age.

The onset of arthritis and not being able to hear as well as she used to signaled that she was getting older. At first, she ignored the changes and then denied them. When she finally faced what was happening, she was a bit angry. My sisters, nieces and I recognized that she increasingly required help, but she didn't want it or think she needed it.

My mom is sharp as ever at eighty-nine years old, but her body is slowing down. Even with a great diet and few vices, the list of declining abilities marches on. Her arthritis and inflammation are sometimes so painful that it's hard for her to get out of bed. We've found that technology has been an incredible aid in assisting her with physical problems and encouraging mental stimulation.

When I got her a cellphone, it was an enormous struggle. She hated it and decided she would never figure it out or enjoy it. That changed the first time she opened an attachment photograph I sent her of my new puppies. It spurred her on to learn more about using all the features of the phone. She quickly taught herself to download pictures and scroll through her growing digital photo library.

Mother wanted nothing to do with electric carts at the grocery store. It took a while to convince her to use one. When she finally relented, after encouragement from us, riding instead of walking saved her feet from the soreness of the hard, concrete floors and spared her knees from the excruciating pain of her arthritis. No longer worn out from picking up a few groceries with a pushcart, she goes down every aisle now and takes her time filling up her electric cart basket. After she mastered driving the electric cart at the store, she purchased her own. It's a stylish, aqua-colored scooter that folds up like a suitcase, making it easy to put in the car or take on an airplane. She has us lift it for her.

My sister and nieces took a trip to New York and tried to get my mother to accompany them, but she struggled at the time to get around and was afraid to go. She was disappointed, but a year later when they traveled to San Francisco, she went along with her scooter. With a little advance planning, she had a blast. Everyone was incredibly accommodating, from the staff at the airport to trolley drivers on the streets of San Francisco. Other passengers at the airport approached her to compliment her scooter. Some waved to her as she whizzed around the terminal wearing her glittery sequin jacket.

No one had to persuade her to use a walker to reduce her chance of falling. She agreed to it as long as it had a seat so she could use the seat like a tray to carry things around the house. The walker is also great on the patio. She can roll it right up to her flower bed, rest on it and enjoy the fragrances of her roses and orange blossoms in the spring.

My mom is now adjusting quickly to changes, and we try to help. Her hearing declined so much that we were turning up the volume on the TV unbearably loud, but then she embraced reading closed captions.

Social interaction is a good lifestyle practice for successful maintenance of cognitive abilities, but we do not attend social gatherings right now. We won't have any direct contact with anyone outside our household until we get past COVID-19. My niece set up videoconferencing calls on the Internet so my mom can keep in touch and see people. She even joined other church members to play Bingo on a Zoom call channeled through our TV.

The greatest technology gift for my mom is the tablet. It opened a new world for her; she reads, works puzzles, plays games, and watches her favorite soap opera on the screen. She taught herself to take pictures with it, pull up e-mails, and surf the web for world news like what's happening with the British royal family.

Although new things may give her pause, little sets her back. Modern technology is complicated, with innovative discoveries rolling out every day, including many that help with physical and mental challenges.

My mom's attitude has changed from weariness to embracing anything that improves her quality of life. Don't count her out from mastering all the newfangled technology. At almost ninety, she's just getting started.

—Jonney Scoggin—

17

MedMary and Me

*We all have a path to take; sometimes it's hidden under
the weeds, so you might have to work a little.*
~Mike Dolan @HawaiianLife

O n a sunny Florida morning, I was first in line. Standing outside the locked doors of the medical marijuana dispensary, I knew the drill.

At nine o'clock, the doors would open. I would hand the armed guard my caregiver's medical marijuana photo ID card, which depicts me and names my husband, Paul, as my patient. The guard would walk me to a receptionist, who would take my card and check it against the state's online list of caregivers. Then I would wait. Soon, an escort would unlock the salesroom door and retrieve my card. Eyeing it and then me, he would walk me into the salesroom and up to a counter, where a counselor would take my card, make the sale, and return my card.

Yes, I would pass the scrutiny of four individuals before receiving the medicine!

But why the armed guard? Because marijuana is at high risk of theft by illicit drug users.

On my first trip to the dispensary with Paul — a retired public servant who uncomplainingly lives with Alzheimer's disease and an assortment of other poor health conditions — the handgun riding on the hip of the uniformed guard had been as startling to these two octogenarians as the number of Cannabis strains and their delivery systems had been surprising. Three strains — indica, sativa, and hybrid — are available in tinctures with droppers, topical creams, nasal sprays, oral syringes, edibles, and capsules of varying strengths. With so many possible combinations, it's no wonder the sales force is comprised of trained counselors.

But why medical marijuana? Other pain medications had not relieved Paul's chronic nerve pain enough, and marijuana is a more attractive alternative than a potentially addictive opioid. Therefore, Paul's doctor had enrolled him in the state medical marijuana program.

Afterward, I had doggedly worked my way through the multi-step process of obtaining the photo ID card that allowed Paul to purchase and use what we playfully dubbed MedMary. But when the purchase process overwhelmed him, sending his counselor to the waiting room for my advice, I paid the extra fee for the caregiver's card that allowed me to go behind locked doors and make the purchase for him.

That's when doing business solo, and in the presence of an armed guard, became my standard operating procedure. And so did fielding jokes from friends, who teasingly referred to me as my "pothead husband's drug runner."

Paul's nine-times-a-day dosage schedule now included a dizzying array of ten prescriptions for pills and capsules, three for eye drops, and twelve over-the-counter nutritional supplements and digestive aids overseen by eight doctors. Add to this list a dentist for his teeth, an optometrist for his eyeglasses, and an audiologist for his hearing aids, and Paul helps to support a huge chunk of the health-care industry.

How do I juggle Paul's daily medicine schedule and numerous doctor appointments with my household duties and personal tasks? With commitment and a fair amount of lunacy.

But my lunacy is organized. I fill Paul's seven-day pill tray and check off his medication chart with each dose given; cross items off a crowded to-do list; maintain an appointments datebook; stay connected to church, family, and a small number of friends; squeeze in a regular exercise program; participate in a caregiver's support group; practice prayer and gratitude; and welcome bedtime every night.

Now in the dispensary waiting room, I checked Paul's bottle.

Good, enough capsules to last through tomorrow. Then I spotted the electronic card reader on the counter. Good again. Since neither Medicare nor health insurance pays for MedMary, I had welcomed the recent e-mail announcing that my debit card would satisfy the dispensary's cash-only rule.

"Carole?" called my escort. I stood and followed him into the salesroom, where a smiling counselor waved me to her counter.

"Good morning," I said, showing her Paul's bottle of capsules. "Three bottles, please."

Her smile faded. "Oh, my!" she said. "I'm afraid we're out of those."

Apologies followed, but the fact remained. The dispensary had none of Paul's medicine in stock, and she didn't know when it would be available.

What to do? I started my drive home. Then I remembered a different grower's dispensary several miles away. Did I have enough time to go there and get home before Paul needed me? Yes, because that morning before leaving, I had allowed for an unforeseen delay by setting out his MedMary and a glass of water. "Take this at eleven-thirty," I had said, "and I'll be back for lunch."

If my wait at the next dispensary became too long, I'd bail out and go home to make Paul's lunch — a task too challenging for him. But I wouldn't be out of options; I still had tomorrow.

Thirty minutes later, I checked in with a receptionist — and no armed guard. I was counting the number of customers ahead of me when a wall chart of available products screamed at me in huge capital letters: COMING SOON. And it listed Paul's capsules.

What? Two dispensaries out of stock? When an escort came and walked me behind locked doors to a salesroom, there stood the standard armed guard. With widespread legs, crossed arms, and a serious face, he eyed me and a counselor with a ready answer: Paul's form of MedMary capsules had arrived that morning. "I'll just run and get some," she said, disappearing behind the stockroom door.

Eventually, she returned, bottle in hand. Smiling, I whipped out my debit card. Frowning, she withdrew the bottle. "Sorry, but we don't accept plastic cards."

Oh, no! Different dispensary, different policy—a possibility I hadn't considered.

Defeated? No, determined. "Okay, let's see what I have here," I said, shamelessly spilling the contents of my wallet onto the counter and spreading out my bills and coins as I counted. "Oh, no! I'm short $1.44!"

"Oh, no," she echoed. "Let me go find my manager."

More waiting. But she returned with good news. As a first-time customer, I was eligible for a 10-percent discount.

What? A 10-percent discount? No, a 100-percent miracle! Thanking her, I pocketed the little cash I had left, grabbed the medicine, and hurried home.

"Hi, Paul," I announced cheerily, breezing in just before noon. "Did you take your MedMary?"

Glancing at the filled pill cup on the coffee table, he hung his head. "No, I forgot."

"No problem," I said, handing him the glass of water and the pill cup. "We got this."

After lunch, with Paul medicated and free of pain, I reflected on my harried, clock-watching, eldercare adventure in the brave new world of medical marijuana. No problem, we got this. MedMary and me.

— Carole Harris Barton —

Worth the Effort

Prayer is less about changing the world
than it is about changing ourselves.
~David Wolpe

No matter what I did, I couldn't please my mother-in-law. For the first years of my marriage, I tried everything. Every time she flew across the country for her two-week annual visit, I felt judged. My dinner was not as good as hers, my floor wasn't as clean as hers, and my parenting skills weren't in line with hers. It was as if her disapproval threw a heavy blanket over my spirit.

Part of the problem was my husband, the fourth child after three sisters. They called him "The Prince." That should have been my first clue. I would never be able to meet her expectations. Still, I tried. I scrubbed the floor and she complained I cared too much about the house being clean. I shopped for her favorite foods, but she grumbled that I pushed myself too hard for perfection. I whipped up dinner with her recipes, but she turned up her nose as she ate them. I prayed for her as I sat next to her in church, but she criticized the sermon for being too long. I kept my mouth shut but inwardly simmered.

Finally, I stopped trying. I cheered when my husband drove her to the airport after her visits. I admitted to myself that I didn't like my mother-in-law.

I kept praying for her, though. And then I felt like God said, "I want you to call your mother-in-law and ask her if she wants you to pray with her every week on the phone." That was ridiculous. But the idea wouldn't go away. I followed my heart and called her one Sunday morning. I thought she would laugh when I suggested we pray together on the phone.

But she didn't laugh. She said she'd love me to call every Sunday and pray. So, I did. I didn't know what to say, so I prayed the 23rd Psalm and inserted her first name, making it a personal prayer.

Her health declined and she couldn't come to visit. I continued praying with her on the phone, and the years sailed by. One Sunday after our prayer, she said, "That was great! I love you so much!" I pulled my iPhone away from my ear and stared at it. My voice wouldn't work. I barely recovered and murmured, "Thank you! I love you, too," and hung up.

Soon after, she became bedridden and moved in with her daughter, who was a nurse. A year later, she required full-time nursing care. Through it all, I kept the Sunday prayer calls coming. Her daughter eventually told me, "Mumma looks forward to your weekly calls. It changes her whole countenance and makes her day so much better."

Two years later, my mother-in-law died. Psalm 23 was read at her funeral. I was eternally grateful that I had managed to swallow my anger and humble myself to call and pray with my mother-in-law years before. It changed both of us — for the better.

— Suzy Ryan —

19

Sparkling Sam

I do not bemoan misfortune. To me there is no
misfortune. I welcome whatever comes;
I go out gladly to meet it.
~Muriel Strode

"There's my daughter!" Dad exuberantly announced every time he saw me arrive at the skilled nursing facility where he battled the dementia that was sapping him both physically and mentally. If I'd been employed, I wouldn't have been able to stop by every day. But this was during the Great Recession, and I was one of the many who had found themselves out of work. The timing for my unplanned career break was, in retrospect, fortuitous.

It occurred only four months after my father moved away from western Colorado and his beloved hometown of ninety-plus years to a retirement community in Boulder on the other side of the Continental Divide. I had battled to keep Dad in his home, but family disagreements and the reality of Dad's worsening dementia made that impossible.

Back home, Dad's close friends knew him as Bucky, but at the nursing home he asked to be called by his first name, Sam. Always kind and gregarious, but in a quiet, dignified way, Sam — the newest old man on the block — quickly became a hit among the nursing staff and other patients.

Dad was a retired optician and easily befriended the aged and dying and those caring for them. My father's natural joie de vivre stayed with him throughout his decline. I once read that some dementia patients become even more of who they are at their core — for better or worse — as the disease progresses, and this was especially true of Dad.

Unfettered by the concerns of everyday life — shopping to do, bills to pay — Dad was free to express his true spirit in every moment. The nursing facility's social worker pulled me aside one day to ask, "Has Sam always been this warm and genial?" Indeed, he had, but now even more of Dad's special life force seemed to shine through.

Months before he moved into the facility, I had taken Dad to the Veterans Administration Hospital in our hometown. Because my father was a former soldier who had spent fourteen months as a prisoner of war held by the Nazis in World War II, the VA did its best to provide him with attentive care. This visit was to get an X-ray of Dad's head, which ultimately confirmed his doctor's — and my — worst fears, which was that Dad's brain was shrinking, causing increased memory loss and confusion.

But on that day, as Dad walked back to where I was sitting in the hospital waiting room, he was smiling, and so was the middle-aged X-ray tech accompanying him. Looking into my eyes, she said in all sincerity, "Your father just sparkles." During twenty minutes in a hospital X-ray room, unsinkable Sam's essence had shone through.

There's nothing humorous about watching a loved one lose his physical or mental faculties. But my partner Gary and I joked that Dad had "funny dementia," because, well, he did. My father, who had always enjoyed a good laugh, was becoming an unwitting entertainer.

Despite everyone's best efforts to keep Dad mobile, he gradually lost his ability to walk. After lending us a used wheelchair, the VA Hospital in Denver crafted a custom wheelchair for Dad. A wheelchair wouldn't fit in my sporty import, so Gary let us take his older Cadillac DeVille — a luxurious tank of a car — to Dad's VA appointments. After confirming that the new wheelchair was the perfect fit for Dad, the folks in the VA rehab center told us we could keep both wheelchairs if we wanted them.

"We'll just toss them in this Cadillac we borrowed and hit the road," Dad declared in all earnestness, prompting chuckles from everyone nearby.

Dad's residence in Boulder was across from a small park and, when weather permitted, I wheeled him around the park's duck pond. During one of these outings, when my father's dementia had become quite advanced, he glanced over his shoulder at me. Sensing that he wanted to say something, I stopped the wheelchair and leaned down.

"Do you want to sit here while I push you around the park for a while?" Dad asked sweetly.

I didn't know whether to laugh or cry. This wonderfully caring man, who forgot he couldn't walk, just wanted to help, like he had during his entire life. I gulped and gave Dad a hug. "I'll keep pushing because I need the exercise. How about that?" He agreed that was a fine idea, so we continued our journey.

I didn't learn until after Dad passed away, at age ninety-four, that he had promised at least two of the female nursing-home residents — and maybe more — that if they could bust him out of the joint, he'd take them to Hawaii. My father, who often mentioned his 100-percent fidelity and deep love for Mom, had become a nonagenarian Lothario! It spoke to his love of life that despite being a widower for fifteen years, Dad still dreamed of fun in the sun and travel to an exotic locale that he had never gotten to visit.

Dementia tried to steal everything from my father, but it couldn't touch his indefatigable spirit. I fully expect to see Dad someday on the other side. I'll just need to look for an iridescent soul who joyfully calls out, "Hey, there's my daughter!"

— Tammy Parker —

Sacrificial Service

*It is under the greatest adversity that there exists
the greatest potential for doing good,
both for oneself and others.*
~Dalai Lama

I pulled the brush through my mother's brittle gray hair. As I worked, more and more hair filled the brush. I stopped and looked at the balding patch at the back of her head.

Mom's eyes opened. "Why did you stop?"

I dragged the brush once more across her scalp, and her eyes closed again as she enjoyed the attention. I simply wanted to help Mom feel like her old self — to give her a sense of normalcy. But nothing seemed typical anymore. Since she'd chosen to stop fighting the lung disease that had plagued her for decades and taken to her bed, nothing seemed normal. Now our lives were full of hospice workers and terms like "end of life," "palliative," and "transition." Dad and I were "caregivers" now.

I finished and asked, "How's that, Mama? Feel better?"

"Oh, yes, thank you." She gave me a slight smile.

I helped her back into bed.

"Can you trim my nails?" She looked at her hands. "They seem to get so much gunk in them. I'm not sure from where."

I knew how the "gunk" had accumulated but remained silent as I retrieved the clippers and nail file. Months spent in bed, without the benefit of a proper hand washing, tended to add build-up under the nails. She was unable to go to the bathroom now and used a potty chair beside the bed. As I bent to my work, I pushed down my nausea.

"Ouch!"

"Oh! Sorry. It's hard to do this on another person. I have to use my left hand on this side and, well, I'm not sure how those nail techs do it." I smiled, but she held onto her scowl.

"Be careful! A bleeding finger would just add to my ailments." She leaned her head back on the pillow and closed her eyes — the signal she didn't wish to discuss it further. Her hand stayed out, ready for service.

I sighed and kept going, more careful this time. She could at least be a little grateful.

As I continued my task, I tried to focus on making Mom feel like a normal, healthy person. I'd spent almost every day — at least several hours each day — with my mother for the past two months doing such tasks. I had become manicurist, hairstylist, cook, entertainer, confidante, and nurse.

Even when I did have time to spend with friends and my husband, I was often too exhausted to make conversation, laugh, or even focus on anything except Mom's last days.

I worried about my dad as well. Because we'd decided to keep Mom at home, he spent every hour with her, rarely sleeping, always worrying. I'd sent him off a time or two for errands to simply get him out of the house, but he never stayed away long. I could sense the fear in him. What if she died while he was gone? What if I needed help with her, and no one was there? I'd noticed his hair had grown just a touch grayer, and his waist had thickened from stress eating.

Finishing my task, I smoothed lotion over Mom's hands and tried to think of a conversation topic. When I opened my mouth to say something, I noticed she'd fallen asleep. I carefully put her hand back on the bed and tiptoed away, relieved for the moment.

Giving care to someone means giving of yourself, letting go of everything you want to do, or even need to do, to be there for this other person. I thought about how we strived to provide a normal life for my mom, to make her final days peaceful. We added to our worry by attempting to remove hers. Caring for my mom meant pushing past every grumpy moment and pretending things were okay.

I wish I could say I did what I needed to do every single time without feeling bitter, angry, or resentful, but I can't. And I think that's okay. We need to accept not being perfect in these situations. I didn't do this task of caregiving flawlessly. I failed at being a good nurse. I went home almost every day and vented my anger, fears, frustrations, and hurt to my husband. And some days I felt like the worst daughter because of that.

But we all need to find ways to cope during these stressful times. Friends told me time and time again that caring for my sick mother would be the hardest thing I'd ever done, and they were right. It wasn't because of the physical labor — although that was tough — but because of the emotional scars and exhaustion.

Yet I'm grateful she could stay home and live her last days in the place she'd built with my father. I'm thankful my job allowed me to spend so much time with her — to mother her the way she'd mothered me.

After her death, I skimmed through a journal she'd written in those last few months. In many entries, she wrote things like, "I'm glad Sue is here," "Carson is such a good husband," and "They are taking such good care of me." When I read these sentiments, all the hard stuff seems to matter much less because I know we did the best we could. Every swipe of the brush through her hair, every time I wiped her face or fed her lunch, and every smile I mustered was a bit of sacrificial service for me but a lot of joy for her.

— Sue A. Fairchild —

Gorgeous!

Mothers are always on stand-by.
~Pam Brown

My mother was nearing the end of her seven-year-long battle with Alzheimer's disease — a battle no one wins. What a hideous disease it is: a slow, steady, downhill progression toward the end of a life. But there still can be moments that are very heartwarming, moments that show you that the person you love is still in there.

One of those moments occurred a few months before Mom died. My son Michael and my daughter-in-law Crescent had just learned they were having a baby! They wanted to share the news with their grandmother despite her dementia. This would be her first great-grandchild.

At this point, Mom had been unresponsive for months. She would look at you, but there was no recognition, just a blank stare.

Mike and Crescent went to her house. They sat on her bed, they hugged her, they held her hands. No response. Then they said they had something so important to tell her that they made a special trip to her house so they could tell her in person. They began to tell her their pregnancy news. No response. They told her they were so excited, and they wanted her to know because they knew she would be excited too. She looked at them with that blank stare. Then they started questioning her. Do you have any ideas for names? What do you think we should name our baby? Do you have any favorite names? Still nothing. But they kept on talking and questioning and… and she blinked.

She looked directly at them and asked, very clearly, "Do you know if the baby is going to be a boy or a girl? The name will kind of depend on that." And then she faded away.

They were blown away. She could hear. She could understand. She had asked a logical question.

A few months later, and just two days before she died, I was sitting on my mom's bed and talking to her. By this time, she was in a fetal position, not moving, and although her eyes were open some of the time, she made no eye contact whatsoever. Just a blank stare off into space. Seeing her like that was very difficult and I was near tears the entire time, but I just kept talking to her and joking with her. I never took my eyes off her. I told her I loved her. I told her she was beautiful. I told her she was the best role model any daughter could ever have. I told her she was the best mom in the whole world.

Then I started to talk and joke about me and kept up this constant barrage of questions. On and on just to see if I could break through that barrier of the disease and find my mom.

"How about me, Mom? Do you love me? Are you proud of me? Am I the best daughter you ever had? (Being her only child, that was a no brainer!) Am I the worst daughter you ever had? (Also a no brainer!) Am I pretty? Am I as beautiful as you are, Mom? Do you think I'm pretty?"

Then I stopped talking. The room was quiet. Mom looked directly into my eyes. She was absolutely there. She was connecting with me. And she spoke. She said, "Gor-geous."

She hadn't spoken since Mike and Crescent had told her about their pregnancy a few months before. Her voice was so weak, and it was so hard for her to speak that she broke the word gorgeous into two syllables and she took a breath between them. But her word was very clear. When she spoke, she answered the question I had asked her, and she made sense. Somewhere, somehow, some way, I had broken through and connected with her. For a split second, she was my mom again. She knew me. I was her daughter being silly and pestering her, as usual!

And then, just a quickly, she was gone. Back into the thick fog of

Alzheimer's. Her eyes glazed over, and she stared off into space. And then her eyes shut. She never uttered another sound. And two days later, she passed away.

They say that hearing is the last sense to go. My mom, a trained psychologist who had her Ph.D., always said that. They say you should never stop talking to people just because they can't respond, or it seems like they can't hear. Mom was adamant about that. They are right. Mom was right. What better proof does anyone need than these two examples that hearing is still there at the end? So, always keep on talking, singing, joking, pestering, laughing. Never stop.

What a gift Mike and Crescent got when my mom responded to them. She heard them and they knew that they had gotten through to her, if only for a minute. Although she did not live to meet her great-grandson, she knew he was on the way and that brought them joy.

And somewhere deep down, she knew me too. She knew I was there. She knew I loved her and she knew… that I was gor-geous!

— Barbara LoMonaco —

Next Steps and Tough Choices

The Visitor

*We must learn the power of living
with our helplessness.*
~Sheldon Kopp, No Hidden Meanings

When my plane left Orlando Melbourne International Airport in Florida, I was on a mission with little chance of success. I had to persuade my ninety-one-year-old mother to move from her rented house in upstate New York to an independent-living facility. Mom was dead set against the move. But recent close calls with her gas range, iron, and wood-burning stove proved she could no longer live alone safely.

As the plane sped northward, I recalled how strong-willed Mom could be. Three years earlier, I had taken her to the hospital for a knee replacement. The morning after the operation, a nurse called to report that, at 5:00 a.m., Mom decided to go home. She ripped the drainage tubes from her knee and the IV from her wrist and hobbled seven floors down to the parking lot to look for a taxi. Luckily, an orderly spotted her and returned her to her room.

After landing, I confirmed an appointment for Mom and me to tour an excellent independent-living facility near her home. Her name had finally come up on the waiting list. Her consent was required for admittance. She had to be in by Thursday, or she would lose her spot. I had three days to make this happen.

When I arrived at Mom's, I took her grocery shopping. She pushed the cart up and down each aisle, selecting her favorite foods. Her elbows bent sharply as she grasped the cart handle. She was no longer the four feet, eleven and a half inches she claimed to be. At the checkout, I searched for her SNAP card in umpteen zippered compartments of her massive purse until she retrieved it from her pants pocket.

The next morning, I rose early to prepare breakfast. When I heard footsteps on the stairs, I slid a golden omelet onto a serving plate next to tomato slices garnished with parsley. On another plate, I arranged whole-wheat toast points around a ramekin of glistening marmalade. I filled her coffee mug to the brim the way she liked it. Everything was in place, but I was not prepared for what happened next.

Mom appeared at the entrance to the kitchen wearing her pink sweatshirt and gray jogging pants, her hair a mass of springy gray curls. She stood frozen in place.

"Good morning," I said. "Did you sleep well?" I set her pill dispenser next to her mug and adjusted her rocking chair.

"Good morning," she said. Her eyes had an unmistakable look of fear. "What are you doing in my kitchen?"

"Making us a delicious breakfast."

"I mean... who are you?" It was my turn to freeze. Mom had mild dementia, but she had always recognized me.

"I'm Dave. Your favorite son."

"I'm sorry, but you are not my son. My son lives in Florida. He calls every day. He didn't say anything about coming."

"Why don't you have a seat in your rocker and enjoy your coffee? Breakfast is almost ready."

Her initial fear abated, but she eyed her phone on the counter as she lowered herself into her rocker.

"Don't worry," I said. "Your mind is playing tricks on you." I showed her my Florida driver's license. She glanced at it and handed it back.

"Why are you here?"

"I'm visiting. I'm here to help around the house."

She sipped her coffee. "So," she said, "you're a visitor."

"Exactly."

Mom took her seat at the head of the table.

"Breakfast looks beautiful," she said. "Like something you'd see in a gourmet magazine." She tasted the omelet. "Mmmm, so good! Who taught you to cook like this?"

"You did."

"I'm glad." She smiled.

As we ate, Mom told me how she had raised three sons and a daughter on our dairy farm. When her husband died, she moved into town. I pretended to listen, still shaken by her inability to recognize me.

"One son lives in Florida," she said. "The other two are nearby, but I never see them. My daughter, Bonnie, lives in Oneida and takes me shopping, but I take care of myself. I mow my lawn, shovel my sidewalk, and carry in wood for the stove."

As Mom talked, she relaxed. But my anxiety grew. I had two days to build trust from scratch.

After breakfast, I went to work. My first task was to fix the vacuum cleaner that lay in pieces on her living-room floor. I reassembled it. Mom clapped when it roared to life.

"Thank you," she said. "The cleaning lady comes at 2:00. Now she can vacuum the house."

I examined her microwave but found it scorched beyond repair. The bottom of her electric teakettle had melted, suggesting she had tried to heat it on the gas range. Her ironing-board cover had burned through to the metal. I asked her if she would like me to clean out her junk-filled second bedroom. She agreed. I ordered a dumpster and began filling it.

The house buzzed with activity. Social-services people came and went: Meals on Wheels, the cleaning lady, and a nurse. My sister, Bonnie, stopped by to help me sort through items. Neighbors came to inquire about the dumpster.

That evening, as Mom and I were finishing dessert, I casually mentioned the tour.

"Our appointment is at 10:00 tomorrow."

"I'm not going."

"Your landlord is selling this house. You'll need a place to live."

"I'll find another place when the time comes."

The next morning at 9:30, when Mom was putting away dishes,

I announced it was time for our tour.

"Look," she said. "I know what you're up to. You want to get me down to that nursing home and leave me there!" She lifted the receiver on her phone. "Leave this house now, or I'll call the police!"

"But…"

"I'm dialing. Nine…" The look in her eyes was fierce.

"Okay. I'm going."

I went shopping instead. I returned loaded with purchases and rang her bell.

"What do we have here?" she asked.

"A new microwave, an electric teapot, and an ironing-board cover."

"It must be Christmas. Come in."

I replaced the old items and sipped tea with Mom as she rocked.

"If I moved to that home, could I take my rocker?"

I nearly spilled my tea.

"Yes, but I'd get you a new one." The bottom of her rocker was held together with lumps of glue and bungee cords.

"I've been thinking. All these people coming in to take care of me and now you cooking my meals… I might as well admit it that I'm not taking care of myself."

I made final arrangements for the move and took Mom shopping for a rocking chair. We found one she loved. She refused to get out of it until the salesman told her the store was closing.

Thursday morning, Bonnie helped Mom pack. We checked her into the independent-living facility. She signed. Mom settled back into her new rocker.

"I love this chair," she said. "Wait until I tell Dave that I've moved here. He'll be so pleased."

"I bet he will," I said. "I bet he will."

— D.E. Brigham —

A Small Miracle with a Big Meaning

Miracles come in moments. Be ready and willing.
~Wayne Dyer

y wife Mary was diagnosed with early-onset Alzheimer's disease over ten years ago at the age of fifty-nine. Due to her rapidly deteriorating condition, and because I was working full-time, there was no way I could care for Mary at home. A couple of years after her diagnosis, she moved into an assisted-living, memory-care facility. I always felt guilty about moving her there so soon, and for a long time I wondered if there was any way I could bring her back home to live.

But she was safe and happy where she was, and she loved the caregivers. Ensuring Mary's happiness has always been my number-one goal. There was no way she would have been as happy with just one caregiver all day or only me, even if it could have worked out.

She hasn't been able to communicate verbally for the last four years, except for a few words now and then. We've developed an alternative, a nonverbal connection that works — touching, hugging, smiling, eye-gazing, hand-holding, humming, dancing.

In the past, it was always a joyful surprise when she said a few words or even phrases that seemed appropriate for the circumstances, especially if they resembled "I like you" or "I love you." But then even those semi-coherent verbal moments disappeared.

Then, a couple of years ago, when we were walking the hallways of her residence during my nightly visit, I noticed she was more energetic than usual. She was humming loudly, always a sure sign she was feeling happy. I mentioned I needed to leave soon and would come back the next day. She said the word "home," followed by, "I stay here." It was an unexpected statement, both for the clarity and the context.

I was shocked and didn't know what to say at first, but then I responded, "This is a nice place, isn't it?"

She broke into a big smile and then gave me a little laugh. "Yes, I like it. I love it," she replied clearly, followed by, "Thank you so much." I was flabbergasted with the articulation and apparent understanding she expressed. This type of clarity hadn't happened for a few years and hasn't happened since. It was phenomenal... and exactly what I needed to hear to know she was happy and to assuage any lingering guilt I felt for not being able to bring her home.

A few days after that, she stated out of the blue, "I'm home."

I replied with pleasant surprise, "This is a nice home."

"Yes, it is," she said. "Thank you."

The above quotes may seem simple to some, just snippets of thoughts with few words, but they are very meaningful to me, and I cherish them. While my wife may seem oblivious to her circumstances at times, I believe she accepts her surroundings and is happy, which is all that matters at this point. Little instances like these have a big impact... and they keep me going.

— Marc Alderdice —

24

The Fight that Never Ends

*The day the roles reverse is foreign.
It's a clumsy dance of love and responsibility,
not wanting to cross any lines of respect.
~Lisa Goich-Andreadis*

A mere four months before his death, as we returned, ironically, from our monthly visit to the retina specialist treating his macular degeneration, Dad announced that he wanted to buy a car. This was not a new theme, but this time I asked, "Daddy, why do you want to buy a car?"

"Well, so I won't have to bother you to take me where I need to go."

"Daddy, it is an honor and a privilege to spend time with you and take you where you need to go. I'm happy to do it."

After a deep sigh and a lengthy pause, he conceded, "Well, you are a good driver."

Wow, high praise, I thought, recalling his sardonic comment when I passed my first driving exam as a teenager: "Just because the state of Pennsylvania thinks you can drive doesn't mean I do."

"Thank you, Dad. You taught me."

The first indication of Dad's declining driving skills had come fifteen years earlier when my son, a newly minted driver, pulled up in front of a vacation rental near Williamsburg, Virginia. I could not believe my eyes. Nor could I fathom why my dad had let his inexperienced firstborn grandchild take the wheel on I-95, of all places. My son read my incredulous expression, jumped out of the car quickly, and whispered while hugging me, "Mom, it was better that I drove." *Wow, it must have been scary,* I thought. I hugged him hard, choked down the tirade that I was ready to unleash on my dad, and thanked God they had arrived safely.

Several years later, Dad was in an accident that left him uninjured but totaled his pick-up truck. No one was with him, and the only witness was the other driver. Naturally, he claimed the accident was not his fault. We kept our suspicions to ourselves, for once heeding Dad's dry but pointed comment, heard often throughout our lives, "Well, you just missed a good opportunity to keep your mouth shut."

After a fall that resulted in a head injury, Dad saw a neurologist. Prior to the visit, I spoke to the doctor about our concerns regarding possible dementia and stressed how worried we were about his driving. This man held the power to have Dad's driver's license revoked, and I figured he was our last best hope. I also knew the policemen in our small town. My plan, if he drove without a license, was to alert them so they could pull him over, chew him out, and call me to come and drive him home.

When the letter came from the state revoking his license, Dad threw a royal fit, raging about being the only decent driver in our family and storming into the neurologist's office, threatening to sue him. Mom and I stood behind Dad, begging the doctor with our arms and eyes to stick to his guns. That coward folded. Two weeks later, Dad received another letter telling him that he could keep his license. Dad rejoiced. We felt like crying.

From then on, Mom and I made every effort to be the drivers. On only one occasion did I allow my dad to drive me anywhere. We were out together, running errands, when I suddenly doubled over in excruciating pain. I was in no shape to drive. A few days later, as I lay in a hospital bed recovering from emergency surgery, he said, "I should have taken you to the emergency room. You wouldn't have let me drive unless you were really sick." No joke.

The following year, my parents moved to Tennessee to be near my brother and escape the raw, snowy Pennsylvania winters. Mom and I rejoiced. We knew that Dad would have to take a driver's test, and we were confident that he would not pass. He was eighty-five years old. We were concerned about his judgment, vision, reaction time and insistence on driving in the passing lane, despite annoying every driver on the road. He could not read the overhead road signs until he was almost under them. He told us that if people didn't like him driving in the left lane, they could just pass him on the right.

On that fateful day, he went to his driver's exam alone. When he returned, he was practically dancing a jig. "I passed. And I even went through a stop sign and didn't stop before I turned right." We were speechless.

When he left the room, I turned to my mom and said through clenched teeth, "If he kills someone, you need to tell their family to sue the Tennessee Department of Transportation." I meant it.

Dad, on the other hand, felt like he had a new lease on life. We will never know how often his guardian angel intervened when he went to the grocery or hardware store because none of us would ride with him. When they went anywhere together, Mom raced to the car to get to the driver's seat first. When Dad misplaced his keys, she would hide them if she found them. That merely slowed him down; in a day or two, he would telephone the Honda dealer, ordering new ones. Eventually, she flat-out refused to get in the car if he was driving. He would rant and rave about it, and then grumble from the passenger's seat: "I feel like a vegetable sitting here, staring out the window, doing nothing." We often wondered what vegetables feel like but didn't think probing that subject would help matters at all.

A couple of years later, Mom and Dad moved to a continuing care retirement community atop nearby Signal Mountain. There are just two roads up and down that mountain — a winding one and one dubbed, ominously, "the W Road." The last thing we wanted was for Dad to drive on either of them; the idea was enough to give us nightmares. Since the retirement community provides transportation to doctors, shopping, and social outings, we convinced him to sell the car. He vociferously mourned that loss for the rest of his days.

When Dad's vascular dementia progressed to the point that Mom needed help caring for him, he moved to the memory care unit where he lived the last two years of his life. Mom and Benji, their little dog, visited daily, and he never knew that Mom, ten years his junior and a very capable driver, had gotten a car. The week the title came from the state of Tennessee, she sat in front of me, signed her name on the "sold by" line, and handed it to me.

"Put this in your safe-deposit box," she said, "and if I don't have enough sense to know when I should quit driving, take my keys and sell it." Occasionally, she asks my brother or me to be her passenger, just to be sure all is well.

Thanks, Mom, for ending the fight.

— Capi Cloud Cohen —

25

From a Distance

The highest reward for a person's toil is not what
they get for it, but what they become by it.
~John Ruskin

y story began one weekend when Pop took one of his extended fishing trips and left Mom alone. She and I decided to have some mother-daughter time, with lunch at our favorite restaurant followed by shopping at the mall.

Mom was excited about getting out of the house and spending the day with me. So, when she didn't show up at the restaurant as planned, I was concerned. I rushed to her house and found her unconscious on the couch. The paramedics arrived and determined that Mom, a diabetic, had contracted the flu, which had, in turn, spiked her temperature as well as her blood glucose and ketone levels, resulting in a diabetic coma.

Mom emerged from the coma, but afterward she suffered from mild depression, dementia, diminished eyesight, and diabetic neuropathy that brought burning nerve pain to her arms, fingers, and feet. Pop became her primary caregiver, administering medication, shopping for groceries, and cooking meals. I lived closer to the folks than my brothers and provided them support, accepting but occasionally resenting the age-old adage that women are better caregivers than men.

But when my husband was laid off, we faced our own challenge — a financial crisis requiring me to work a second part-time job. I struggled with finding sufficient time to meet my parents' needs as well as my own but forged ahead while quietly harboring resentment toward my brothers. Eventually, my husband received a job offer and a new career opportunity, which meant moving 800 miles away from my folks.

"Bill has a job offer," I explained to the folks, "but I'm hesitant about moving so far away from you."

"Your husband is your first priority," Mother said. "Don't worry. We'll be fine," she assured me. "Besides, your brothers live nearby and can help if we need anything."

Although my brothers lived close, I wondered about their capacity and willingness to care for the folks' needs, especially the emotional ones. Nonetheless, Bill accepted the position.

"We'll keep in touch regularly by phone," I said, putting on a brave face but still questioning our decision to relocate.

"Don't worry," Mother reassured me again.

We moved and began life anew, establishing ourselves in new careers, buying a home, and becoming entrenched in our new lives. For the next fifteen years, I cared for my parents as best I could from a distance, calling them every Sunday, and regularly sending cards, letters and photographs documenting our lives and activities. I shipped them care packages of home-baked goodies and special treats, as well as birthday presents, cards, and more. We returned home twice a year, spending Christmases and part of our summer vacations with them.

Then the unthinkable happened. We were awakened in the middle of the night to the shrill scream of the telephone ringing. "Pop's had a stroke," said the distraught male voice on the other end. "You need to come home right away!"

Ten hours later, we arrived at the hospital and found Pop in the ICU hooked up to a ventilator. "The prognosis isn't good," explained the doctor. "Your father's stroke was massive and has impacted the left side of his body, including his mobility as well as his ability to speak." The tile floor beneath me felt soft under my feet, and my knees weakened. I fought back the tears, groping with the fact that the healthy, vibrant man Pop had been was gone forever.

A few days later, Pop stabilized and was placed in an in-patient rehabilitation center after which he was placed in a full-service nursing home. Since Pop could no longer care for Mom, my brothers and I faced the daunting task of getting her needs met. We made arrangements with Meals on Wheels and contracted with an in-home elder health provider who checked on Mom daily, making sure she was taking her medication and eating the meals she was provided. After a month, the situation was under control. Bill and I were more than ready to go home. So, we checked out of our hotel and met with my brothers one last time.

"You can't go!" my younger brother demanded. His voice shook in anger. "You're the girl and the one who's supposed to take care of the folks. You're abandoning them and our family."

"What are you suggesting?" I asked, resentment and guilt bubbling in my stomach.

"You need to quit your job and move back home. It's the responsible thing to do."

"Don't you think that's a bit unrealistic?" My eyes widened in disbelief.

"Honestly, no."

"If the situation were reversed, would you quit your job and move across the state to where I live?"

"That's different."

"No, it's not!" I fired back with protest in my eyes. "I wouldn't ask you to upend your life. We're leaving," I said in a sharp tone, turning away abruptly, getting in the car, and driving straight home.

Back home, I wrestled with the decision I'd made, replaying it over and over in my mind, wondering if I'd done the right thing. While at work, I put on a happy face, but inside my self-confidence wavered. I was easily overwhelmed and avoided making decisions. I suffered from insomnia and was always on the verge of tears.

"What's wrong, sweetheart?" Bill asked after one of my sleepless nights.

"I feel selfish and guilty. Maybe my brother was right. Perhaps I should've dropped everything and rushed to the folks' side."

"Hold on just a second!" he said sternly. "Your brother's using your conscientiousness just as he's always done to guilt you into doing what he wants. Caring for your folks is a growth opportunity for him. You did the right thing; you're forcing him to accept responsibility. I beg you, don't own the guilt he's placed on you. Remember, your folks wouldn't have wanted you to disrupt your life. They made that clear years ago."

"You're right. I just wish I had a do-it-yourself eldercare manual, one that would tell me how to care for them from a distance."

"You don't need a manual. Trust your intuition," he suggested.

I put aside my notions of selfishness and guilt and discovered myriad ways I could care for my folks from a distance. Although Pop had lost his ability to speak with me over the phone, I knew he'd want to hear my voice and maintain our father-daughter connection. So, I prepared audiotapes detailing my activities, emotions, and thoughts and sent them to him. I sent them books-on-tape to help them wile away the hours. Despite her diminished eyesight, Mom could still quilt, so I sent her fabric and quilting patterns. I called her every week and regularly sent flowers, cards, and photographs.

Over time, I became comfortable being a long-distance caregiver. I learned not to be so hard on myself, accepting that each person cares in his or her own way. Just because I hadn't relocated in order to physically care for my parents, I hadn't abandoned them. My brand of care and kindness was bringing light and love into their lives in a unique way, and they were better for it.

— Sara Etgen-Baker —

26

The Journey Through

Sometimes the hardest thing and the
right thing are the same.
~Author Unknown

I sat on the edge of her narrow bed as she fretted, reliving memories. I wrapped my hands around hers and listened to her regrets. Together, we shared her sorrows and cried.

The progression to the nursing home included a valiant attempt by my brother to care for her at home after our father died. Her diabetes and history of heart attacks had led us to believe she would go first, but now she was the one who was alone.

Mom had never lived alone before, but she made do with the help of my two brothers, who lived close by. I had left over thirty-five years earlier on a route off the family map — college. Now I lived three hours away.

Then one day, she became confused, slurred her words and couldn't move one side of her body. An ambulance rushed her to the hospital, and a stroke was confirmed. After the hospital, she went to rehab. Upon discharge from rehab, we were informed that she would require twenty-four-hour care.

My younger brother had promised Dad he would look after Mom. Without hesitation, he moved in, quit working, and abandoned his nights out with friends. They both survived on one small Social Security check. Mom resisted any discussion of leaving her home to move closer to me. I tried to hire outside help, but according to Mom, the first candidate was "too talkative," the second "stank of smoke," and the third "didn't know what she was doing." Three strikes, and I gave up. It was obvious someone from the outside was not going to satisfy her requirements.

The demands of caregiving wore through my brother's good intentions. He pushed Mom to do more for herself. She pushed back with helplessness. She complained of boredom, sitting in the house all day while he watched TV. Visitors dwindled after they were met with his gruff greetings.

I visited every other weekend to provide a small break, but I was like the "weekend parent" who entertained her by taking her shopping and out to eat. My brother rarely took advantage of this opportunity to visit friends or do something for himself. When we returned, he made a point of being disinterested. If he talked at all, it was at me or over me.

I left money so he could take Mom out, but he felt safer with her at home — and I understood why. Though Mom could manage her personal care at home, she required help in a public restroom. And I had to admit, by the end of each outing, my patience was exhausted. Mom had always been adamantly self-sufficient, but now she was unable to drive, couldn't find the words she needed to express herself, needed a walker to steady her steps, and depended on others to cook her meals and dole out her medications. It was a maddening cycle of wants and needs on both sides.

As I drove to each visit, I brainstormed ways to give them both what they needed. Upon my arrival, there was often silence until I spoke. The air felt charged with irritation and resentment. A slow fuse seemed to be burning, with a bomb threatening to explode. I wanted to turn around and run back home.

Following each visit, I analyzed the events, trying to determine what I could have done differently. The worst part was the guilt attached to the relief I felt as I headed out their door. Once home, I couldn't sleep and obsessed about what to do. Urgent calls for help — from each of them at different times — sent me flying across the 150 miles on rescue missions that often yielded more dissent than assistance.

Mom wasn't happy. My brother wasn't happy. I wasn't happy. Mom and I discussed alternate plans. She was eager to try something else. I moved her into an apartment with full-time care provided by a younger relative. Housing and meals were part of the pay, along with a modest stipend. But within days, the demands of Mom's care unraveled the plan. The challenges my brother had faced were more complex than I had understood. Yet he still offered to take over her care again. However, Mom wanted him back as her son, not as her caregiver. The inevitable loomed.

A doctor's order confirmed Mom's need for a nursing home. My parents had owned their doublewide trailer in the woods of upstate New York and had a tiny sum in the bank. There was no pension, and the life insurance barely covered the funeral expenses. Because she required the assistance of Medicaid to cover the costs, there would be no choice of facilities. We were thrilled when a small agency, close to home and recommended by a niece who had experience there, had an opening. Mom's Social Security check was transferred to the nursing home, and a lien was placed against her house.

The staff was caring and friendly. Mom soon discovered common acquaintances with both the staff and other residents. She chose her nicer clothes and jewelry for dinner and group events. As she became more comfortable in her new setting, the knot in my stomach began to loosen. Mom had never seemed to be a "group person." But as I watched her interact, I realized that may have been due to the isolation of her home in the woods, along with my father's tight control over our family, rather than her true nature. As she chatted and laughed with others, it occurred to me that she was experiencing what I had experienced when I went to college — the camaraderie of shared group living! This was her "dorm" of sorts, and these were her "classmates." For her, it was a new life adventure rather than a dreaded ending.

Things went well for several months until another stroke further reduced Mom's independence. I tried to focus on the positive but soon realized her need to express her sadness and grief. As I listened, she taught me how painful regret is. I silently vowed to live my life more fully now. Initially, our hours together had been about reliving the good times and avoiding the hard ones. But, ultimately, the only way past pain is through it. We shared that journey, too, and grew closer.

Each time I left, Mom's sad face followed me out the door. Then, one day as I turned for a last wave, she sat smiling at me — glowing with contentment! On that trip home, my sadness slipped away. Soon after, a phone call in the night informed me she had passed on. A howl escaped from deep inside me. But the gift of her last smile eased my grief and helped me past the pain. That beaming smile remains the image of her that I carry in my heart.

— Susan K. Shetler —

You Can Get Through This

Peace is a day-to-day problem, the product
of a multitude of events and judgments.
Peace is not an "is," it is a "becoming."
~Haile Selassie

From the time I was a child, my mother made it clear that she did not like nursing homes. I remember her saying that nursing homes were places where "the smell of urine wafts through the hallways, broken men rock back and forth in their wheelchairs, and forgotten women wail with piercing, cat-like screeches." Whenever my mother said this, she would shake her finger at me and add an ominous warning: "If you ever put me in one of those places, I'll haunt you!" I knew my mother's wishes and wanted to abide by them.

Fortunately, my mother lived near me, and for many years it was easy to check on her and help with her care. But with each passing year, my mother experienced a decline in her physical ability and mental acuity. After ninety, when she was diagnosed with dementia, she needed more assistance with the normal activities of daily living and required close observation because of lapses in her memory. With each new day, it seemed like she needed more care, just for her own safety.

During this passage of time, I, too, had "matured." My children were grown and had moved to distant states. I now had grandchildren, and it hit me one day, like a knock on the head, that I, too, was getting older. I had my own mobility issues and health concerns, and a voice in my head started asking, "If something happens to you, what on earth will happen to your mother?"

As the days passed, it became clearer that some changes were needed. If I had to go out for groceries, and my mother didn't want to go, I couldn't leave her alone. When I slept, my mother was unsupervised, and she could get out of bed and wander off.

Fortuitously, while I was wrangling with what to do, a brand-new nursing home was built in our town. I toured this facility and discovered that they could provide a private room for my mother. They also had a staff that was very professional and well-trained. I tried to convince myself that this new nursing home was the best and safest place for my mother, but I kept hearing my mother's words and seeing her finger shake in front of my eyes.

I did talk to a staff member at the facility, and she walked me through a long list of confusing choices. From what I gathered, for our situation, there were three options: full-time in-home care, an assisted-living facility, or a nursing home. Full-time care did not seem like a viable option in our area. My mother's physician had already indicated he didn't think she could manage in an assisted-living center because of her dementia. He felt she required more observation and care than an assisted-living center could offer. That left only the nursing home. Logically, I understood this was the best option, but I was still reluctant to set a move-in date because I knew my mother's wishes.

I wrestled with the pros and cons for months.

Then one day, I happened to talk with an old friend whose parents had passed away in a car accident. She listened to my concerns and was very simple in her guidance, but she helped me to narrow my focus. She distilled all my thoughts down to one concern, and I think she helped me make the right choice for someone I loved.

This friend told me that deciding about care for a loved one is never easy, and there are never clear choices that are perfectly right or wrong. She told me to make an informed decision about my options and to be sensitive to my mother's needs and wishes, but in the end my decision should come down to one word: safety. Simply put, she said, "When safety issues are apparent, you can't wait. You have to decide for safety because you know your loved one needs to be and would want to be in a safe place."

I knew she was right. My mother needed to be in a nursing home. I think I made this decision in my brain long before my heart would accept it, but my friend's words really clarified the situation for me. She was right, and she ended our conversation by saying, "You can get through this."

I finally set a move-in date for my mother to move to the nursing home.

As soon as my mother was settled in her new room, she took the change in surroundings as an opportunity to move to a new residence in her mind. Mentally chopping off several decades chronologically and moving two states east geographically, she retreated to her child-hood home where there were sweet voices and friendly faces. It was a world where she could visit with her deceased parents, sister, brothers, friends, and two husbands.

My mother resided in the nursing home for about three years before she finally passed from this world at the age of ninety-four while sleeping in her bed. According to her wishes, I arranged to have her body transported to the town where she grew up, so she could be buried in the place she loved so dearly. Here, as she desired, she was interred beside my father, her first husband.

Years have passed, but to be honest, I sometimes still see my mother shaking her finger at me, and I hear her saying, "If you ever put me in one of those places, I'll haunt you!" But I still believe I made the right decision. I know my mother was safe and comfortable until she drew her last breath.

I have concluded that parents should be careful about what they say to their children. Sometimes, their words linger with their children and interfere with decision making. Few people are able to live out their years as they originally envisioned or planned.

When it comes to eldercare, I believe you must make the best decision you can, at the time, with what you have available — but always keeping your loved one's safety as a priority. Whatever decision you make, if you make it carefully and with the best intentions, you can live with it. I did.

—Billie Holladay Skelley—

28

Better for Everyone

God gave burdens; he also gave shoulders.
~Yiddish Proverb

During the final chapter of my father-in-law's terminal illness, an unspoken question hung over us. Though neither my husband nor I would express it aloud, it sat there like a squatter, almost taunting us, asking, "When all this is finally over, what happens to Mom?"

Looking back, my husband and I should have addressed these concerns years before. No one lives forever, and in the case of my in-laws, my mother-in-law was not only a typical 1950s housewife, completely dependent upon her husband, but also foreign-born. Her spoken English was excellent, but her writing skills were not. In her seventy-five-plus years, she had never paid a bill, written a check, or handled any correspondence. She did not have a driver's license, and hence had never been to the grocery store, doctor's office, or even the hairdresser's alone. She was completely dependent upon my father-in-law.

Nature eventually took its course, and my father-in-law passed away in early June. That very same day, my mother-in-law came to stay with my husband and me. I will never forget the car ride from my in-laws' home to ours. I was sitting in the back seat, looking at my husband's profile as he negotiated the traffic, and next to him was this petite, gray-haired lady. All I could think about as my eyes settled on her suitcases crammed on the floor next to me was that life as we had known it would never be the same.

That summer was one of the most difficult periods of my life. Every weekend, my husband would travel to what had been his parents' home and continue the Herculean task of cleaning out a half-century's worth of clutter. My in-laws grew up during the Great Depression and saved everything — furniture, clothing, envelopes, rubber bands, empty jars…. Every drawer, closet, and corner within the four-story home was packed with "stuff." The Salvation Army was a godsend, and representatives from that organization made many visits to pick up donations that ranged from two sets of kitchen furniture to a rowboat that we discovered under the front porch.

Once my father-in-law had passed, my mother-in-law refused to ever cross the threshold of that home again. Therefore, while my husband labored at clearing out the old homestead, I had the "pleasure" of my mother-in-law's company. As she had never been alone in her life, she insisted upon being with someone — namely, my husband or me — at all times. This forced camaraderie with my mother-in-law was all-consuming, but I tamped down any stresses I felt. Wasn't this what family was all about?

While weekends were challenging enough, work presented another set of obstacles. As my mother-in-law refused to be alone, and both of us worked full-time, we faced another dilemma. Thankfully, we both were working at a nonprofit hospital at the time, and the administration was very understanding. I would arrive at the hospital by 7:00 am. For the next ninety minutes, I feverishly responded to e-mails, returned phone calls, and managed my calendar. By 9:00 a.m., my husband would drop his mother off in my department, and she became our "senior volunteer."

I will forever be grateful to my office colleagues who were more than gracious and kept my mother-in-law busy stuffing envelopes, affixing labels, and counting charts. My husband would take his mother to lunch at 1:00 p.m., and I would drive her back home when my shift ended by 3:00 p.m. After a quick run to the grocery store, I would settle in for the night by 4:00 p.m. with my mother-in-law, and this soon became my "normal" routine.

After several months of this insanity, we knew that something had to change. My husband and I were exhausted, our jobs were in jeopardy, our marriage was suffering, and my mother-in-law was miserable. At that point, I started to re-think our decision about an assisted-living arrangement for my mother-in-law, something that I had vowed I would never consider a mere six months earlier.

As luck would have it, a five-star senior community was situated three miles from the hospital where we both worked. The assisted-living facility had a sterling reputation, spacious apartments, and a nursing unit on-site. In addition, German immigrants had founded the community nearly a century ago, which was the same culture and heritage that my mother-in-law had brought with her to the United States many years before. That afternoon, unbeknownst to anyone, I made a call to tour the facility myself. Again, this was something that I never thought I would ever pursue for a loved one — that's what families were for — but I was truly grasping for a lifeline.

Pulling into the parking lot, I was pleasantly surprised by the beautiful landscaping, the festive holiday decorations, and the numerous birdhouses that graced the grounds. I walked to the main entrance, which was spacious, spotless, and protected with a high-end security system. Once inside, I noticed comfortable chairs artfully arranged in the large sitting area; several residents were enjoying the late autumn sunshine streaming through the large windows.

Studying the residents, I noticed that some were reading, some were working on a large jigsaw puzzle, and others were involved with a word game. Everyone seemed engaged, and no one was sleeping. While I was observing this almost idyllic afternoon, a woman from the culinary team brought pitchers of iced tea, pots of hot tea, a bowl of fruit, and a plate of homemade chocolate cookies to a table, and began arranging glasses, cups, plates and napkins.

As I was lost in this reverie, Noreen, one of the sales representatives, greeted me, extending her hand. At that moment, I burst into tears, much to my embarrassment. Ever the professional, Noreen recognized caregiver burnout, handed me a tissue, patted my shoulder, and began our tour. For the next half-hour, we toured several apartments, met dozens of residents, and visited the chapel. An hour later, I was so impressed with the community that I wondered why I had waited so long to pursue this option.

The following weekend, Noreen met me again for another tour, and this time my husband and mother-in-law joined us. To my sheer amazement, my mother-in-law seemed excited about the possibilities this new living arrangement might offer and agreed to a two-week trial stay. That two-week stay lasted fourteen years, and my mother-in-law became one of the all-time longest residents of the community. She also confided to me that she had never been happier.

Looking back, I can now see clearly that no matter how hard my husband and I tried, it truly takes a village to care for the elderly during that final chapter. We were just two people, and we alone could never have created the camaraderie, fellowship, and support that are the hallmarks of such a caring community.

— Barbara Davey —

29

What Took
You So Long?

*To care for those who once cared for us
is one of the highest honors.*
~Tia Walker, The Inspired Caregiver

"I don't know what to do anymore. We have to run to their house every day to fix something Dad has broken." Hearing the frustration in my sister's voice was heart-breaking. I knew I was being asked to help. Living nearly 400 miles away made this difficult.

Yet this phone call led to many conversations and visits. I loved traveling back home. My dad had an endearing, witty personality. Each time I would arrive, he would say with a grin on his face, "What took you so long?" as if I were late for an appointment.

Five years prior, my dad had been diagnosed with Alzheimer's. He first noticed something was different when having difficulty with small tasks on his computer, which he had done thousands of times. Even remembering how to turn it on and log in became frustrating. His doctor suggested he see a specialist, who confirmed the diagnosis of Alzheimer's. He and my mother continued their daily routines as if nothing had changed. But things did change.

Talking about future events that might transpire due to Alzheimer's is difficult. Many conversations with our parents ended with the response, "We are old. All old people forget things." Yet, through my research, I knew this wasn't just about forgetting. When my mother admitted he hadn't picked her up at the hairstylist, which was in their neighborhood, I knew things had deteriorated. It turned out that after Dad had dropped her off, he'd driven around for two hours trying to locate the house they had lived in for years.

My dad was proud. We knew the conversations would be tough and hoped they would go better than they did. First, I tried to get them to visit an assisted-living facility, explaining the situation. "We think... it might be best to move into this type of setting. Then, as your situation worsens, someone will be there to help Mother."

On the day of the appointment, they refused to go. After many weeks of trying to work through other possible arrangements, my siblings and I decided for them. The plan was to have them come to visit me and not let them go back home. They would live permanently with my husband, my children, and me.

This was a heartbreaking decision. Taking them from the life they had known and from their friends and church family was not only gut-wrenching but also came with risks. Changing the environment of an Alzheimer's patient is known to escalate the symptoms. However, we worried more about my dad becoming a statistic on Silver Alert, both parents being killed in a car accident or, even worse, having an accident that killed someone else.

I cherished those months with my dad. I took him to the barbershop and on drives around the neighborhood, and we had many conversations on the front porch. One conversation still pricks my heart. "Can I go back and visit just once? I just want to see everything one more time," he pleaded. I felt like I had taken away everything he knew and loved. He died four months after the move.

Alzheimer's is a difficult road for everyone involved. However, there is one thing we must keep in mind as we navigate this journey. Recognizing and accepting our responsibility to love and care for our parents who are affected by this life-altering disease should be the priority. My dad was a planner and rarely procrastinated. He taught us to do the same. We did what we needed to do—a compromise that wasn't ideal but kept them safe.

Next Steps and Tough Choices |

I look forward to seeing my dad again. And when I do, I'm sure I will hear him say, "What took you so long?"

— Darla Czeropski —

30

Time for Memories

Memory... is the diary that we all carry about with us.
~Oscar Wilde

I t was heartbreaking. My friend's elderly mother was upset about moving into an assisted-living apartment. She was in her mid-eighties and had been living in a two-story house for more than forty years, but with declining health she could no longer manage.

She had been struggling to get up and down the stairs and couldn't keep up with the housework or yardwork anymore. Her long-time wonderful neighbors had always helped but had recently moved away. Everyone was getting older, and life had become difficult and lonely, so it was time.

Her family packed up some of her furniture and personal items and had them delivered to the apartment. Even though her daughter was there trying to help her get settled, her mother wouldn't stop crying. My friend tried to console her, but nothing was working. So she picked up the phone and called me. "Do you have an hour or two to come over to see if you can cheer up my mom? She likes you, and I don't know what else to do."

"I can be there in twenty minutes," I said, writing down the address and directions.

The apartment building was brand-new, and her one-bedroom apartment was quite lovely but small, especially compared to the house she was leaving. It had a compact kitchenette with a fridge, sink, and a few appliances, including a dishwasher, microwave, and coffeemaker.

There was space for a small table with one or two chairs but no stove. Many of the seniors preferred eating their meals in the communal dining room, where the food was prepared for them.

Every floor had a snack area with fresh fruit, coffee and tea, and usually a few tasty pastries. There were handrails along the hallways to assist those who needed a bit of help walking, and everything was set up to accommodate walkers and wheelchairs.

There wasn't much of a view, but the building was within walking distance of amenities such as a medical clinic, grocery store, and hair salon. Regular field trips were organized for those who wanted to venture out, and there was usually some kind of daily entertainment. All in all, it seemed quite nice.

When I arrived at the apartment, most of the furniture had already been delivered and set up. It was fairly crowded, even though there was a lot less furniture than she had in her house. I saw pictures leaning up against walls and bedding still in bags.

We put on the kettle to make tea and had a little visit while waiting for the water to boil. "Your place is lovely," I told her. "But it must be hard to leave a home you've lived in for so many years."

She looked at me with tear-filled eyes and whispered, "I don't like it here. It just doesn't feel right."

I assured her we would start getting things organized and put away, and maybe it would start to feel more like home. Her daughter and I set up the bedroom, making the bed and arranging some personal things on her dresser. I looked at all the pictures and paintings that needed to be hung and asked, "Which ones would you like in your bedroom?"

She pointed to an old-fashioned oval picture of flowers and asked me to bring it to her. She gently caressed the curved glass and said, "Oh, I just don't know. I've always liked this, but maybe you think it's tacky."

I took a closer look and realized it was a cross-stitch of flowers made with buttons and pieces of fabric and jewelry interwoven throughout the artwork. I had never seen anything like it. "Did you make it?" I asked.

She told me that her own mother had made it and incorporated special mementos such as an earring that once belonged to her grandmother.

It included a button from her uncle's military uniform — an uncle who had died in the war. There was a piece of lace from a wedding gown and a tiny satin bow from a baby's christening outfit — all special keepsakes from her family's history, spanning five generations. Each unique item became part of the creation, adding sparkle and texture to the homemade work of art.

"This is really incredible," I said, and then I noticed the look on her daughter's face.

"I've seen that picture my whole life but never knew the history behind it. She never told me," she added softly. "But I guess I never asked."

That became the first picture we hung up — in the bedroom where she could see it as she fell asleep and first thing in the morning when she woke up. She also agreed to take some time in the next few weeks to write down the history and tuck it behind the frame so it could be shared with future generations.

She told us more family stories as we set up her new home, putting a homemade quilt on her bed and draping a crocheted afghan over her sofa. We placed family photos and knickknacks on the shelves and tried to arrange everything to her liking.

It was a small fraction of the treasures she had in her old house, but we showcased the special antiques and family heirlooms that were near and dear to her heart. More importantly, we put her favorite artwork and photos where she could see and enjoy them.

We gave everything a final dusting and took her downstairs to the dining room, where she was introduced to some of the other seniors living in the complex. Her daughter agreed to stay for a few more hours to help transition her mom into her new home.

I went back to my own family feeling good about what we'd accomplished that day. A little bit of time and elbow grease had helped make the new apartment feel like a home, but listening to a lifetime of memories turned a sad time into a special walk down memory lane.

— Lori Kempf Bosko —

31

When It's Time

If we are facing in the right direction,
all we have to do is keep on walking.
~Buddhist Saying

Ray curled our fingers together as we walked toward the theater. What could be more romantic than a Johnny Mathis Christmas concert? My heart stirred with love and pride as I looked over at my husband. After sixteen years of marriage, I still found him movie-star handsome. "You look lovely tonight," he said to me, and then, "The moon is up, nearly full. Perfect for tonight."

We chatted about the weather, unusually warm for December, about one of his daughters who had called that afternoon, and about our plans for Christmas Day when his children and mine, with their children, would gather in our home for our traditional family gift exchange. Once we were settled in our seats, Ray again reached for my hand. My heart leapt with joy. He hadn't done that in months, if not years. I was once again with the man I had fallen so madly in love with.

I was sure Ray was the love of my life when I married him. But each year of our marriage grew harder, the moments like tonight rarer. This sweet, good-natured man became more and more anxious and argumentative. Eventually, we learned the reason why: Alzheimer's.

When Ray got his diagnosis, I immediately enrolled us in classes and support groups at the Alzheimer's Association. I pored through books that offered recommendations for dealing with issues such as when to take away the car keys and how to take control of the finances. I read memoirs by men and women who knew firsthand the kind of devastating loss and loneliness I experienced caring for my husband. Ray began taking an experimental drug to dissolve plaque in his brain. We developed close friendships with other couples dealing with Alzheimer's and sometimes went to dinner with them.

Then going anywhere out of our routine became too confusing for Ray and increased his anxiety. I noticed a bone-deep weariness growing in me and a worsening depression that manifested daily in a headache and extreme fatigue.

In support groups, the question of when it was time to place a loved one frequently came up. Reluctantly, I looked down the terrible road ahead of us. "I'll place him when he wanders," I said. But, according to our neurologist, 40 percent of people with Alzheimer's never wander. Even well into mid-stage Alzheimer's, with his short-term memory and problem-solving skills mostly gone, Ray could walk miles without losing his way.

"I'll place him when he is incontinent," I said. But his medical team included a wonderful urologist, and when Ray had mild incontinence, medication adjustments took care of the problem.

"I'll place him if he gets too obstinate," I said. But as he grew more obstinate, I could see that his world was becoming so confusing that he would naturally be more anxious and prone to angry outbursts. *It is the disease, not him,* I reminded myself, although I cringed at his frequent criticism.

My shoulders grew rounder, my blood pressure went higher, and my heart raced despite my efforts to do everything recommended for caregivers' self-care. Other caregivers were also developing health issues but made light of the statistics that at least 50 percent of caregivers die before their loved ones with Alzheimer's. We simply continued to focus each day on providing the best life possible for our spouses.

Occasionally, I saw a glimmer of the man I had married. We had been ballroom dancers, and one day when a waltz played on the radio, I pulled him into dance position and counted 1-2-3 until he had the beat and moved with the music. My spirits soared. Then, abruptly,

Ray sank onto the couch, exhausted. His eyes grew blank again. Mine filled with tears. The music played on.

At a funeral for his best friend, Ray became his charming, social former self. He remembered most of the man's extensive family and chatted and laughed with everyone, calling many of them by name. I watched, amazed and delighted. There he was, the man who had been waiting for me when I walked down the aisle.

The next day, Ray sat hunched in his recliner, looking even sadder than the evening he learned of his friend's death. "I didn't talk to anyone at the funeral," he said.

"You did, sweetie," I assured him, my hand on his shoulder. "You were great. You talked to everyone."

"No, I didn't," he said despondently, not believing me.

"I don't know how I can go on another day," I wrote more and more often in my journal.

At my annual physical, my doctor ordered an EKG, compared the results to a baseline EKG, and was alarmed by the differences she saw. I felt more and more overwhelmed. I increased therapy sessions from monthly to weekly, and the therapist and I examined many issues. This was my second marriage, Ray's third. We had no children together. Ray needed a very structured, quiet environment. He now found even visits with family and close friends a strain. I wasn't ready for my world to shrink. And my health issues frightened me.

One day, I lunched with the daughter of Ray's close friend Molly, who also had Alzheimer's. We had visited Molly a number of times in an adult foster-care home located in the neighborhood where Ray had lived with his second wife. The first time we visited her, Ray had said, "I could live here. It's so peaceful and quiet." I'd been stunned, more fully realizing what a limited world he wanted and needed.

"They're moving Mom to a room off the dining room so they can watch her more closely," Molly's daughter told me.

"So, the big front bedroom is vacant?"

"Yes."

I caught my breath. Was it time? When I met Ray, he owned a restaurant and ran a large golf program in our activities club. Now, his needs had changed. He might be happier with the structure of the foster home, living in a neighborhood he remembered better than the places we had lived together. And I could heal. I agonized over the decision. Then, with the help of his children, I placed him.

He has been there more than three months and tells everyone he is content. He describes the walks he takes past large, lovely homes and along a canal, and talks about his friendship with Molly.

Today, as we strolled together in his neighborhood, I thought about how lucky we are. Ray is happy. My health is improving. Yet a part of me still feels like maybe I let him down in some way. Some of my caregiver friends continue to care for their spouses at Ray's stage of Alzheimer's. I don't know if I will ever feel like I did enough. Placing a loved one is such an individual choice. My heart goes out to all those making the decision that it's time.

— Samantha Ducloux Waltz —

Strategies and Tips for Coping

32

Grandma's External Hard Drive

To ease another's heartache is to forget one's own.
~Abraham Lincoln

I was determined to find a way to help my mother after she had a series of mini strokes. She remained quite normal in many ways, but although she could remember many things that happened years before, her short-term memory was almost nonexistent. She didn't recall things like leaving the gas on under the teakettle, which made her a danger to herself. After she was diagnosed with dementia, her doctor suggested moving her to assisted living.

My sister flew to Los Angeles from Alaska and helped me with the move. It was a big adjustment for Mom, who had always been independent. She peppered us with questions like, "How long will I be here on vacation?" and "What happened to my apartment?" Somewhat living in the past, she was once again a young woman in her mind, concerned that her mother wouldn't know where she was. Questions and concerns like that consumed her, and all we could do was repeat the same answers.

Other than that, she was the same loving woman she always was — never mean or rebellious like some dementia patients. But if she couldn't find answers to the questions, she became agitated. For her, it was like being in a room without doors or windows, while the answers were just outside. Sometimes, the door opened, but only for a short time before it slammed shut again.

Mom was eighty-seven at the time. I jokingly told her she was an "old duck," and her mother would be about 140 if she was still living, but she couldn't relate to the timeline. How could she? She had lost the ability to put things like that into perspective. I assured her that her furniture was in a safe place and never balked at the twenty calls a day I received as she repeated her questions over and over. She continued to worry about my grandmother knowing where she was and when her "vacation" would be over. I soon realized she thought she was staying in a hotel.

In a moment of inspiration, Grandma's External Hard Drive began as a list tacked to the wall of her apartment in assisted living. "Answers to My Questions" was written across the top of the bright yellow sheet in bold letters. My sister and I considered everything she asked on a repetitive basis and added them to the list along with answers. Later, we found it helped to give her a second list that she carried in her purse. Like Sophia on *The Golden Girls* TV show, the purse was always with her, and all it ever carried was the list. She consulted it many times a day. Although the page became quite tattered, I could see how much it calmed her.

Eventually, the list evolved into a little book created from index cards, and that's when my son dubbed it "Grandma's External Hard Drive." It was much more elaborate than the list. The cover had her photo, her name and ANSWERS TO MY QUESTIONS in bold lettering. Each page had one question with the answer or explanation printed in large letters. The facing page had a photo of a family member or group of family members with their names and relationships printed below. Altogether, the little book was about thirty pages. The cards were laminated back-to-back and bound into a book form so she could flip the pages. Later, I went to using little 4x6 vinyl photo albums and sealed each page with tape so the index cards could not be removed.

After she moved to a nursing home when she was ninety, she had one book for her purse and one for the front desk. I also kept two or three spares at my house because she fingered the pages so often that the books had to be replaced when they wore out. The mere fact that she could open her purse and find the answers her mind couldn't retain gave her peace of mind. If her book disappeared, she could go to the desk to see the other one there. She used to show people her purse and say with pride, "This is where I keep my important papers."

As time went on, other residents of the nursing home began to covet Grandma's External Hard Drive, and her books would disappear without explanation until one would be found in someone else's room. Everyone wanted one, and with their impaired memories, it didn't matter what information was in the book — they just wanted one of their own. One day as I was visiting Mom, a man I'd seen many times sat at the far end of the table. He never spoke, but he often grunted. We were looking through her book as she pointed to various family members and said their names. Suddenly, the man moved closer and looked at me with hope in his eyes.

"When will I get my book?" This man hadn't uttered a word in three years. The caregivers were amazed. One even had tears in her eyes.

"Soon," I promised him. On my next visit, I brought him one of the books, knowing it didn't matter that it was my family, not his — my mother's questions, not his. He had a book.

I suggested to the home that it might be a good idea to contact the families of their residents to see if little books like Mom's could be made for them. Many didn't want to put the time into doing something like that for their mother, father, aunt or uncle, and that made me sad. Others thought it was a great idea, and soon several residents had an answer book.

I cannot tell you how many books Mom went through over the ten years she used them, but until she passed away nearing her ninety-seventh birthday, she always kept her purse containing its precious book close to her.

"Honey," she would say as she clutched her book, "thank you for making this for me." Then she would give me a kiss and add, "I love you."

When I think about the peace and happiness that book brought our mother, and some of the other residents who either had a copy of hers that they had purloined or one made by a loving family member, I am filled with joy that my sister and I created that first book.

— Morgan St. James —

33

Sam

Doctors diagnose, nurses heal,
and caregivers make sense of it all.
~Brett H. Lewis

I'm my mother's sole caregiver. I shop, cook, and clean, and I can manage all that. But as she ages, my mother requires more care. I now schedule her doctors' appointments, provide transportation to medical offices, consult with physicians, fill prescriptions, review test results and file reports.

Remembering and managing the flood of information from all the doctors and following their orders is wearing me down. There's this "ologist" and that "ologist," and each one adds another medication to an ever-expanding list. Did the internist say he wanted to see my mother in three months, six months or tomorrow? Or maybe that was the dermatologist. What did the orthopedist say the diagnosis was? Spondylo... lo... what? I'm pulling out my hair. How many pills did the gastroenterologist prescribe? Did she want my mother to take them before breakfast, lunch, dinner or with a glass of wine? Maybe the wine is for me.

How to keep my sanity? How to handle my stress? How can I provide good care for my mother if I'm losing my mind? Help!

Sam to the rescue! Who? Not a who. A what! Sam is a spiral notebook.

During one medical visit, lightning struck as I watched the physician's assistant tap the doctor's words into an electronic device. I realized then that I may not be tech-savvy, but I can write. The physical act of writing calms me down and keeps me focused. I got a notebook.

Always at the ready, Sam the notebook needs no downloading time or passwords. He never malfunctions, crashes or needs to recharge. And no worries if I drop him.

Tucked into my tote, Sam accompanies me to all my mother's appointments. Some doctors give me a sidelong glance when I pull Sam out of my bag and open him. I shrug it off. Better to get a fisheye than to give up my Sam. "Did you forget your tablet?" a doctor often asks as I begin to write. I smile, wave my notebook, and answer, "I didn't forget it. I've got this." In a keyboarding world, writing is an odd sight, but I'm sticking with my ballpoint. When the doctor states the diagnosis, I say, "Could you please spell that?" Sam graciously offers me a blank page to write it all down.

"Let me see when the last visit was," the cardiologist says. By the time he clicks onto my mother's file, waits for the information to download and searches the data, I've already flipped through Sam and found the date. "August 20th," I tell him.

"My computer is a little slow today," he explains.

Well, not Sam! While the doctor continues waiting for the records to appear on the screen, I tell him my mother's weight, blood pressure and EKG results. He thanks me for the report. I thank Sam.

I'm all for technology, but a simple notebook makes a big difference in my life, giving me control and a way to cope. Sam is my partner. He's the lifejacket I wear to survive choppy medical waters. With him I'm able to track all the different doctors and keep straight everything they tell me. Information is literally at my fingertips, easy and organized. No longer feeling so overwhelmed with caregiving responsibilities, I provide better care for my mother.

Now that I'm aging and have more doctors of my own, I'm thinking about starting another notebook — for me. One with a red cover would be nice.

— Hannah F. Garson —

34

The Bobblehead Dog

*Common sense and a sense of humor are the same
thing, moving at different speeds. A sense of humor
is just common sense, dancing.*
~William James

Shortly after my grandmother was diagnosed with Alzheimer's, her behavior began to change drastically. The woman I had grown up with, who followed a daily routine, cooked marvelous meals, and had a strong faith, was suddenly acting more like a child. She was crying when confused or overwhelmed, forgetting faces, and getting angry at people who were trying to help her.

I watched as my grandfather tried to help her, but she was quite stubborn when it came to eating, showering, or taking care of her body. I offered my own help but was met with the same resistance.

One day, my grandfather took her out for a drive, and they stopped at a garage sale. There, they found a bobblehead dog that my grandmother quickly grew fond of.

My grandfather bought it for ten cents, and they returned home for lunch.

As usual, when they sat down to eat, my grandmother refused to try anything. My grandfather suggested she ask her new dog what he thought about her eating lunch.

My grandmother leaned toward the dog and asked, "Should I eat my lunch?"

She bopped the dog on the head, and the dog, being a bobblehead, nodded its head up and down.

Delighted, she started to eat.

This became a daily routine — her refusing to do something and the dog encouraging her. From showering to eating to brushing her hair and getting dressed, the dog motivated her to take care of herself. It was a tremendous help to my grandfather.

Sometimes, when we've tried everything, the solution can lie in getting a little creative. Who knew that a ten-cent bobblehead would prove to be an effective healthcare aide?

— Catherine Graham —

35

Our Secret Game

Trapped by reality, freed by imagination.
~Nicolas Manetta

My father called and said, "I need help with your mother. Would you please come over?" Fearing the worst, I rushed to my parents' home.

Upon arriving, I found them seated on barstools at the kitchen counter, taking their nightly medications. This was not the emergency I had anticipated, but from the frown on Dad's face I saw he was frustrated. Mom was scowling at him and I could tell she was not cooperating. "She won't take her medicine because she wants to know what each pill is for, and I don't know!" Dad said with exasperation.

"Well, Momma, what is wrong? Why won't you take your pills?" I asked gently. Mom glared at me as if I were now the enemy as well.

"He wants me to take these pills, and I want to know why I am taking them," she snapped.

"Well, Mom, they will make you feel better." She glared at me. I realized we were at an impasse.

I cautiously crossed over into her world — the world of dementia. It is a place I can visit and she cannot escape. I picked up the first pill. "This one is for your heart," I explained.

Mom glanced at me. "I didn't know I took a heart pill."

"Yep," I replied and handed it to her. In amazement, I watched as she took the tablet from my fingers and proceeded to swallow it. One down and only eight to go.

"This one is for your brain. This one is for your nose.

"This one is for your hair. This one is for your toes.

"This one is for your knees. This one is for your eyes.

"This one is for your ears. This one is for your elbows."

There was an occasional question. "I take this for my nose?" she asked.

"Yes, ma'am," I replied.

Content with my answer, the game continued. I was afraid we would run out of body parts before she had taken all the medication, but finally the last pill had been swallowed.

"You did a great job, Mom. I am so proud of you," I patted her on the back. A smile spread over her face, and she replied, "I am proud of me, too."

Dad looked at me as if I had just performed magic, and then he grinned and asked, "What just happened?"

"Mom didn't act out to be mean, Dad," I explained. "She just needed answers, and I provided answers for her. By making it fun, perhaps it seemed more like a game, and she played along. Understanding that Mom can no longer return to our reality is important, and crossing over into her reality was my only choice to defuse the situation."

Tears glistened in Dad's ninety-year-old eyes as he thanked me and then added, "It's just so hard these days. I need to be more patient with her."

Mom and I continued playing the game for months. As outside caregivers assisted more, I occasionally walked in and found Mom resisting them. Once I arrived, Dad would wink and we'd use our secret method to bring Mom around again.

— Brenda Creel —

36

Coloring Love

Creativity doesn't wait for that perfect moment.
It fashions its own perfect moments out of ordinary ones.
~Bruce Garrabrandt

Over the phone, Mom's voice sounded flat and disinterested. "I just watch TV all day," she admitted. A few weeks before, she'd moved from her Arizona home to an assisted-living complex. At age eighty-five, Mom was still in "independent living," but I worried about her more and more.

Watching television? All day long? She sounded nothing like the person I remembered, a woman who'd worked full-time, led a Camp Fire group and was known to do the ironing at 3:00 a.m. Even with the normal slowdowns that aging brings, I couldn't imagine her or anyone else staying inside a studio apartment for weeks on end.

At first, I pressed Mom to tell me if the facility offered any physical-fitness activities. "Aren't you allowed to go outside and walk around? Go out and get some sunshine?" It seemed incredible to keep older folks cooped up inside.

But Mom just laughed. "Honey, it's already 110 degrees here in the Valley." In the background, a laugh track roared its approval. I thought about trying to convince her to break down and finally get hearing aids. She practically yelled into her phone, "Who wants to go outside and get roasted?"

Fair enough. The heat was one reason I'd moved all the way to Oregon. I pushed a little harder. "Isn't there anything else to do besides watch the boob tube?" Growing up, I was often reminded that too much TV made you lose brain cells.

"I guess so." Mom paused. "They did hand out these little tablets. You know, they're like computers. We're supposed to do some sort of video thing," she said. "But I can't remember how to work it." She sighed. "So, I just watch TV."

"Speaking of TV," I said, "do you mind turning yours down a little?"

Mom put down the phone. After a few moments, the background noise subsided. "There. That's better," she said as if it had been her own idea.

I wasn't ready to let go of my worry. "Goodness, you must be so unhappy — and bored. I wish I were there to help you." At that moment, I did feel pretty helpless. I wanted Mom to be the active woman I'd always known. And to be honest, I was scared. Would I slide into the same rut as Mom? How long before I'd park myself in front of the flat screen and wile away the days watching *Wheel of Fortune,* too? My own mother was proof that my golden years were coming much sooner than I expected.

But Mom just chuckled again. "No, I'm not bored. And really, I'm not unhappy — although I'd love to be out shopping at Pier 1 again. I do wish I had something to keep my hands busy."

"It costs a bundle to live there, Mom. Can't they at least offer something to occupy your time?"

A lightbulb seemed to go on. "You know," she said, "when they deliver our meals, they put the tray on a chair outside my door. And lately they also leave some pages with pictures to color."

"Do you like coloring the pictures?"

"Oh, yes. I mean, I would if I had some colored pencils."

Now, my own lightbulb came on. That same day, I rounded up a couple of adult coloring books, a nice set of pencils and even a little battery-powered sharpener and shipped them off to Mom in Arizona.

A few days later, I phoned Mom again. Her voice bounced with enthusiasm. "I just love the books and pencils," she said. "Thank you. I especially like the book with the cats wearing hats."

"Glad you like them. I got some for myself, too." Joy surged through me. "Now, you won't have to sit and watch TV all day long." I felt strong and wise, as if I'd just told old age to take a flying leap.

Mom paused. "Oh, I still watch TV," she said. "But now I can watch and color at the same time."

"Well, don't forget to get up and move around a little. I worry about you sitting so much."

"Okay, okay," Mom said. "Honey, I gotta run. My favorite game show's on."

As much as I wished Mom would learn how to do the video chat, the set of watercolor pencils and coloring books spoke to her in a way that kept her mind and her hands occupied. She wasn't ironing at 3:00 a.m. anymore, but she was doing something creative again, and I wasn't worrying about her as much. Maybe I'd figure out a way to help her with the video chat, and then she could share some of her masterpieces. I switched off the TV and picked up my new pencils, ready to color my own worries away.

— Linda S. Clare —

More than Just a Blanket

The excellence of a gift lies in its appropriateness rather than in its value.
~Charles Dudley Warner

When my mom reached the point where she needed daily care, we moved her to the local nursing home. Initially, she was not pleased with that decision, and she felt betrayed by her family and her doctor. For that reason, as a family, we tried hard to make her room at the nursing home feel as comfortable and home-like as possible. The facility allowed us to have a mini fridge in her room, and it was so exciting for her to still be able to offer someone a Pepsi. We also stocked it with baked goods so that she could offer some "goodies" to her visitors. She also had a bookshelf with some of her favorite knickknacks, books and photo albums.

Some of the staff members were excellent and treated her with great kindness. To others, she was just another resident and, some days, just another burden. Mom became annoyed when some would call her "Granny." She would often voice her annoyance to family and say, "I am NOT their granny!" Mom felt that they didn't take enough personal interest to even learn her name. She also questioned me many times on whether she paid to stay there. I told her that she did. She generally retorted, "Well, it sure doesn't feel like it. They treat you with more respect at a hotel!"

The management at the nursing home tried to make every resident feel important and unique, and their efforts did not go unnoticed. They had a photo and the name of each resident beside the door of their room. In the newer section of the building, each room had a glass bookcase built into the wall beside their door, and residents and family were able to display photos or other personal items that had special meaning to them.

One resident was a former mechanic and had several wrenches and other small hand tools on display. For anyone with the time to listen, he would tell stories about how many antique trucks and tractors he had brought back to life with those old tools.

But Mom still felt as though she was nothing more than "the Granny in Room G240."

Then my sister discovered she could have a blanket made at Walmart with some of Mom's favorite photos printed right into the material. She carefully chose photos that reflected Mom's life over the years, and she gave it to Mom for Christmas.

Mom was thrilled when she saw it but didn't want it on her bed. She wanted it hung on the wall so she could look at it while relaxing in her reclining chair.

What none of us anticipated was the interest it generated. The blanket was large and covered a good portion of one wall, so it was easily noticed. It became quite the conversation piece. It was a helpful distraction when Mom needed to be poked for a blood sample. It also inspired friendly chats while monitoring her blood pressure or with staff as they cleaned her room. Mom would proudly point out her husband, children, grandchildren, great-grandchildren, parents, siblings and in-laws.

Whether it was our imagination or not, it also appeared to us as though the staff took a little more interest in Mom as a person and not just someone who occupied a bed. "Dorothy, is that your husband?" meant far more to Mom than "Granny, it's time for your pills."

The conversations made Mom feel as though the staff was genuinely interested in "who" she was. She became very fond of some of the staff.

But equally important was the fact that she could lie in bed and see her blanket. She said it made her feel as though the family members she dearly loved were all in the room with her. As her health declined and she spent more time in bed, it became even more important. When she opened her eyes in the morning or closed her eyes at night, the first and last thing she saw was her family.

Although the blanket never provided the physical warmth that was originally intended, it provided an emotional warmth that was even more important.

— Brenda Leppington —

The Man Under the Bed

The disease might hide the person underneath,
but there's still a person in there who needs
your love and attention.
~Jamie Calandriello

Her dementia diagnosis came when she was sixty-one years old. My strong, smart, human-resources executive, president of the local Rotary Club, graceful, kind mother had Lewy body dementia. It's the second most common type of progressive dementia, after Alzheimer's disease.

There had been many falls, some hallucinations, some checkbook mistakes, and incidents of leaving the garage door open all night. Mom had trouble sleeping, her hands would tremor, and she was getting lost going to familiar places. When the diagnosis came, I moved from San Diego to New York to be with her on this journey. She had taken care of me, and now it was my turn to take care of her. After all, she was my best friend.

We moved Mom into an assisted-living facility because her doctor was concerned about her safely navigating the stairs of her two-story home. I visited her every day and managed her care. A few months after she moved in, the phone rang.

"Kris, there's a man under my bed," she said.

Now, mind you, the average age in the assisted-living facility was

Strategies and Tips for Coping | 123

eighty. She was sixty-one. If there was a man under her bed, he must have been quite limber, perhaps a former gymnast.

Here's a key lesson I learned: Do not argue with the person with dementia. It will only agitate them and you. Instead of telling her, "There's no man under your bed!" I went into her reality, met her where she was, and started asking questions.

"Okay, Mom, is he banging on the bed?"

"No," she said.

"Is he yelling while you are watching television?" I asked.

"No!" she responded. "He's just under there."

Then I reached into my caregiver bag of tricks — a bag I didn't know I had but kept adding to throughout my mom's dementia journey — and pulled this out: "Well, Mom, he's under there to make sure you go to lunch on time. Why don't you go to lunch, and when you come back, he'll be under Mary's bed telling her to go. He's the under-the-bed-go-to-lunch guy. He works there!"

I held my breath and crossed my fingers.

After a few seconds, Mom responded, "Oh."

I had validated her thoughts and feelings instead of arguing with her, and most importantly, I let her know she was safe. I went into her world, and it worked.

Within the first year of her diagnosis, Mom called me in a panic. We had written appointments on a large calendar in her room, but she soon had trouble keeping track of numbers, dates and seasons.

"Why aren't you here? It says I have a doctor's appointment at 10:00 on Wednesday. It's 10:00!" she exclaimed.

For a second, I panicked. Had I forgotten an appointment? No, Mom had. Many short-term memories disappear for people with dementia, while memories of old remain. We had been to the doctor on Wednesday at 10:00. It was now Thursday. She had no memory of what had happened the day before. I tried to alleviate her concern with humor, but I did not correct her.

"I'm sorry, Mom. The doctor called and cancelled today's appointment. He's going to Aruba!" I exclaimed. "They are always going on vacation! How about I come over, and we'll go to lunch instead. We'll see him when he comes back." It was another holding-my-breath moment.

She relaxed a bit. I am not saying this tactic will work every time, but it is another key stashed in that crucial caregiver bag of tricks, ready for you to try to unlock your loved one's mind. I call it using the "two S's": I would tell her I was *sorry* and that she was *safe*.

One day, I walked into the facility to visit her, and she was very angry. Mom said that I hadn't been visiting her. I had abandoned her there. Didn't I love her?

I felt such pain sear. I *had* been there. Almost every day. But she didn't remember. So, I knelt down to her eye level and gently said, "Mom, I am so sorry I haven't been here. I've been crazy at work doing great things! You would be so proud of me!" And I immediately changed the subject to distract her.

I learned so much during my mom's four years with dementia. It was painful, but there were beautiful moments of togetherness as well. Taking care of her gave me a new passion and purpose in life. I now work for the Alzheimer's Association, sharing those life lessons with others and striving to end the disease that took away my mother. I know she is proud of me.

— Kristen Cusato —

A Rewarding Day

May you live all the days of your life.
~Jonathan Swift

I was so blessed for all the special moments I had with my mother. When she was eighty-two, she thought she was bothering me by asking me to take her to the many doctor visits she had, but it was a privilege for me to spend quality time with her.

I tried to make an adventure of our days together, combining her doctor's visits with running her errands. One day, while we were driving and deciding where to eat lunch, I pulled up to a stoplight and saw a large arcade sign.

I looked at the colorful sign and asked my mother, "Have you ever played Skee-Ball?"

"No," she replied.

I turned at the light.

The venue was mostly empty except for a children's birthday gathering in the back corner. I ordered the special lunch buffet with pizza and salad, and it came with fifty tokens for the arcade games. The cashier had a large smile for my mother as she placed a cup of tokens on the counter. Mom's blue eyes looked down at the shiny golden tokens.

I said, "Arrrgh, 'tis a fine treasure! We are rich!"

It was 2:00 p.m. The lunch buffet was almost gone so the employees made a fresh pizza for us instead.

There was loud music playing and someone in a mouse costume

encouraging the little children to dance. My mother was delighted by the dancing mouse and cheerful music, and we swayed along in our seats. We laughed as the kids tried to follow the mouse's moves.

After we ate, it was time to use those golden tokens. Mom loved playing Skee-Ball and collecting tickets. She moved from game to game like a child. She had fun watching as one machine spewed out seven tickets again and again! She giggled about the super long strand of tickets and placed them around her neck like a necklace. I handed her token after token for the next game to be played… until we ran out of tokens.

When we went to trade in our handfuls of tickets at the automatic counting machine, Mom placed them into the wrong slot. Actually, it wasn't a slot at all, just an opening in the machine where two parts came together. A man had to come and open the whole thing up to get them out! He was very good-natured about it, and we all had a good laugh.

We stood at the redemption counter for a long while as my mother tried to decide what to get with her tickets. Finally, she decided on a toy whistle with the image of the mouse on it. The man gave her an extra one for me, so we had fun blowing them together.

I keep that whistle on my desk, a souvenir of a wonderful experience with my mom as we embraced her willingness to make the most of every day.

— Sheryl L. Fuller —

The Evaporation of Memory

Worry never robs tomorrow of its sorrow,
it only robs today of its joy.
~Leo Buscaglia

"I t's my turn to care for my mom," said my partner, Erika. "You know I've been telling you this for months. This is something I really want to do...." That was her opening line to me after she put a down payment on a house in Naples, Florida. I could either go with her or stay in Los Angeles by myself. I decided to go.

Erika's mom had a stroke in 2013. Aside from her memory issues, she's in pretty good shape for being ninety. She doesn't complain and she doesn't demand. But a large chunk of her brain has evaporated. It's not dementia or Alzheimer's; it's just the residual effects of her stroke.

Over the past two years, we have seen Erika's mom gradually decline. She is becoming more reclusive, sleeping more, and doesn't often want to leave the house. Food, television, and listening to the standards are her main forms of pleasure.

Her short-term memory issues make it impossible for her to retain much information beyond the previous five minutes. We can engage her momentarily, but then the activity flitters into some frontal-lobe abyss. At times, she can recall the particulars of her past two husbands, but even those memories are evaporating.

Being a caregiver wasn't something that I had planned or hoped for. It just sort of happened to me. I'd volunteered for many years at the Culver City Senior Center in Los Angeles, so I knew quite a bit about the aging process and the challenges of being a caregiver.

I try to come up with ways to keep her stimulated. I decided it would be fun to do karaoke with her. She loves the older songs and can recall the lyrics vividly. It gives her a momentary distraction to remember the good old days and sing along with the tunes. Sometimes, we play simple card games like Fish and Old Maid. Those games are easy for her to comprehend, and they gave her some joy.

I have also purchased some children's books for her with print that is large enough so she can read them easily. The plots are simple, and the graphics are engaging. They seem to give her some joy.

If we engage her with recollections of growing up, her memory is intact. But it's sometimes frustrating to converse with her because she rarely initiates any conversation. If she does, she will often ask the same questions over and over. But with my improv background, I just roll with it.

"Did you make this?" she asks. I can't cook a thing, but I always say yes. She seems happy with that answer, and I can pretend that I am a gourmet chef.

If we just roll with her train of thought, it seems to work well. There's no point in correcting her or trying to make her recall the truth of the situation.

I am grateful that Erika's mother is still here and provides some semblance of company. But it's hard to see a loved one deteriorate. Time will tell regarding her care as things progress. I hope I have the strength and patience to continue.

— Mary McGrath —

41

Who Am I Hurting?

Your own self-realization is the greatest service
you can render the world.
~Ramona Maharshi

M y mom was in her early eighties when we first noticed her memory problems. They were minor things, and a gentle reminder would usually set her back on track. She would comment that she hadn't seen her neighbour for several days, and I would remind her that she was away visiting her son. She would respond, "Oh, yes, this old head of mine is getting forgetful."

Over time, as her mobility worsened, her memory did, too. As a family, we made the difficult decision that it was time for her to be placed in a nursing home where she would receive daily care. We tried to make her room in the nursing home look as much like "home" as we could.

Mom was an animal lover and enjoyed the company of her cat, Chico, who helped her through losing my dad. I decided that she needed another Chico, but pets were not allowed in the nursing home. I was thrilled to find a battery-operated cat that would squirm, meow, open and close its eyes, and wash its face. Mom was thrilled when I brought "Chico." She was amazed at how lifelike it was for a toy cat. She would regularly remind me to bring batteries on my next visit because "Chico is slowing down!" We would install new batteries, and he would immediately meow and begin to wash his face. Mom commented about how wonderful it would be if we could do that to humans, too! She used to laugh and say how nice it would be to hear "Dorothy, time to change your batteries" rather than "Dorothy, it's time to take your stack of pills!"

She still enjoyed phone calls from her sisters. Her family was very tight-knit, and family reunions were full of laughter from start to finish. My aunts and uncles had a unique sense of humour. If I walked into Mom's room and saw her on the phone laughing so hard that she was crying, I knew that she was talking to one of her family members.

My mother and father had a marriage that most would envy. They were each other's best friends and enjoyed spending time together, whether it was travelling in their motorhome, visiting friends and family, or going to antique tractor shows. Mom was devastated when Dad died of leukemia when she was seventy. I would often find her starring at their wedding photo. It was generally followed by, "I miss him so much."

Over the years, as Mom's memory continued to fail, I struggled with the reality that my mom and best friend was slowly disappearing. On one visit, I was wallowing in self-pity. When Mom asked, "Can you buy some cat food for Chico?" I responded, "He is just a toy. He doesn't need food." When she mentioned that she should phone her sister, I reminded her that her sister had been gone for four years. When she said she needed to get home to make supper for Dad, I asked her if she didn't remember that he had been gone for twenty years.

I was angry. But I was angry at the world, not my mom. Unfortunately, we often hurt the ones we love most.

Mom just stared at me and then said, "I loved my life. I look back, and I wouldn't have changed a thing. I loved my family. I loved your father. I love my three girls." I held my mom and told her that I was sorry. Those weren't gentle reminders; they were comments reflective of me putting myself first.

After a few minutes, Mom said, "If I think hard enough about it, I know that they are all gone. That is why I like to pretend that my life is the same. Chico is sleeping on the couch. I talked to Edith yesterday. Lorne will soon be home for supper. I loved my life, and I just want to relive a life where I wouldn't have changed a thing. Who am I hurting?"

That conversation changed everything. My visits took on a different tone. I would tickle the chin of her toy cat and ask her what Chico had been up to. I would take old photo albums, and we would look at each page and reminisce. I found that her memory was extremely good as long as we moved back in time about twenty years. She recognised everyone in the photos and always had a story to tell. I found a stack of old letters from her brothers that she had saved and took them to her one by one. She would read the letters as though they had just arrived in the mail and be excited to share the news with me. I no longer reminded her of who was dead or alive. What did it matter?

Did I hear the same stories over and over? Of course, I did. But I also had my mother back. She returned to the same witty, kind person who was always excited to see me… and ready to have coffee and a visit.

We were able to visit and share stories until a week before she died. I am so grateful for those last years. Yes, she was confused at times. But I never tired of hearing her repeatedly tell me how much she loved me and that I was "such a great kid."

If I could give her one final message, it would be, "You weren't hurting anyone, Mom. Thank you for giving me the opportunity to relive some of the happiest years of my life, too."

— Brenda Leppington —

42

Tips for the Transition

Caregiving is a constant learning experience.
~Vivian Frazier

G iggles from the hallway piqued our curiosity. I imagined any number of funny scenarios as my elderly mother exited the bathroom and entered the living room where my sister and I sat anticipating an amusing story.

"What are you laughing about, Mom?"

Inquiring minds wanted to know.

"I'm wearing two pairs of pants. Isn't that funny?"

This was not any scenario I had imagined. I was not amused; I was anxious.

Two pairs of pants! Who knowingly puts on two pairs of pants? Didn't she notice how hard it was to pull the second pair over the first? Wasn't she uncomfortable? It was 4:00 in the afternoon. Surely, she had gone to the bathroom before then, so why was she just noticing? I couldn't stop the questions swirling in my mind.

Mom's contagious laughter eventually drew us in. We began to laugh with her, albeit nervously. This latest faux pas added to the growing list of strange behaviors, leaving us wondering if something more than old age was creeping in.

Was it more than fatigue and the dark of night that caused her to take a wrong turn on a familiar road home? Did mixing up her morning and evening medicines indicate something other than a little confusion? Why couldn't she remember that every item in the Dollar

Tree store cost one dollar? We began to have more questions than answers. Unfortunately, when the answer finally came, it wasn't funny at all. My mother had Alzheimer's disease.

Keeping my mom in her home was top priority, so my siblings and I muddled through making plans for her care. We got some things right and some terribly wrong. Unmet expectations, lack of knowledge regarding her disease, and juggling our emotions and personal lives soon wreaked havoc on our relationships.

Years later, when my ninety-nine-year-old father-in-law passed away, we welcomed my mother-in-law into our home. Determined to do things differently, we had a better grasp of ways to make the transition easier on all of us. These baker's dozen tips can create a smoother transition whether you're caring for a loved one in their home or opening yours.

1. *Use empathy before practicality.* Put yourself in their shoes and imagine having to condense a lifetime of memories and physical belongings into a new, smaller living space. The transition may be harder on them than you realize. Make sure their favorite mementos are seen or stored. Sending the message you value their life's journey helps to allay fears for what may lie down the road.

2. *Validate their feelings of loss.* Whether it's their spouse, health, mobility, or friendships, surrendering life as they knew it affects their emotional stability and the harmony of your relationship. Understanding the difficulty of adjusting goes a long way in creating paths of eventual acceptance to this new stage of life.

3. *Establish boundaries for privacy, whether physical space or topics of conversation.* They may not be ready for help with their financial decisions, and you may not want their two cents about your children or grandchildren. Discussing when to join the family versus enjoying their space will avoid guesswork and the frustration of unmet expectations. Be faithful to uphold visiting or caretaking times whenever possible to earn future trust.

4. *Acknowledge the emotional issues that will arise with role reversals.* After spending your life raising children, you may resent providing care for your parents. They may not be ready to turn over decision-making and they may not want your advice. You may feel anxious or unqualified to plan for their future. Feeling trapped can spiral into self-pity for either one of you. Reaching out for counseling can help you cope, whether individually or in a support group.

5. *Establish parameters for what you can and cannot offer physically, emotionally, and spiritually.* You may enjoy providing meals but are unable to help with housework. Is laundry doable but helping with a bath out of the question? Deciding beforehand what you will and won't be able to perform will determine when outside help is needed.

6. *Listen to their stories.* One day, you'll want someone to listen to yours. Asking questions to reveal new details in a familiar story may surprise you. Take advantage of the time to get to know your loved one as a person, not just a relative. Consider preserving their voice with a recording or write down their stories to pass on your family's heritage.

7. *Practice good communication.* Send "I" messages instead of "you" messages. "I need some time to process" sends a completely different message than, "You're talking too much." Truth spoken with love can ease the angst about bringing up difficult conversations. Reflecting feelings sets the example to have them respect yours. "I can see this move is difficult for you. It's hard on me, too. I wish there was another way, but I'm glad we can learn to make the best of it."

8. *Talk about the future.* What health issues would necessitate the next level of care? Is there a will or medical directive? Who gets the family heirlooms not mentioned in the will? Asking about future desires today may prevent frustration in the future.

9. *Work together to find creative solutions to everyday challenges.* Amazing gadgets wait to be discovered on the Internet. From putting on socks

to opening jars, chances are there is a product to increase your loved ones' independence, lessening their feeling of being a burden.

10. Don't take things personally. Practice overlooking offenses. This time together may provide opportunities to heal past hurts, giving one or both of you the opportunity to find forgiveness. You may even discover a friendship side of your relationship.

11. Preserve relationships outside of the caregiving circle. Connect socially with family and friends and find ways to protect time with your spouse, even if it's just going for a daily walk. Whenever possible, maintain interests or hobbies for a refreshing break. Look into adult day care if necessary, whether in a group setting or your home.

12. Learn to read between the lines and offer help when you see it's difficult for them to ask. Stubborn pride can emerge and create tension on either side of this new caregiving connection. "Is there anything I can do for you today?" offers them a graceful way to ask for assistance without feeling like a burden.

13. Practice your faith. As a Christian, I gain strength knowing help is only a prayer away. Meditating on encouraging Bible verses helps keep my focus on the positive, knowing God will be with us as we navigate these uncharted waters. Hope in a greater power keeps me hanging onto possible endings for our future together.

Growing old isn't for the faint of heart. Eldercare creates opportunities to share in both the joys and burdens of aging. Patience, understanding, and love are needed in abundance to make eldercare more of a joy and less of a burden. Here's to a smooth transition from caring *about* your loved one to caring *for* them.

— Cindy Richardson —

Chapter 5

Blessings & Gratitude

43

Faucet Fairy

Enjoy the little things, for one day you may look back
and realize they were the big things.
~Robert Brault

"This may take some time," I warned my husband Tom as I helped my mother out of the car. We had pulled off the highway for a bathroom break. It was February, and we were traveling from our home up north to our new home in a warmer, sunny state. Mom, who was in her nineties, would be living with us. We looked forward to the milder climate, away from snow and icy sidewalks.

Since we had only been on the road for an hour, we still had miles to go before we could escape the cold and ice. Mom gripped my hand tightly as we inched our way to the restroom. I had my free hand under her elbow for added security. Our steps in sync, we slowly covered the slippery terrain of the parking lot. I glanced back at Tom and noticed he was walking our small pup, Shadow, to a nearby tree.

Spotting a large area of slushy water in our path, I had to re-route Mom around it. That detour added five minutes to our trek. Finally, we arrived at the door of the rest stop. Stomping our feet, we maneuvered inside, still clutching each other. Her tight clench on my fingers loosened a bit as the warm flow of air relaxed us. I looked around for the bathroom, frowning as I realized it was clear across the building.

Our caution continued due to wet areas on the floor. Once again, we took tiny, careful steps, working as a team. We were a five-legged unit if you included Mom's cane. Arriving at the bathroom, I relied on that cane to keep Mom steady. Opening the door, I guided her through and led her to a stall.

"I will be right outside the door," I assured her.

Mom hadn't been in a modern public bathroom in a long time. The few outings she took were to her doctor's office, and the bathroom in that office resembled one found in a house.

"There's no way to flush!" she called out to me.

"It will flush itself when you step away from it," I told her.

"It may be loud," I added.

At that moment, the enormous roar of the flush filled the room. It was intense. When it was over, I listened for Mom's reaction.

"Good golly!" she exclaimed.

I giggled a bit at that one. I had to give through-the-door instructions when it came time for her to unlock the door.

"Lift and slide it, Mom," I said, crossing my fingers.

She struggled long enough for me to panic a bit. Mom's hands were weak, and arthritis interfered with her abilities. I looked at the dirty floor and hoped I wouldn't have to slither under the locked door in order to free her. As I was evaluating whether I would even fit, I heard the click of the lock, and the door opened.

I led her over to the sink. "Where are the handles for the water?" she asked.

"Just wave your hands under the faucet," I instructed. "The water will come out."

She looked at me as if I had grown two heads. Slowly reaching her hands forward, she jerked them back as the water appeared.

"What in the world?" she repeated over and over as she watched the water cascade.

"The soap is over there," I pointed out. "Again, just wave your hand underneath, and it will come out."

Mom flashed a hand under the dispenser. The soap deposited onto the sink. She gave me an accusatory glance.

"Try again but hold your hand still and catch the soap as it comes out."

After six attempts, the soap hit the target.

"I can get the water to flow by myself now," she told me with authority.

I smiled at the pride in her face as she accomplished the task. She approached the hand-towel dispenser confidently, with her arm already outstretched. Her wave was rewarded with the appearance of a paper towel. Her face beamed.

Once again, we linked arms and hands and began the long journey back to the car. But this time, Mom had a bit of a spring to her step.

"I will have to tell Tom about the fancy contraptions in the restroom," she told me. "He won't believe it! Who knew life could be so easy? What a blessing."

Her words made me smile as I realized how correct she was. For caretakers of the elderly or disabled, these "fancy contraptions" are indeed a blessing. The world has bestowed these gifts of convenience in small increments, unnoticed by most of us. But once you walk hand in hand with someone who can't turn handles or push the button on dispensers, it all comes into clear focus. Kindness and caring, compassion and empathy for the needs of others have appeared in many forms. Caretaking is not easy, but looking around I see that help has been arriving. Mom is right... what a blessing.

— Marianne Fosnow —

44

Sing an Old Song

*Music washes away from the soul the dust
of everyday life.*
~Berthold Auerbach

I've been a daddy's girl for sixty-eight years. I was born mid-century to a post-War World II veteran and his lovely wife. They had two daughters, Diane and Sharon. I am Sharon, four years younger than Diane. I discovered later in life that Walt Disney also had two daughters named Diane and Sharon. Like the Disney girls, we grew up in a *Father Knows Best* kind of America.

Even with that great start, we eventually had tough times. First, my sister Diane passed away in 1999. My mother followed her four years later. So, for the past eighteen years, it's been only my dad and me. Of course, I created my own family along the way — a husband, three daughters, and four granddaughters — but my father and I are the last of our original family.

After he lived on his own for almost two years, we decided my father should move in with us. After all, our girls had grown up and moved out. We had the space, and it just made sense. So, at seventy-eight years old, he came to live out his golden years with my husband and me. Amazingly, he stayed for sixteen years. For fifteen of those years, his health was great. He drove his car, walked every day with his buddies, and maintained an active, healthy life.

In January 2020, we made the decision to place Dad in an assisted-living facility. It was difficult because he had been a part of our day-to-day lives for sixteen years, but he needed more care than we could give him. Dad made the move with a good attitude and adjusted well. We were able to visit him often, take him out to lunch, and remain a part of his life.

Two months later, COVID-19 hit. They locked down his facility. No one was allowed inside, and residents were not allowed to leave. It was hard on him, and it was hard on us. We were only allowed "window visits." We had to make an appointment to sit outside in front of a window and peer inside while speaking on our phones to each other. It was difficult to see each other, and Dad even had trouble getting in and out of the little chair.

Since Dad lived on the first floor, I opted to visit him through his own window. This was a feat because I first had to make my way through the azalea bushes to get close enough to the window to see inside. Still, we were able to occasionally visit for a short while.

It is hard to explain how I feel about being cut off from my dad. Even as an adult child, feelings of sadness and loss exist when lifelong connections are severed. Yes, we can talk on the phone daily, but the human interactions of touch, facial expressions, and occasional hugs are greatly missed.

A few days after Christmas, I got a surprise from an unexpected source. This surprise has brought me much joy and a new connection with Dad that I never would have anticipated. You see, my dad loves music, specifically classic country music. In fact, he once wanted me to join him in a father/daughter country vocalist duo. He had the backup band and everything. But that's another story for another time. Needless to say, Dad loves old country songs from his younger days.

When he moved to assisted living, I let him take along my little Amazon Echo, a smart speaker device that plays music on demand. He loves using it because it connects him with all the music of his past. All he has to say is, "Alexa, play Willie Nelson," and instantly he is able to hear Willie Nelson singing, "Blue Eyes Crying in the Rain."

During this past "COVID-19 Christmas," my daughter gave me another Echo because I had given mine to Dad. I set it up next to my big, comfy chair where I sit every morning to sip my coffee. That's when I noticed the screen read, "Recently played: Keep on the Sunny Side." I thought, *I didn't play that song.* Then it occurred to me, *Dad just played that song!*

Next, he played, "One Day at a Time," and I realized I was getting these notifications because we were on the same account. Tears came to my eyes as I thought of him alone in his room listening to his old songs. Through this little device sitting on my side table, I was given a view into what my dad was thinking and feeling. It was evident that he was trying to cheer himself up with his music.

When I told my daughter about this, she said she once asked him, "What do you do to cheer yourself up?" And he responded, "I sing an old song."

That is just what this man does. I can be sitting in my chair reading or working on my computer, and I will see the screen light up with another song notification. Instantly, I will feel an emotional connection. I know my ninety-five-year-old father is sitting alone in his little room, reminiscing about his life so long ago with Mom, Diane, and me. And those old songs from long ago bring him much comfort, as they do for me.

— Sharon Carraway Jones —

45

I Found the Right Gift

When you are grateful, fear disappears
and abundance appears.
~Tony Robbins

Walking along the Lockport Canal, I spotted two women coming toward me. The elderly woman had a cane in her right hand and moved slowly. I noticed white hair poking out from underneath her hat. The woman next to her strolled along at the same pace. Upon a closer look, I decided they must be mother and daughter.

The daughter looked tired. Her shoulders sagged. I remember the pressure I had as I tried to take care of my aging mother. I was a wife and mother who worked full-time and felt like I was losing at the juggling act.

The two moved to a bench by the water. I stood at the railing observing but unable to hear any conversation. The daughter reached into her pocket and handed her mom a snack. They both laughed.

I began to think about my mom. My mother had helped me grow into the person I've become. She offered life tidbits along the way. "Friends will come and go out of your life. You just have to adjust."

I remember when my mom left the stove on, so I removed the handles. Problem solved. The front door was open, and I put a sign on the inside. "Mom, lock the door." That solution failed. It remained unlocked.

How could I leave her to fend for herself? The answer was simple:

I couldn't.

I knew I had to act to keep her safe like she protected me when she took my tiny hand and walked me to kindergarten.

I talked to my brother and sister. Together, we tried to come up with a solution. A few weeks later, my sister-in-law came up with the idea of a college student.

Living close to a college, I contacted someone in Student Services. I asked for a responsible student to live with my mom free of charge.

The college worker said hesitantly, "I'll see what I can do."

I hung up the phone feeling like I had reached another dead end. The surprise phone call came a few days later.

"I may have someone for you, Joanna. She's living in New York City but is originally from Ghana," the college rep said. "Do I have your permission to give her your phone number? She's here only for a day."

"Sure, and thank you," I replied.

Within a few minutes, the call that changed my mom's future came through. We met at a local doughnut store. I didn't want anyone to know where my mother lived.

Driving to the destination, I was filled with doubt. *What was I doing? Am I crazy allowing a complete stranger into my mom's house? Will this even work? What questions should I ask?*

My desire to protect my mom pushed me forward as I sat at a red light.

Walking into the doughnut shop, I saw her before she saw me. On the table sat the college's admissions manual. *Could she be as nervous as I am?* With every step I took forward, I felt another pushing me back.

"Hi, I'm Joanna," I said, extending my hand.

"Gifty," she said and smiled.

We both felt a little awkward, but I asked, "Tell me a little bit about yourself."

"First of all, thanks for seeing me. I hope you are an answer to my prayer."

I was hoping the same.

"I'm originally from Ghana, but my family lives in New York City now. I'm hoping to go to college to be a nurse, but I can't afford the dorm," she said with a tear in her eye.

"Let me tell you what I'm looking for," I said. I took a deep breath and slowly let it out. "My mom has dementia. She's in the early stages. I need someone to be my eyes and ears. Someone responsible, someone who will care for her. That person would get a free room and use of the Internet living with my mom."

More tears from Gifty. Then she spoke. "I know you don't know me, but I'm very responsible. I would never do any harm to your mom, and I want so badly to be a nurse."

I believed her. I don't know why, but I did.

She continued, "In Ghana, I was taught to take care of my elders with respect. My grandmother has passed, but I helped take care of her."

We chatted a bit more, and I asked for references. I know the people could have been relatives, but something told me to trust my gut. I felt Gifty was telling the truth.

She was prepared. She handed me a list. "These are people from New York City who can vouch for my character."

"Who are they to you?" I asked.

Pointing, she said, "This one is a former employer, and this one is my current employer."

"And this third one?" I asked.

"A friend. I thought you'd want to know me as a friend, too."

I told her I'd get back to her after I spoke with her references. The words I heard to describe Gifty were "dependable, honest, trustworthy and genuinely kind." Now I had to make a decision. My instinct said yes.

My mom's past words swirled in my head. "Joanna, be open to meeting new people. There's a lot of good folks around."

I think back to waiting on my mom's porch. A car stopped in front of the house and out came Gifty pulling a suitcase behind her.

She smiled. "What should I call your mom?"

"Everyone calls her Nana. It means grandmother in Italian."

"Can I call her Nana? I miss my grandmother."

"I'd like that," I replied.

The first night, I was nervous. Was Gifty everything her references said? Was I copping out or finding a good solution?

Unannounced, I stopped by the next day and peeked into the large picture window. There sat my mom eating lunch with Gifty. I moved away from the window and rang the doorbell so I wouldn't startle anyone when I used my house key.

"It's me — Joanna!" I shouted.

Gifty met me at the door. "Are you hungry? I made lunch for your mom. There's plenty."

I joined them at the table, where conversation flowed freely.

Gifty was more than her references. She was truly a gift.

When Gifty graduated, I contacted the college to find another responsible student to live with my mom.

My mom lived ten years in her own home before she died. My siblings and I were able to keep my mom safe and cared for. We welcomed four nurses, three teachers and one student who decided to put college on hold. I am thankful for all of them.

A simple walk by the canal that day, observing another mother and daughter, helped me see I had done the best I could.

— Joanna Montagna Torreano —

Meeting
Ms. Smolinsky

Music is the moonlight in the gloomy night of life.
~John Paul Friedrich Richter

I had relocated to the Midwest after living on the West Coast for more than thirty years. For months, I unsuccessfully sought new friends and new employment. I was lonely and depressed, and I wondered if I was too old or unlikable to fit in.

One day, I decided to stop feeling sorry for myself. It was time to do something worthwhile and make a contribution. I recalled seeing a call for hospice volunteers at the local hospital.

Could I handle comforting someone who was soon to die? What would I say? Did I have the strength to put my feelings of sadness aside and enjoy each moment spent with them? Then I recalled the wonderful individuals who visited my own mother when she was dying of cancer, and how she looked forward to their arrival each week. Yes, I could handle this; I knew it in my heart.

That very day, I contacted the hospice supervisor, and we met that afternoon. They explained that a thorough background check was required, and they would contact me once the report came in.

It took a bit over a week until I heard that they would welcome me as part of the Hospice Volunteer Team. But first, I was sent to the hospital's lab for blood work to be certain I had no communicable diseases. So, off I went to what I laughingly call The Vampires. After drawing the blood, they said I'd hear from someone within three days.

Tina, the hospice volunteer supervisor, called me two days later and asked me to come into her office to discuss the different patients and my availability. I found their greatest need was for volunteers at nursing homes, so I readily agreed to meet with my first patient, Ms. Smolinsky, the following day at Rolla Manor Care.

I had no idea what to expect for I was told only that Ms. Smolinsky had Alzheimer's. After checking in with the head nursing station, they led me to a community room and told me to wait while they alerted Ms. Smolinsky that she had a visitor.

While waiting, I scanned the room full of women and men who seemed pleased to see me. I had brought my keyboard with me and they seemed curious about it. I introduced myself, saying I was there to visit Ms. Smolinsky. I decided I might as well entertain them while I waited, so I set up the keyboard. I played a very simple song I thought they might recall, "Twinkle, Twinkle, Little Star." I knew it was the right choice when a few sang along with me.

I noticed a few nurses and aides had gathered at the doorway to watch. The staff joined in the singing as I played the second song, "Joy to the World." Then, Ms. Smolinsky entered. I ceased playing as they led her to my side. She spoke in gibberish, so I could only nod my head and smile. It seemed we weren't going to have any meaningful conversations.

How was I to comfort my patient? When I looked into Ms. Smolinsky's eyes, I saw a spark of interest. But in what? Oh, yes, of course, she wanted me to play more music. That had to be it. I played another song. More guttural sounds came from her mouth, and she placed her hands onto the keyboard. What could she want? She pushed her fingers onto the top of the keyboard and bounced them up and down. Then it dawned on me: She wanted to play. I didn't know what to do, for I figured she'd pound on it like a child.

She became louder with her unrecognizable words and more forceful as she pounded on the keyboard. I asked her, "Do you wish to play, Ms. Smolinsky?" As if she understood, she nodded. What did I have to lose? If it gave her happiness, we could listen to the pounding of keys for a few minutes.

I stepped aside, and Ms. Smolinsky took my place before the keyboard. I readied myself for the inevitable when I heard the most beautiful, concerto-style music fill the air. I glanced at my patient and saw her lost in another world — one full of beauty, passion and magnificent sound.

The room was silent, all eyes focused on this miracle we shared. Our hearts and souls were full of joy as we were one with Ms. Smolinsky. What a grand present she had brought to us this day.

When she tired of playing, I gave her a huge hug. And as I smiled, our eyes locked. I saw life in those eyes. I saw purpose. And, most of all, I saw her as a valuable person who, on that day and many more to come, would enrich all of us with her talent.

Thank you, Ms. Smolinsky. I know none of us who witnessed the outstanding music shall ever forget the gift you brought to us.

—Monica M. Brinkman—

Screen Time

*A grandma and granddaughter always share a special
bond, which is engraved on their hearts.*
~Author Unknown

"I don't want to make the texts. Show me how to do a selfie."
That's how my grandma started our first iPhone training
session.

My ninety-one-year-old grandma needed a better
mobile phone because she was never home. She thought it would be
foolish to keep paying for a landline when all she needed was a phone
she could carry in her purse. Her old flip phone for emergencies was
no longer cutting it. So, I got my grandma an iPhone with an orange-
striped case — orange because it's her favorite color — and added her
to my plan. Every month, she mails me a check, and when I don't
cash it, she scolds me.

We sit side by side on the couch as I go through her new phone,
starting with the basics. She handles the phone like one would a live
bomb, unsure how it's put together and afraid to touch the wrong thing.
As a girl of sixteen, she learned how to drive a '36 Nash with the stick
shift on the floor. Throughout her life, she's navigated everything life's
thrown at her — wars, civil rights, divorce and the loss of her only child,
my mother. By comparison, this is minor, but she's nervous, afraid she's
too old to learn. Still, she loves the orange case. She's quietly focused
and determined, and I know she'll navigate this, too.

We've gone through the screens many times. We practice calling each other. Each time, it gets a little easier. She touches the screen so softly that it doesn't register the movement of her smooth fingertips. I tell her not to be afraid — she won't break it. I remind her to hit the Home button if she gets stuck because home is where you go when you don't know what else to do. She taught me that.

Soon, she's mastered making and answering calls. As a kid, we would only call at certain times because long-distance calls were expensive. We had a signal. The phone would ring once, and then my mom would call her back. Now, with unlimited voice and data, she can call whomever she wants whenever she wants, but she has fewer people to call. I enter in all her numbers and show her the contact list, which she never uses. She doesn't need to. She has all the phone numbers memorized. Each year, her contact list gets smaller, but she holds on tight to the ones who are left.

When I show her the photo gallery, she lights up. She can't believe that she can look at all her pictures anytime she wants and, more importantly, whip them out at a moment's notice to show her friends. With the exception of the photos in frames on her walls, most of her printed pictures are in boxes in the storage locker or passed on to family or friends. She figures out the camera right away, and we take selfie after selfie before settling on a good one to send to her friend — the only other person in her group who has a smartphone. For a brief moment, I think about showing her how to edit the photo to add filters and funny hats but decide to save that for another day. I know she would love that.

During the next lesson, we introduce a few apps. I thought she would be excited about *Candy Crush*, but she's more amazed that she can get a weather report whenever she wants one. We Uber to a restaurant for lunch — an exercise to keep her freedom since she gave up her car. Instead of being buried in her phone during the ride, she collects the driver's story, offering advice and encouragement. Next to her, I put away my phone and join in the conversation. The three of us arrive at the restaurant as friends. She can't stop talking about what a nice young man he was and how she hopes he asks that girl to marry him. For her, the phone lives in her purse, not her hand. It's not a tether.

When she was born, transatlantic calls weren't a thing. It took effort to see and talk to the people they loved. Now, my son FaceTimes with her. Each time, it thrills her—the surprise of having her boy suddenly appear in her living room. He's tried to show her how to do it, but it hasn't stuck. He doesn't realize that she enjoys the time spent with him, heads bent over a common objective, more than she cares about the lesson in videoconferencing.

Sometimes, I get calls from strange numbers. When I answer, it's one of my grandma's friends telling me her phone is broken. So, after work, I drive over to her apartment and flick the silencing switch back to its original setting. Like magic, the phone starts making noise again. They are amazed at my technical skills. I am happy to have solved a problem so easily. These impromptu tech-support visits always end with a shared meal around her kitchen table, the one we've moved from her house to apartment after apartment over the years.

I've tried multiple times to show her how to text, but she always refuses. The letters are too small and in the wrong order. After a lifetime of working in bakeries and butcher shops, she doesn't know the QWERTY keyboard. She has no use for it now. Her patient fingers, the ones that once taught me how to thread a sewing machine and build a house of cards, aren't steady anymore. It's okay. As she repeatedly tells me, she doesn't want to make the texts. She needs to hear our voices to know we're all right. So, when my phone rings, I know who it is. She's the only person who calls me instead of texting.

— Meadoe Hora —

48

Those Three Additional Years

All that we behold is full of blessings.
~William Wordsworth

"Call me and let me know how his surgery goes," I instructed my brother before I hung up the phone. My seventy-two-year-old dad had been having back problems for about two years. It had gotten so bad that he walked hunched over, in constant pain. The folks at his work moved his desk closer to the door so he wouldn't have to walk as far and gave him a parking spot right in front.

My brother and I hoped this surgery would fix the problem by taking the pressure off his fractured discs and give him a chance to regain mobility. And maybe even golf again!

The surgery went well. With me in Nashville and them in Cincinnati, I had to rely on my brother to share information. Finally, I was able to call Dad. He was groggy but said he already felt better. The sharp pain was gone, replaced by the normal temporary pain of surgery.

I went to bed hopeful. He would be going home the next day, have a few weeks of recovery and physical therapy, and that would be that.

The next morning, my brother called me. The physical therapist had come to the room to help Dad get out of bed and walk a bit before being discharged. Dad threw a blood clot. It went to his brain, and they were airlifting him to University of Cincinnati Medical Center.

We jumped in the car and drove as fast as we felt comfortable. It was five hours of calls, updates, questions, and sobbing. They said it was a massive stroke, and they weren't sure he would make it. How unfair! He was young and healthy. It was a fairly routine surgery.

As we pulled into the parking lot, Dad was in ICU and alive. We met with the team of doctors who showed us images of Dad's brain and the extent of damage from the stroke. More than three quarters of his brain had been affected. We heard a litany of words and had no idea what they meant: aphasia, hemiplegia, agnosia, apraxia. Basically, they didn't know what effect the stroke would have on Dad or what, if anything, he would be able to do or understand.

The next day, Dad woke up, and we were able to briefly visit him. He was alive but not out of the woods. My husband and I stayed with my brother for almost a week, visiting, waiting and watching Dad to see if the doctors could determine the extent of the damage and what type of recovery we could expect. From what the doctors could surmise, Dad was now paralyzed on his entire right side and could no longer talk. We were told to be hopeful that these things could be reversed with therapy.

By the end of the week, the social worker at the hospital had found a bed for Dad at UC Drake, a stroke-recovery facility in Cincinnati. My brother and I had high hopes that this team of doctors would be able to reverse some of the damage from the stroke. Though he might not play golf again, walking with a cane wouldn't be terrible. And if he learned to talk again, even a little, we could take it slow and help him find the right words for the situation.

Once he moved to Drake, a team of doctors and therapists worked to determine the extent of his disability. They evaluated the paralysis and the aphasia. We learned quickly that we could ask Dad if it was sunny, and he would say yes. Wait a few minutes and ask him if it was sunny, and he would say no.

The paralysis on the right side was extensive. Physical therapists worked to help him relearn how to walk. It was heartbreaking to see my dad lifted and supported, struggling and sweating to try to take steps. The therapist had a series of pulleys and straps to help Dad.

I waited at the end of the hall watching as she worked to get him to take steps. It reminded me of watching a child learn to walk. The instability. The wobbling. Dad would get frustrated and angry, and then quit. We were never sure if it was because it hurt physically or if he was just embarrassed.

The occupational therapists worked with him so he could try to feed himself and perform routine hygiene. His speech therapists sat with him, pointing at pictures of common items like eyeglasses, combs, shoes, and books, trying to get Dad to repeat the words.

Days turned into weeks and months. I was traveling to Cincinnati and staying at his apartment while visiting. I took over his finances so that his bills were paid. My brother and I met with our family attorney to shift power of attorney and medical power of attorney to us so we could make decisions for him.

After about six months, Dad had given up. He had stopped trying to walk. He had stopped trying to talk. With this realization, my brother and I also had to face the fact that Dad would not be able to live independently anymore. I researched nursing homes and found one that was highly rated. Dad had Medicare, and we had to apply for Medicaid based on his income (which was now only Social Security).

Figuring out the Medicare and Medicaid systems and taking care of Dad's finances was like a full-time job. Now I feel equipped to plan for my husband's future and mine!

Over the next two and a half years, Dad was in the nursing home. My brother took him on outings to the casino, restaurants, and baseball games. We rented a hotel suite for Thanksgivings and Christmases and had our holidays there. We picked up Red Lobster food for him for his birthday and even met halfway between Cincinnati and Nashville to have meals and visit. We decorated his room with things from his apartment to make it homey, and my brother visited and brought meals to him three to four times a week. I visited as often as I could but always felt it was never enough.

This past spring, his nursing home went into lockdown due to COVID. A staff member tested positive, and Dad was taken to the hospital two days later. Three weeks later, he died. Because of COVID, my brother and I were only able to visit him a few times. And because of COVID, his funeral was a quiet affair.

I miss him terribly but am forever thankful for the three additional years we got to spend with him. We could have lost him with the stroke. While it wasn't easy, having him here a little longer was a blessing and provided memories I cherish.

—Julie Gwinn—

49

The Social Butterfly

Aging is an extraordinary process where you become
the person you always should have been.
~David Bowie

"You are not moving me into a nursing home, young lady!" My tiny mom sat in the passenger seat of my car with her arms crossed, refusing to exit.

"Mom, this is not a nursing facility. It's the independent-living, senior apartment complex you applied for two years ago. You're free to come and go as you wish."

Mom sat like an obstinate child. Cajoling didn't work. Sweet talk didn't faze her. So, I used my teacher voice and ordered her out of my car. I buzzed the office intercom.

"See! They lock you in!" Mom was convinced she was about to become a prisoner.

The property manager greeted us with a wide smile. "Welcome, Virginia. We've been expecting you."

Mom put on her happy face like a kindergartener being praised. We walked through an elegant vestibule, past a large birdcage where parakeets flitted. A lobby area with comfy plaid couches, overstuffed chairs and a large-screen television had a homey feel. Tables, chairs and stocked bookcases invited residents to linger in the lobby. Mom gave me the side eye and whispered, "I am not visiting people I don't know."

I nodded. "You won't have to."

From the office to the elevator, we strolled a long, glass-enclosed hallway. Outside, the green space, teeming with flowers and bushes, was home to bunnies and even a box turtle.

"I do like to walk, and I don't like to feel closed in. Nice," she admitted to herself.

The manager explained that the four apartment buildings were connected by these corridors, so she would be able to walk in comfort, regardless of the weather.

After Mom settled in, she called me several times a day. "Do you know they have line dancing here? But I'm not joining!" She'd never been a joiner. When I had Tupperware parties, she refused to attend because she didn't feel comfortable in a crowd. I was amazed when she mentioned amenities such as card-making, book clubs, and free bus transportation to shopping centers and grocery stores.

I felt a sense of relief. I had been my mom's sole transportation for many years. I was about to get a break. Mom used her sweet voice to entice me.

"Honey, if you have time, could you come take me to the grocery store?"

I hopped on it, even though I wished she'd hop on the free bus.

"Can you come over and help me straighten my drapes?" I could hear the smile in her voice.

I dropped by whenever she called. I brought leftovers and bags of homegrown tomatoes for the residents. I took her shopping and on evening rides.

One evening while carrying her groceries to her apartment, I looked at the sign-up sheet on the bulletin board. "Why isn't your name on the bus list? I thought you said you were going to the mall this week."

Mom waved me on and said, "I might, and I might not."

I called my grown daughter and asked if she had seen her grandma lately.

"Of course, I have. I see her almost every other day. I always take her to the mall and grocery shopping."

I phoned my adult son and encouraged him to stop by his grandma's.

"She might be feeling lonely, you know?"

"How could she be? I've seen her almost every other day. She asked me to program her television remote. Then the VCR wouldn't rewind. When she called to tell me her thermostat wasn't working, I had to convince her not to touch it because it's a heat-pump system. I took her for ice cream last night. She wanted me to put something high up in a closet. Next week, she'll call me to take it down." He chuckled.

The next day, Mom asked me to take her to McDonald's for a fish sandwich.

That evening, my daughter called to tell me she'd taken Mom to McDonald's.

"Not true!" I said. "I took her this afternoon for lunch."

"Well, I just took her for a chocolate sundae."

While we all imagined Mom suffering from loneliness, she was busier than ever yanking all our strings, orchestrating which one of us she would see on different days at different times.

Little did we know that Mom, who had been shy all her life, was becoming a social butterfly in her later years. As it turns out, she had joined all sorts of clubs and had even made a best friend in a Bible study group.

When the office manager called me into her office to show me a photo of Mom and three other residents wearing white cowboy hats and silver badges, I couldn't believe it. Mom brave enough to stand before a group? Dressed in costume?

"This was our monthly residents' meeting. There was a theft in our building. Someone stole the large-screen TV last night. So, because your mom is always walking the halls, we deputized her and these other two women and this man as our residence watch committee. Did you know your mom has even tried kicking up her heels on the dance floor?"

Really? I walked into Mom's apartment. "What have you been up to lately?"

"I've been busy working as a deputy," Mom beamed, showing off her badge and photo. I expected her to run to the closet and pull out her boots.

Mom, a late bloomer, was like a lovely wild rose that finally blossomed in her elder years.

—Linda O'Connell—

50

Ray of Light

Give thanks for unknown blessings
already on their way.
~Native American Saying

I wasn't sure if Dad was going to remember my name. I hesitated just before I reached the door to the house. The wood was weathered, with streaks of stripped paint. Around the corner, a dusty RV peeked from beneath a canopy. The sun's rays struggled to shine through the misty morning. With my eyes closed, I grasped the loose doorknob, bracing myself before seeing him.

Dad wasn't actually my father; he was my best friend's dad. I had lived across the street from them when I was a teenager. However, I had spent more time at their house than I did at my own. After a while, it was only natural to see him as a father figure.

I had quickly learned how stern a man Dad was. He once scolded us for feeding peanuts to squirrels. He lectured about how they would rely on us for food, thus forgetting how to forage for themselves. He claimed the squirrels would then die on their own, and the whole ecosystem would be disrupted. I wished I could say he was joking, but there was no overt humor in that man's body, and we never dared to giggle at his words — at least not in front of him.

Any time we protested his lectures, he'd reply, "It is what it is," and we knew the conversation was over. We didn't understand what it meant other than there was no point in arguing.

Despite his demeanor, Dad had welcomed me into his home. I

had an open invitation to dinner any night and frequently took up the offer. He gave me an escape from my primary home when things became overwhelming — an invaluable resource for a teenager.

I had been traveling around the country when I learned that Dad had Alzheimer's. Growing up a poor black man in the South, he had worked hard to save money for when he retired so he and Mom could live in their RV and travel the country together. This had inspired me to take up my own adventure, often traveling the same routes Dad had scouted.

He was forced to give up his dream of traveling shortly after his condition became a reality. His mind was no longer as sharp as it once was. His Alzheimer's made him lose focus on current tasks and delayed his reaction time — a lethal combination when it came to driving. He was forced to relinquish his RV keys.

I entered the house expecting to be greeted by the aroma of warm cigars and the intoxicating sound of smooth jazz I was accustomed to as a kid. I was disappointed to meet the smell of impersonal cleanliness and a cold silence.

I stepped into the living room to find Dad resting in his usual recliner. I hardly recognized him. His face was sunken, and his hair was completely white. He somehow seemed shorter than he already was. His eyes drifted toward me. He stared for a long second as the wheels in his head struggled to turn. He was searching for some kind of memory — some kind of information — about who I was.

Then he raised his arms toward me, waving me closer. For the first time in my life, I witnessed tears filling his eyes.

"You're here," he choked out, his voice now a permanent whisper. "It has to be thirty years since the last time."

His concept of time no longer existed. It had only been a couple of years since I last visited him at some RV park along the highway. However, just having him understand that it had been a long time was enough for me to see that he recognized who I was, despite not knowing my name.

"Are you here to stay?" he asked.

"I'm here to stay," I replied.

The rest of his words were slow and jumbled. I had to decode what he was trying to say for most of the conversation. Although he had forgotten how to smile, a ray of light rose in his eyes as I told him stories of my travels. They were resonating with him, and I was sure he had a lot of his own stories that we both wished he was able to share.

Months went by in a routine — helping Dad eat, watching TV, going on short walks. Dad could hardly speak anymore. His words became too scrambled and nonsensical for me to decode. The doctor told us that his decline could take ten years. Well, Dad was a stubborn man who thrived on proving people wrong. I imagined him saying, "I'll show you," as he aged ten years in five months.

My own exhaustion was weighing on me. Caring for someone you love while simultaneously trying to process that his life was coming to an end was no easy feat. With Alzheimer's, the grieving process never fully begins. Every time I thought Dad was reduced to just a physical form, a ray of his personality would shine through, giving me hope again. Lingering grief, longing to be on the road again, and the guilt of feeling those emotions were draining me.

"I'm sorry, Dad," I told him one day when I felt particularly over-whelmed. "I'm sorry this is happening."

He placed his weak, weathered hand on mine. He leaned toward me, using what little strength he had left to tighten his grip. "It is what it is," he said as clearly as ever before — one of those rays of light.

I mulled over those words. I hadn't heard them since I was a kid. I never paid any mind to what they actually meant until that moment. I squeezed his hand, finally understanding. He was saying there was no point in dwelling on things. Sometimes, we just had to accept reality instead of trying to change it. In those moments, we needed to make the best of what we had.

I took a deep breath. I understood.

I drove him around in my car, elated to be back on the road after so long. The taste of the crisp air lingered on my lips. The rhythm of classic jazz drifted from the radio. I peered into the rearview mirror to see a ray of sunshine cutting through the misty air, illuminating Dad. He gazed out the window — his head bobbing to the music, eyes in awe of the towering pine trees. For a second, it even looked as though he remembered how to smile.

In that moment, Dad didn't need to form words or remember names. He just had to feel. He felt the euphoria of the open road that we were both familiar with. Our adventures were no longer epic journeys across the country. Now, they were mild outings, driving a few miles around the house and, on more ambitious days, venturing to the highway.

It wasn't the ideal situation, but it is what it is.

—London Alexander—

51

Painting Ships

*When we are engaged in pursuing our passion, we feel
better about ourselves and have a more positive view
of the world around us.*
~Dennis Houchin

When I was a child and too young for school, I spent a
lot of time at my grandfather's house while my mom
was at work. What I remember most was how he loved
painting ships — old sailing vessels.

As I grew up, I saw him often, but we hardly spoke. We picked
him up for church, where he played the piano, and then took him
home. I noticed that he didn't really paint much anymore. He had quit
driving, and he began to walk with a cane. My sisters had cleaned his
house for a little extra money because he couldn't do it well himself.
After some time, I started cleaning for him. Then, about a year ago,
he had a heart attack. He was in and out of the hospital for a while,
but he recovered and went back home, still weak from his condition.

When I started cleaning for him, we began to talk more. We
discussed life, our interests, and what I was thinking about doing in
the future. He told me stories that were only funny when he told them.
However, when COVID-19 hit, he had to stay home a lot more. We
couldn't risk him catching it as he was weak enough already, moving
around his house in a wheelchair. He only went to church when he
felt up to it or when the weather made it easier to push his wheelchair.

When I showed up, he wanted to talk a lot. At times, it distracted me from cleaning, but I figured he was lonely and enjoyed the company. I knew he was probably getting bored in the house by himself all the time, and I noticed that he wasn't doing much other than watching TV. I asked him why he didn't start painting again. I could tell that he was indifferent to it since it had been a long time since he had painted. I made it a point to casually mention it when I came over, telling him often that I thought he should paint again.

It worked! He started sending me to the store to get tubes of acrylic paint, canvases or poster boards, and even a shark magazine. He asked me about colors and showed me his paintings when I took breaks from cleaning. I loved the ship paintings he did, the way he painted the water and the ancient vessels.

He seemed happier, and I was glad that he was doing something he enjoyed because he wasn't as bored anymore. It seemed like it brought back some youthful part of him.

Cleaning for my grandpa has brought us closer together. He can't go outside much due to the virus or how weak he gets, so I know how important it is that he doesn't feel too isolated. He has started asking me for help with his Chromebook, and despite his nearly seventy-five years of age, I refuse to discourage him from it. He's still figuring it out day by day, but I'm glad I get to discuss it with him. Days like these are precious, and I enjoy the little moments.

— Amanda Pillow —

52

The Unexpected Gifts of Caring for My Aging Mother

*The closest thing to being cared for
is to care for someone else.*
~Carson McCullers, The Square Root of Wonderful

I help my mom out of the car and walk her to the salon doors where her kind stylist greets us and takes her hand to lead her back to her station. My mom has her weekly hair appointment scheduled again after months of being in quarantine due to COVID-19.

I visit my mom as often as possible, helping her with household chores and having long talks. Since our options are limited on where we can go, I take her for long drives just to get her out of the house and give her a change of scenery. We'll often pick up carry-out food and picnic at a park while watching the sun set beyond the pond, which is one of our favorite things to do.

Most of her sight was stolen from her two years ago, along with her freedom, when she suffered optic-nerve strokes in both eyes. For years, she had struggled solely with painful neuropathy in her legs that continues to make walking difficult, but now my mom is battling two demons that are trying to take her active life away. But she won't back down or give up the fight. She just needs help being victorious.

Leaving my mom in good hands, I pull out of the salon parking lot and head to the grocery store to pick up some things she needs. Then I park the car next to her first-floor patio so I can bring her groceries through the door and into her kitchen, where I'll put them all away. I don't have much time before I need to go back and pick her up.

Once I pick her up, I'll swing by the repair shop to pick up my daughter so she can leave her car there for maintenance work and get a ride home. After I drop my daughter off at our house, I'll run my mom back to hers. I'll try to hurry her out of the car and into her place gently but assertively, reminding her that I have one more kid to pick up today. She understands, so she moves as fast as her body will allow.

I race to pick up my son from soccer practice, now late, so he calls wondering where I am. I tell him I've been with Grammy, but I'm on my way. He understands. My kids have grown to accept that caring for my mom sometimes interrupts my caring for them.

This is my life, full of caretaking and parenting and trying to balance the demands of both as best I can. My days, once filled with the priorities of marriage and kids and work and friends, have expanded with my mom now lingering at the top of the list.

She needs me to write her checks, file her papers, and drive her to her doctor's appointments. She needs me to tell her what color her pants are, label her lipsticks, and find her phone, wallet or any other important item that has gone missing. She needs me to be her eyes in a world she now struggles to see.

It's amazing she still lives alone, able to cautiously move around her place with the help of low-vision adaptations that make everyday life a little bit more manageable. She still dresses impeccably and has many close friends in her senior-living apartment building. Before COVID-19 hit, she had a full social calendar, including a book club she started (she listens to audiobooks regularly), exercise classes over at the assisted-living building next door, movie nights in their building's gathering room, and weekly dinners out with her gaggle of girlfriends.

She's a wonder, my mom. I'm so proud of how she doesn't give up. I often feel the overwhelming ache that comes with watching one's own mother suffer, hoping and praying for healing, for answers, for anything to help her steer this new, complicated course.

I notice her weariness; she's worn down from all this trying. I tell her how amazing I think she is. I can only hope my words help her believe it's true.

My mom tells me she feels like a nuisance, always interrupting my busy life. But she doesn't realize all she's given me during this challenging season for us both. Our relationship has grown in ways only millions of minutes spent together can do. It's transformed into something nourishing and affirming, giving and forgiving—adding new beautiful depths of understanding of one another we did not have before. We've been afforded the precious time to peel layers of our history back for each other to see, revealing hidden stories we never had a chance to tell. There's no need for eyesight when one is truly listening.

My mom has been able to see me despite the loss of her sight, maybe even because of it. Since spending so much time together, she's been folded into the fabric of my life, deeply aware of the details, applauding it all and cheering me on.

And I believe she knows that I see her, too. I see her strength and perseverance in rising up every day to live a life worth living. I see all the details of her long history, full of incredible challenges and amazing triumphs. I am grateful for the chance to take in the view. There's so much there I hadn't seen before, and I know she feels the same way about me, too.

And although she would give anything to have her sight back, her life restored to what it was before, at least something good has come from it. We have grown so much closer through it all.

One day I get an e-mail notification from the Nextdoor online community, and I click to read it. "My mother recently passed away, and I'm looking for a good place to donate her visual-impairment equipment." I gasp quietly, tears filling my eyes as I'm struck by the grave reality in front of me. I tell this woman how sorry I am for her loss and that I'm interested in the equipment for my mother.

I pick up my phone and call my mom to tell her I might have some new equipment for her to try. I don't share the rest of the story.

She's well aware of how it ends. There's no need to remind her while she's still fighting to write the last chapter of her own.

And as I prepare my kids to begin writing their own stories while helping my mom finish hers, I create intricate pages woven with gifts I cherish in the middle of mine.

— Christine Carter —

Final Memories

Forever is composed of nows.
~Emily Dickinson

helped give my mother her shower. Her wrinkled skin had a
soft sweetness to it, like the wrinkled folds in my baby's thighs.
I brushed her fine silvery hair, her curls now gone, and was
soothed by knowing that she had done the same for me in times
past.

As I helped her dress, she moved her white visor from the bed.
"Bad luck, dear. Never put a hat on a bed."

But I knew none of us could be protected from the curse of
letting go. She didn't know our plans for her as she ate tiny pieces of
sweet potato, her lunch laid out by Lovelace, the kind aide from Sierra
Leone. Soon, we would move her to a home. We won't say where we
are going, only "Mom, let's get ready to go outside." She does best with
simple instructions. Memory loss doesn't allow for planning beyond
the present moment. "Next" is immediately forgotten, along with the
minute before. We will direct her to the car and strap her in to keep
her safe. She is ours to take care of now.

I took her to dinner one last time at the little hotel a block away
from her apartment. It had been my home when I would visit—a
retreat from the battleground of old age. I would return to my room in
the evening and become a civilian again. There, I told myself bedtime
stories of happy memories growing up to soothe my sorrow.

Sometimes I'd hand those memories to my mother to make her

smile until they quickly flew away. I described our family vacations on Martha's Vineyard when all was right in the world. We mastered poker in the comfy, dusty living room; stacks of pennies were our chips. We drove to the end of the island where there was a Native-American outpost, bought pumpkin pies and rock candy, and played family tennis on a red clay court with cracked white lines and a hole in the sagging net.

The "Vineyard" is where my mother wants her ashes scattered. "High in the sky, if you can. I want to be able to look down on all of you!" That was six months ago when she confessed, "Deary, I think I have about six months of memory left, but then I will no longer remember that I can't remember, so promise you won't worry."

I returned to her home after we moved her. We packed up her things, touching her as we sorted through blouses and sweaters, casserole dishes and mugs, books, photos, jewelry, and perfume. I brought her familiar blue-and-white dishes to my kitchen, comforted by the delicate blue lines around the border that outlined our childhood dinners.

And now her new "home" is a small but sunny room at Symphony Manor. On Thanksgiving, her memory of my sister's visit only lasted as long as the sweet taste of pumpkin on her tongue — gone with a swallow. When I visited for the first time, she shrieked with a quiet joy, pushing her walker toward me. "Oh, deary, you're here!" I too shrieked inside, weeping with both relief and sadness.

We found a corner to sit where I showed her photos on my phone, reminding her of her life before. She smiled gently, holding my hand. "Sweetie, your hands are so cold." She had lost so much, yet her devotion as a mother was instinctual. Even her dementia couldn't rob us of that. We filled two hours together traveling from her bedroom to the lobby to a chilly excursion outside, walking two minutes to where the sidewalk ended and then back again. I escorted her to lunch on the memory-care floor where her grilled-cheese sandwich was cut in bite-sized pieces. I couldn't stay — not because I didn't have the time, but because I *couldn't*. When I hugged her goodbye, it was clumsy as she let go of her walker. I stood and watched her back as an aide guided her away. She was a foreigner lost in her own home.

Over Passover, I called to wish her a "Happy Pesach." Her phone rang but no one answered. Cherise at the front desk assured me, "I bet she is at the afternoon Happy Hour." My mother was never a happy-hour kind of gal. But perhaps in the last chapter of our lives, we maintain a graceful farewell by continuing to experience what we have never done.

When I did reach her by phone, I turned our conversation into a walking meditation. I spoke very slowly and loudly, taking small methodical steps around our living room as she tried to understand me. Each step matched the slow expression of my words stretching out the spaces in-between like a rubber band — hoping that I wouldn't snap with impatience. I continued to slowly circle my living room after saying goodnight. I didn't know how many tomorrows my mother would have, but in this last chapter she had finally found a sweet peacefulness in today. She had no worries because worries must be held to be remembered. There was no choice now; her mind only allowed for the present. I breathed and sat, grateful that my mother's gift to me as I turned sixty-one was the beauty of the moment.

— Priscilla Dann-Courtney —

Chapter 6

The Lighter Side

54

The Great Escape

Mirth is God's medicine.
Everybody ought to bathe in it.
~Henry Ward Beecher

As I pulled up to my grandparents' home, the flashing lights of the police cars in the driveway were as comforting as they were frightening. I only lived about three miles away, but when the call came that my grandmother was missing, it seemed like it took me forever to get there.

Grandmom was in the middle stages of Alzheimer's. Though she still appeared to recognize me, she was often confused as to exactly who I was. My grandfather was the only person she distinguished with any certainty — and even then, it was iffy. On this day, she was taking a nap, so Grandpop took the opportunity to go down to his basement workshop. When he came back upstairs about an hour later, she was gone.

A quick search through the house and yard yielded nothing. Could she have walked to the shopping center a few blocks away, or had she ventured into the woods behind the house? Grandpop was frantic. He called 911 and then my dad, who called in the rest of the family to pray and search.

We scoured the woods calling her name. "Helen!" "Mom!" "Grandmom!" We tried any name we thought she might respond to as we walked back and forth through the acres of woods separating my grandparents' house from the houses on the next street.

Decades before, my grandmother, her sister and brother had each bought a lot and built homes. To get to each other's house, you just had to follow a path through the woods. It was easy if you knew the way but could be confusing if you didn't know where to turn. Both her siblings had passed on, so we were concerned that she might be "living in the past" and trying to find her way through the woods to the homes that had once belonged to them.

My parents went over to the shopping center across the street to look for her. Running errands there was another familiar routine from her past.

My sister and I knocked on the neighbors' doors up and down the street to ask if anyone had seen her, but it was the middle of the day and most were not at home.

After a few hours of frantically searching, my grandfather stopped in his tracks, turned and ran up to the neighbor's back door. He had a hunch. The time of day was right. Maybe, just maybe…

Years ago — before Alzheimer's — Grandmom and Mrs. Carmichael, who lived next door, would often sit together in the afternoons drinking coffee, eating cookies and talking. They were the best of friends, having been neighbors for more than forty years. They shared stories about children, grandchildren and great-grandchildren over coffee. They laughed and cried over coffee. Gardens were planned, recipes were swapped, and a lifelong friendship was forged over cups of coffee.

Grandpop opened the back door and entered the Carmichael house. Sure enough, there they were, sitting by the window drinking coffee, eating cookies, and laughing — watching all the excitement going on outside. They were wondering what all those people were doing traipsing through the woods, yelling at each other. In fact, when my grandfather walked in, they offered him a cup of coffee and told him to come see what was going on in the back woods. They were having a grand time!

As worried and upset as he had been, he couldn't be angry. Mrs. Carmichael also had Alzheimer's. Something must have "clicked" for both of them that afternoon. They didn't answer the front door when we knocked — probably because they were having too much fun watching everyone run around out back! Somehow, these women, who hadn't cooked in years, managed to make a pot of coffee and found a bag of cookies. We have no idea what they talked about during all those hours. Maybe there was just the comfortable familiarity of a past memory that felt "right" for both of them that day. Maybe it was their way of saying goodbye. Both women had been limited in their ability to get out and about. Mrs. Carmichael had recently lost her husband, and her family was not able to provide the twenty-four-hour care she needed at home.

Not long after this incident, Mrs. Carmichael went to live in an assisted-living facility. Grandmom still had good days, but the disease took its course as Alzheimer's will do. She was no longer able to be left alone. Her health was failing quickly. As it turned out, this was the last time these two dear hearts shared a cup of coffee, some cookies and a good chuckle. Looking back all these years later, we can laugh about it now, too. We know that, somewhere, there is a heavenly coffee klatch with Grandmom and Mrs. Carmichael pouring coffee, passing out cookies and regaling the angels with the tale of The Great Escape: A Coffee and Cookies Caper.

— Donna Anderson —

55

A Memorable Outing with My Parents

Every survival kit should include a sense of humor.
~Author Unknown

"Ready to go?" I asked loudly as I assisted my elderly parents out of their condo and down to the parking garage. I pushed my mother's wheelchair to the car, while my father stood unsteadily behind us.

Now, the athletics began. I hoisted my mother out of her wheelchair and pivoted her into the front seat. She grabbed madly at the car door, which I was anchoring with my weight so it didn't knock her down or slam shut on her fingers. Lift, twist, wiggle, push and fasten the seatbelt.

Then it was my father's turn. He was easier to get into the car since he was self-propelled, but he was also always far more impatient. First, I had to move my mother's seat (with her in it) forward so that my 6'2" father, with his long legs and bad knees, could jam himself into the back seat. But before that, he had to move a child's booster seat out of the way so that he could sit down.

By the time I had wrangled both my parents into my car, I was drenched in sweat. As usual, we were running late. No matter how early I arrived, it seemed we were always behind.

"Where's my purse?" my mother asked, distressed. I stopped the car and retrieved the handbag from the roof of my car.

Now on the road, my mother (who no longer had a valid driver's license) started her running commentary. "It's clear here. No, don't go. The bus is stopped." She also read out loud every road sign she saw. "Right lane merges. School zone. Monday to Friday 4:00 to 6:00 p.m., no left turn."

"Where in the clinic are we going today?" my father asked.

"B Wing, Ground Floor, Room 35a," I replied loudly.

"You have to speak louder. I can't hear you."

I turned the radio from inaudible to off.

"B WING, GROUND FLOOR, ROOM 35A," I bellowed.

"Okay, D Wing."

"It's green," my mother helpfully interjected.

"Dad, do you have your hearing aid in?" He only ever had one.

"No, it hurts to wear it," he explained.

"How long has it hurt?"

"About ten days now. But it's slowly getting better."

My mother interrupted again. "Watch out for that pedestrian!"

I slammed on the brakes. "What pedestrian? Where?"

"Over there, on the other side of the road."

As I sped up again, I asked my father, "Why didn't you tell me sooner about your ear, Dad?"

"Sorry, can you say that again?"

"You should go see the doctor," I offered.

"Can you repeat that, please?"

"I'M GOING TO TAKE YOU TO THE DOCTOR, DAD!"

"Slow down!" my mother cried out in alarm.

Finally, we arrived at the medical building. The parking lot, which I had been promised would be large and free of charge, was neither. I drove into the next residential street and parked in a no-parking zone just behind a huge dump truck. Getting my mother out here promised to be a challenge — a concrete curb with miles of grass before we got to the actual sidewalk. I foresaw problems.

"Dad, I'm going to back up the car so we can get Mom out on the concrete."

Dad was already out of the car, unfolding Mom's wheelchair. "No, it'll be fine. I'll put the chair on the grass."

"No, Dad, I really think I should move the car."

My father waved me off dismissively. And, of course, my mother who could hardly move on a smooth surface got her feet stuck. I did my best to hold her up, but down she fell. I felt terrible. My mother assured me she was unhurt. Somehow, my father and I wrestled her into her wheelchair.

Suddenly, a police car pulled in behind my car. The cop approached the driver of the dump truck, and they commenced a heated discussion. By now, I was livid. I told my parents to go ahead while I dealt with the parking issue.

I approached the cop and said in a completely non-deferential tone of voice, "I have two disabled parents, and the parking lot is full. Where the heck am I supposed to park?"

"You can stay here, but only if you have a disabled parking permit," he replied helpfully.

Thankfully, I had not one but two of those, and so the day did not get worse. Or so I thought.

While waiting for the doctor, who (surprise!) was running even later than we were, I texted my sister, "OMG! Mom just fell getting out of the car. I dropped her. My fault. But she seems to be fine."

My sister texted back immediately. "Well, at least she didn't break her hip this time like she did when she fell last Christmas while visiting me. I win!" With that zinger, I instantly felt better. Better to laugh than to cry over spilled mom.

Our appointment finally over, I instructed my father, "You push Mom to the car. I'm going to pull it out so we can get Mom safely into her seat from the road."

This time, he agreed. I congratulated myself on my genius strategy — not only to get my mother safely into the car but also to ensure that my father would have something to hold on to while he was walking. He had terrible balance and was too proud to use a cane.

As I hurried to the car, I did a visual check behind me. Dad was slowly pushing Mom toward the car. All was well.

I moved the car and waited… and waited. Boy, Dad was even

slower than I expected. Then I saw my parents come around the corner. Slowly. Dad had a bloody tissue in his hand. As he got closer, I saw that his knee was bleeding profusely. Blood was running down his knee and into his sock. His light-coloured shoes were spotted red. His blood thinners were doing their job only too well on this occasion.

"Heavens, Dad! What happened?"

"I tripped over the sidewalk. One section was higher than the others. I didn't lift my foot high enough," he replied ruefully. It was the neuropathy in his feet, bad balance combined with reduced sensation.

"Are you okay, Dad?"

"I need a bandage."

I agreed silently. Fortunately, as the mother of small children, I had a plethora of bandages in various shapes and sizes at hand. We patched my father up as best we could, although I wasn't sure he appreciated the Dora the Explorer design he was now sporting.

"Okay, that'll get us home. So… what happened to Mom when you fell?" I asked.

"Well, the wheelchair kept rolling. She ended up on the grass."

I looked at my mother to see if she was okay. She was reacting the way she always reacted in these situations — laughing her head off at my father's fall. I guess she was just fine.

What did I do? What I always did in these situations — I texted my sister.

— Marina Bee —

56

Guess Who's Sleeping in My Bed

*Unselfish and noble actions are the most radiant pages
in the biography of souls.*
~David Thomas

My mother-in-law's name is Helen Louise, but we affectionately call her "Ma," or sometimes behind her back: HELL-N. Read further, and you will understand why.

Helen was the mother of six children; she has survived all but three. She was married three times and widowed three times. She had successfully lived on her own since her last husband passed away in 2002.

I have tried to find the goodness in her, but I would have better luck striking gold in my back yard. Helen and I were long acquainted before I married her oldest son, Larry, but our chemistry was lukewarm at best. However, despite her lack of gratitude and appreciation, I made a promise that we would take care of her and see that she had everything needed to be safe and comfortable.

Helen was showing signs that she was struggling with living on her own. She resided in a two-story, forty-year-old home nestled in an established neighborhood about ninety miles from Larry and me. From time to time, a grandchild would stay with her for a few months and then decide to leave to recover from her overbearing personality. Helen's neighbors would periodically check on her and give us a call if they saw anything suspicious. With us living so far away, we needed to get as many eyes on her as possible.

Each time we went to visit, there were increased signs that things were starting to spiral out of control. Her ambulation was faltering, and meal preparation was, in a word, gross. Plus, after a diagnosis of dementia, her short-term memory was slowly diminishing. One day, a neighbor called to tell us that Helen was seen flagging down a car passing by her house and asking the driver for a ride to her granddaughter's home just a few blocks away. The neighbor did not recognize the driver and was not sure Helen did either. But away she went.

It was evident she was on a collision course with disaster. I suggested to my husband that we must move his mother closer to us. We were the most logical choice to oversee Helen's long-term care. Larry pounced on my suggestion, probably fearing that I was having a senior moment of my own and might change my mind. I saw relief in his eyes as he realized that he did not have to navigate the journey alone.

With lightning speed, Larry secured her house, notified the family and neighbors what was happening, and packed the items that she could bring with her. He scooped her up and plopped her in our guest room within a few days. After all, we designed our home to accommodate an aging population. It is all on one level, with open spaces, and expanded hallways and bathrooms. We would make this work.

We decorated her bedroom with pictures and other memorabilia so that her new surroundings looked familiar to her. She had a perfect view of our beautiful flower beds that lined the perimeter of the back yard. The kitchen was stocked with her familiar foods and snacks.

The master bedroom and bath were on the south end of the house. The family room, kitchen, and a small dining area were in the center or core of our home. Helen's accommodations were on the north end with her private bath nearby. She had easy access to the deck that stretched almost the length of the house, where she could sit and enjoy the fresh air and sunshine.

Just a few days after we moved her in, I had to leave for an overnight business trip. My anxiety level was a bit high because we were still trying to work out the routines and schedules to accommodate Helen's needs. Before I hit the road, I made sure the house was organized and she knew where things were, such as coffee, TV remotes, towels, etc. Larry and I reviewed our checklist to confirm that we were prepared for any contingency.

Later the next day, I checked into a hotel and settled in for the night. A quick call home assured me that all went well during the day. Helen was settling in and seemed to enjoy her new surroundings. Mother and son enjoyed a nice dinner together, watched the evening news, and were getting ready to retire for the night. I told him that I was scheduled to head home around mid-morning so I could join them for dinner. We said our "I love yous" and ended the call.

The next morning, I made a quick call home to review plans for her to go to an adult day-care center where she could stay until I returned. All my husband kept saying was: "Oh, my God. Oh, my God. Jesus!" I went into panic mode thinking all kinds of catastrophic things were happening, like Helen fell down the basement steps, set the house on fire or, worse yet, left the house during the night and was missing. It was none of these things.

It was the deep breathing that stirred him during the night and woke him up. When he rolled over thinking that I had returned much earlier than expected, there *she* was! Sometime during the night, my mother-in-law had wandered through the house to our bedroom, where Larry was sound asleep, and crawled into bed with him.

As one could imagine, I had no words. My mouth was open, but nothing was coming out. Finally, I uttered one question, "Was she on *my* side of the bed?" With hesitation, he whispered, "Yes," which was all he was able to get out.

"I will be home in two hours," I said quickly and hung up.

Now, we have a lock on our bedroom door. In the short time since she has been with us, we have put in place several things to help her sleep through the night and maintain our sanity. A nice cup of chamomile tea, with a small dosage of a sleeping agent or a soothing lavender bubble bath, have wonderful results for her.

We know that we will get to a place of needing more care than we can provide. We are prepared to make that decision when the time comes. However, it does not lessen our pledge to make sure she is in good hands and getting what is in the best interest for her wellbeing. Failing this, Larry and I will take turns monitoring her travels when she's on a late-night prowl.

— Cheryl Edwards-Cannon —

57

Grandma's Big Surprise

Humor is merely tragedy standing on its head
with its pants torn.
~Irvin S. Cobb

I f we'd been anywhere but central Illinois, I would have thought the loud crashing sound was an earthquake or the explosion of a nuclear power plant. "Sweetie." I turned toward my husband and gently rocked his shoulder back and forth. "Sweetie." His grunt offered no reassurance that he had awakened. "Sweetie, did you hear that noise?"

"Hmm?"

"That noise. Did you hear it?"

My husband rolled over. He pulled the flannel sheet up over his shoulder. "It's probably nothing. You're just not used to sleeping in a different place."

I got out of bed and slipped into my terrycloth robe. A different place, yes, but nothing I hadn't been used to. Once a month for the past few years, I traveled four hours from home to stay with my in-laws for the weekend to assist them at home. In all those times, I had never heard a crash like that.

My husband was one of three siblings living close enough that they could care for their aging parents. We all took one weekend a month, and one of the nearby granddaughters took a weekend. They needed help with heavier housekeeping, grocery shopping and some meal preparation.

Usually, I came alone, but this time we made it a family affair, bringing the kids and grandkids along and having a giant sleepover, much like we had done many Christmases at the farm when our own children were small. Mom and Dad were in a zero-step condo now, so worries about falling down a flight of steps or tripping over a threshold were eliminated. Still, something had caused that noise. My husband might have been able to sleep through it, but I felt the need to investigate.

As I opened the guest-room door, I heard whispers. I glanced in the kitchen at the green digital numbers above the oven: 5:30. The familiar smell of apples, cinnamon and pine invaded my nose as I entered the living room where I found my granddaughters snuggled in their sleeping bags together next to the fireplace.

"Girls, are you okay?" I asked.

"We're scared. Grandpa may have fallen. Our moms went to check on him."

I noticed the quilts tossed aside on both the loveseat and the sofa. I said a quick prayer of thanks that my daughters worked in healthcare. I knelt and hugged my granddaughters.

"I'm sure everything will be okay. Your mothers are experts at caring for others."

Just then, my girls came out of my in-laws' bedroom and quietly closed the paneled oak door behind them.

"Is everything okay?" I asked.

Our younger daughter rounded the kitchen peninsula and began making coffee. "That was an experience," she finally said. "We were pretty sure Grandpa fell, but we didn't know if we should just barge into their bedroom or not. However, we knew Grandma couldn't get Grandpa off the floor if he fell, so we decided to go in. Grandpa fell on his way to the bathroom, and he came down pretty hard."

"He'll have a bruise, for sure. He ended up urinating before he got to the toilet. We don't know if it was before he fell or after, but we cleaned him up and the floor, and got him back to bed. Grandma was thankful, but Grandma…" My daughter shook her head as she reached up as though trying to cover her eyes.

I could hear the dripping as the coffeemaker worked its magic, and the smell of the fresh brew permeated the air. As though beckoning her, Mom entered the great room, pulling up the zipper of her pale pink housecoat as she entered. She had taken the time to apply wine-red lipstick, and not a hair was out of place on her head. She sat down on the stool at the end of the kitchen island. She rested her elbows on the granite countertop and cupped her chin in her hands and laughed.

"Well, girls," she sighed as she paused, "now you've seen every-thing—your grandpa without his pants and your grandma without her hair."

Everyone laughed. Apparently, our girls never realized their grandma wore a wig.

—Deborah Young—

58

An Affair to Misremember

Humor is the great thing, the saving thing. The minute
it crops up, all our irritation and resentments
slip away, and a sunny spirit takes their place.
~Mark Twain

Walking alongside someone with dementia is a difficult journey with very few glimpses of light. But humor can be found along the path if we're willing to look at things in a different way.

For years, my mother's dementia had been easy to navigate, only affecting her short-term memory. As long as we called continually to remind her of things or wrote notes on her calendar, she could function within her assisted-living facility. Then the 2020 pandemic hit, and the routine that governed her life no longer existed. She ate meals alone in her room, not in the dining hall. She couldn't meet with other residents to play cards. Visits with family were through a window, talking over a speakerphone. Even walking in the corridors was discouraged, and then only if she wore a mask. Her dementia spiraled rapidly, and my sisters and I tried to navigate the sudden change.

Mom began to talk about our deceased father in the present tense, as in, "Your father and I had an argument last night, and he didn't come home," or "Your father left for work, and I'm not sure when he'll be back." She would call us in tears, saying that her sisters (both deceased) had visited but then left without saying goodbye. It soon became apparent that Mom's distress came from feeling abandoned. Isolated in her room away from friends and family, her mind was trying to make sense of it all. My sisters and I would often express sympathy for her imagined situation and then try to distract her with news from the family.

This worked most of the time, but one morning my mother called me and yelled, "I suppose you heard all about it. Your father's left me for another woman."

Surprised at her angry tone, I answered, "No, I hadn't heard that."

"He did. He dropped me off here and left. Hasn't been back. He must have taken up with some tart."

She was obviously very upset, but everything I'd read warned me not to tell someone with dementia that their loved one had died. It would only make them grieve all over again. I struggled to think of the right answer to calm her down.

"You're not saying anything," Mom snapped at me. "Have you met her? This woman he's having an affair with?"

Against all advice, I blurted out, "Mom, Daddy's dead."

Silence echoed from the phone. Then, "What?"

"He's been dead over thirty years." I steeled myself for her grief.

Instead, she muttered, "That's better, isn't it?" Then she chuckled. "I guess that explains why he hasn't visited me!"

— Kim Stokely —

Let Me See That Smile

A smile is a curve that sets everything straight.
~Phyllis Diller

Istarted my first job as a nurse's aide at one of the local nursing homes in town the morning after I graduated from high school. I was planning on a career in the medical field, so I thought the experience would be helpful in the future. I was eighteen years old and had never worked in a facility like this. I had no idea what I was getting into, but I was anxious to learn.

The first month or so, I used any spare time I got to learn more about the patients and the institution. We had always known it as Oakhurst Sanitorium. It had been built during the tuberculosis pandemic and had quite a history. I concentrated on the medical histories of the residents. It was important to know, for example, who was diabetic, had heart problems or seizures. I wanted to be ready to help just in case anything happened. I also realized as I was studying these records that most of the residents who lived there were much more than simply elderly folks who were having trouble living on their own. The majority of them had lived at the state mental hospital before they'd been moved to Oakhurst. I guess they needed the room for younger folks, so they brought the elderly to us.

Needless to say, it was a life-changing first job. Every day was a whole new series of very different happenings.

One morning, I arrived at work at 6:45 and was just starting to get everybody up for breakfast when I noticed a horrifying odor that required immediate attention. Not one but two nasty accidents had happened. This meant that breakfast was going to be a little late, and I'd have to really hurry to get all my morning tasks finished in time for lunch.

I kicked it into high gear, got everything and everyone cleaned up, and then headed toward the kitchen to get the breakfast cart. When I turned the next corner, I noticed that all the handrails had been taken down and were lying on the floor along the walls with little piles of loose screws in all the appropriate places. I looked down the hall and saw Gerald, muttering constantly to himself as he unscrewed the next set of screws with his thumbnail.

"Good morning, Gerald," I said. "You have really been busy this morning. But it's time for breakfast, so let's get you back to your room and get ready. You must be starving after all this work."

The first thing I noticed when we walked in was that Gerald's room-mate was lying on his mattress in the middle of the floor. Apparently, Gerald had begun his morning projects with Harry's bed. It was completely dismantled and lying in a pile in the corner of their room. This definitely meant another delay. I decided to get Harry up and get them both ready to eat and worry about the bed and handrails later. Once again, I started toward the kitchen, ready to duck at every turn. The rest of the journey was uneventful. It looked like it was finally going to be time to eat. Relieved, I returned to the ward and began to pass out the breakfast trays.

All was going smoothly until I got to Bill's room. I was shocked to find that he was bleeding, and it was everywhere. I called the charge nurse and rushed in to see where he was injured. As I approached him, he turned and looked up at me with a big smile, which revealed a gaping hole right in the front. In his hand was the missing tooth.

"I've been working on this tooth for weeks," he said, "and I finally got it out."

It turned out he was a retired dentist before he got dementia. He was thrilled with his accomplishment. Once again, I called for the charge nurse and proceeded to clean him up so I could get back to the tasks at hand while also making a mental note to check and make sure that Bill's breakfast included some oatmeal and applesauce — soft stuff.

When the morning finally ground to a halt, I was really looking forward to a quick break. I headed to the office to grab a cup of coffee. As I was pouring in the cream and looking forward to a quiet afternoon (what else could possibly go wrong?), I heard someone come in behind me. I turned around and was greeted by a big, toothless grin.

"Good morning, Laura," I said. "What have you been up to all morning?"

"I've been helping you," she said proudly.

"Fantastic," I replied. "Tell me everything you've done so I can scratch it off my list."

That proud smile stretched from ear to ear as she opened her apron and said, "I washed everybody's teeth for you."

There must have been sixty pairs of false teeth in there. All were spotless, but they were also "mouthless," with uppers and lowers all mixed up together and no clue as to whose mouth they belonged in. My dream of a quiet, uneventful afternoon had just taken a sharp turn, and the race was on. It was almost time for lunch, and this was undoubtedly going to take a while. I spent the rest of the morning and a good part of the afternoon matching teeth to gums and checking to see if the smile that they were smiling was actually theirs.

— Cheri Bunch —

60

The Perfect Apartment

A well-balanced person is one who finds
both sides of an issue laughable.
~Herbert Procknow

When my dad was in his early eighties, he began planning to move from his downtown apartment in Denver back to his roots in southern Illinois, closer to family. Dad considered himself a hermit, burying himself in his books and poetry writing, and only met with people on his own terms as he chose. He'd also given up driving a few years earlier, so his requirements to move were that he needed to live close to a grocery store, a fast-food restaurant or coffee shop, and a thrift shop, preferably without too many nearby neighbors.

My sister Sylvia was thrilled to let him know that she had found a perfect apartment for him — at least as far as location was concerned. The downside was that it was in a huge senior citizen's complex with a number of four-story apartment buildings. Knowing how friendly Midwesterners are, Dad was immediately concerned that the other inhabitants would be nosy and bother him when he just wanted to be alone and do his own thing.

After viewing the apartment, Dad decided it was beautiful and the price was right, so he would take his chances on nosy neighbors and move in. A few weeks later, my sister and I found ourselves lugging boxes of books, several suitcases, and other items to set up a bachelor household on the third floor of the apartment building. His apartment was at the end of the hallway, so he only had a next-door neighbor on one side and another across the hallway. We met a few residents during the move, and they all seemed very pleasant. I could see Dad's fears about nosy neighbors starting to fade as the day went on. We said our goodbyes and left Dad to spend his first night alone in his new place, feeling very positive about how things had gone.

At the crack of dawn the next morning, my dad was on the phone hopping mad, yelling that he had to move.

"What happened?" Sylvia and I asked simultaneously in shocked voices.

Dad was fuming. "Things were going great last night. I unpacked some boxes and had a little supper. About 10:00 p.m., I lay down on the futon to snooze since I hadn't made the bed up yet. I guess I was more tired than I thought and was sleeping hard when there was a loud knocking on my door. I managed to get to the door through the maze of boxes, even though I was so groggy I could barely move. I opened the door, and it was the police — at 3:00 in the morning!"

As it turns out, the apartment walls were pretty thin, and Dad's new neighbor could hear him snoring loudly. Apparently, he snored loudly for several hours and then abruptly stopped. When Dad stopped snoring, the well-meaning neighbor assumed he'd died, so she called the police. Sylvia and I could barely contain our laughter, but it took a while to get Dad calmed down.

He ended up living there for several years. When he was diagnosed with mesothelioma, his wonderful neighbors brought him food and visited him in those last few months, so I think he realized that he had found his perfect apartment after all!

— Cynthia B. Morningstar —

61

At Grandma's Feet

As soap is to the body, so laughter is to the soul.
~Jewish Proverb

"3-3-3-3," I whispered under my breath as I tapped the code at the entrance of the memory-care ward. My grandmother's nursing home was clean, and the workers were kind. Those two blessings made my grandmother's current condition and visiting her bearable.

As soon as the door opened, there was Ethel. She sat in her wheelchair with a glittery party hat propped cockeyed on her white hair.

"Well, hello, Ethel," I said.

"Hi, sweetie," she said, shuffling her feet to bring her wheelchair even closer to me. Ethel half-whispered, half shouted, "It's my birthday today."

I smiled and gave her a warm happy birthday hug. "How old are you?" I asked.

"I'm thirty-two. Thank you very much. Your grandmother has visitors today." Ethel pointed down the hall toward my grandmother's room.

While Ethel didn't know her true age, she was the guardian of the hallway. She greeted every passerby, and she knew all the happenings in the residents' rooms. I had come to know several of the residents by name and enjoyed my weekly visits with them almost as much as my visits with my grandmother.

As I peeked around the corner of my grandmother's room, I

heard my mother's and aunt's voices. They were explaining to my grandmother that the doctor would be in to check on her next week. My grandmother had been in the memory-care ward for nearly six months at this point and always asked when the doctor was coming. It was always on Wednesdays, but this escaped my grandmother's memory like most things these days. I admired the patience my mother and aunt had always shown as they faithfully cared for my grandmother through the years since my grandfather's death.

"What trouble are you ladies getting into today?" I asked. I took a few more steps into the room.

My aunt, mom, and grandmother greeted me with smiles and welcomed me.

"I was just leaving, Cindy, but I'm so glad you came to help your mom out today. Grandma had a bad night, and she's still trying to recover," my aunt said. She touched my shoulder on the way out of the room. "We'll see you tomorrow." She waved goodbye and disappeared around the corner. I heard Ethel greeting my aunt on her departure.

My mom pointed at the wooden chair across from my grandmother's recliner. "Have a seat if you like."

"I'm okay. Actually, I think I'll sit on the floor. Maybe I can put lotion on grandma's feet today," I said. I had wanted to do that during my visit the week before.

"Oh, no. Please sit there," my grandmother said. She motioned to the unoccupied chair. Her frame had shrunk these past few months, and the brightness had dimmed in her dark brown eyes. My grandmother seemed to be only a shell of the person she used to be. Time had not been kind, and her body was failing.

My grandmother was a woman of pride and dignity. She had been her whole life. While she had grown up in poverty and been a working-class citizen in her adult life, she never wanted anyone to have pity on her or see her in a vulnerable state. My grandmother certainly didn't want me to put lotion on her feet. But I was persistent.

I reached into her nightstand. "Grandma, I know you had lotion in here last week. It will feel good on your feet to have me rub them and get your circulation going. Trust me," I said. I pulled out a white tube with a blue cap that had "O-P-A-L" written on the container in a black Sharpie. It was then that the nurse's aide came in to speak with my mother. I had my grandmother's undivided attention.

I sat down at my grandmother's feet and took off her socks. My grandmother didn't protest my actions any longer. I opened the cap of the container and pushed the "lotion" out. A clear gel leached its way out of the tube into my hands. I figured it must have been a special kind of moisturizing gel. I placed my hands on my grandmother's right foot as I rested her foot on my leg. My grandmother smiled as I touched her precious feet, which had supported her while cooking so many holiday meals for the family and hanging clothes outside on the clothesline to save on electricity.

I became fearful that the temperature of the "lotion" might be too cold for my grandmother's feet. I placed my hands together. Then the texture got gooey and started to cling to my fingers. I realized this was no moisturizing gel. About the same time, the nurse's aide and my mother became aware of my misgivings. A large smile busted across the aide's face, and she tried to cover her mouth as she towered over me and held back her laughter.

"Guess this isn't lotion," I said. I looked at my hands. My palms were an ooey, gooey mess. My face flushed with embarrassment.

My mom bent down to pick up the container and read the label. "No, dear, it's ointment for your grandmother's bedsore on her rear."

We all shared in the laughter… including my grandmother. Despite the ointment, or perhaps because of it, it was a good day. Any day I hear my grandmother's laugh, it's a good day. And that day was a very good day indeed.

— Cindy Cremeans —

62

Why My Mother Has Two Phones

I have always felt that laughter in the face of reality is probably the finest sound there is and will last until the day when the game is called on account of darkness.
~Linda Ellerbee

My mother lives with me. She is 101, and she is as attached to her telephone as a phone-addicted teenager. "Where's my phone?" she asked every thirty minutes when she first moved in, which led to a massive search that involved digging through the crevices of her recliner, shaking out the blanket that covers her lap, groping under her chair, riffling through the overflowing contents of her walker, and delving into the pockets of her pants — which is usually where we find it.

It isn't a smartphone, and she doesn't use the camera feature. She doesn't use any features, for that matter. She has a flip phone. All she needs to do is flip it open to answer, which is sufficient for the ten or fifteen calls she gets every day.

Yes, you heard me right. She gets ten or fifteen calls a day!

Sometimes, she talks for several minutes, laughing, answering questions, and ending the conversation with, "I love you, too." When she hangs up and I ask her who it was, she says, "I have no idea."

She got a call the other day from a stranger who said, "Do you want a prayer today?" She hung up on him.

My brother and sister call several times a day to check up on her, and their favorite topic is food. They ask what she had for lunch and what she's having for dinner. She says, "I don't know what Bebe is cooking, but I guess I'll have to eat it, whatever it is."

Mama's phone is her lifeline to the outside world, even when she doesn't know who's calling or even if they only talk about food.

But two phones are one phone too many.

By now you are probably wondering why she has two phones, and this is where I need to confess. She used to have one phone, and I accidentally washed it. I sent it through the washing machine when I put in an armload of her clothes, and the phone came out laundered and dead.

My brother and sister told me to immerse the phone in rice, which I did, but it didn't work. Phones don't often survive a trip through the washing machine.

My mother is on my brother's family phone plan, and when I told him I washed it, he said he would get her another one. In the meantime, she couldn't go phoneless. Try taking the phone away from your teenager, and you know what I'm talking about.

So I got her a TracFone from Walmart, called the relatives and friends who are responsible for her ten or fifteen calls a day, and gave them the new number. Mama was happy again. Five weeks later, my brother's new phone arrived. I called family and friends again and told them to switch back to the old number.

This sounds like a simple thing to do, but it isn't. Her relatives and friends are a decade or two younger than she is, which means they are in their eighties and nineties. Some of them don't hear well. Some of them don't process well. And none of them understands why a woman who is 101 had two phone numbers in two months.

But we finally got it straightened out. Everything was fine for a few weeks, until something terrible happened.

I washed her phone again!

I had been checking her pockets carefully before every wash — until I didn't. So, after ruining her new phone, I reactivated her TracFone, only this time I ordered a phone pouch on a lanyard. She tied the pouch to her walker, and her phone dangles in front of her all day. There is no chance I will wash a phone in a pouch on a lanyard tied to a walker.

I had to call those same friends and relatives and tell them her number had changed again, which confused them. But I finally got the message across, and they began using her TracPhone number. Then my brother sent her another phone because she's on his family plan.

"Now you've got to call everybody and tell them her number has changed again," smirked my sister, who was visiting when the new phone arrived.

"It's not going to happen. I can't deal with it," I said. And that's why my mother has two phones. They both fit in the phone pouch, and she gets to decide which one to answer when somebody calls.

It's a bit of a challenge. She already thinks she's getting a phone call whenever the phone rings on television. "That was the phone on TV, Mama! You didn't get a call!" I tell her from five to fifty times before she catches on and puts her phones back in the pouch.

Sometimes, she answers the wrong phone, and by the time she gets to the other phone, it's stopped ringing. Then I have to call back whoever it was because she can't see well enough to dial.

But it's all worth it if it keeps Mama happy. I think there's even a proverb in the Bible about it: "It's easier for a rich man to ride that camel through the eye of a needle directly into the Kingdom of Heaven than for some of us to give up our cellphones."

— Bebe Nicholson —

63

Navel Maneuvers

The person who can bring the spirit of laughter
into a room is indeed blessed.
~Bennett Cerf

The administrator at the skilled nursing facility where I worked looked at me doubtfully. "I don't know if it is a good idea — having a party for the men that features beer? And then some sort of burlesque show, too? It sounds pretty tawdry."

But I argued on behalf of the men who, as is common in such facilities, were not only vastly outnumbered by the female residents, but also neglected because of that. As activity director, I wanted to have something just for them, something they would really enjoy. Father's Day was approaching, and I thought having a sort-of stag party — an all-guy private affair with a glass of beer and some sort of male-approved entertainment — was just the ticket.

The administrator, a straightforward woman who rarely changed her mind about anything, considered what I was asking. Finally, she said, "I think they could have near beer, but not real beer. And any entertainment has to be approved — I want it kept tasteful." I nodded and then left to consider what sort of tastefully tawdry entertainment for my all-guy shindig I might possibly come up with.

Salvation came in an unlikely form.

Cassie was a sixty-year-old Licensed Vocational Nurse who also worked at the facility. She was a pleasant, grandmotherly sort of woman, the plump and matronly type whom you expected to show up with home-baked cookies, which, in fact, she did often. I was taken aback then when she showed up at my office and offered to entertain the men.

"I'm a belly dancer," she said. "I have been studying belly dancing for twenty years, so I am very good at it. I have the outfit and can provide music — everything."

The thought of this sweet, heavyset woman performing as a belly dancer seemed a bit of a hard sell, but I needed a solution for entertainment, and she was the only solution walking in my office door. "I will have to run it past Donna; she insisted on right of approval. But if she says it is okay, then I think it is a great idea. I sure appreciate you offering to dance."

I kept my doubts to myself, but Donna, our administrator, was enthusiastic about it. "We can have the papers out to do a story! I can just see the title: 'Nurse dances for residents on Father's Day.' It will be great publicity!" And so it was set: There would be near beer and belly dancing for the men for Father's Day. I just hoped that our male residents liked it.

The day of the party, I met with the lady from our small, local paper who had come to cover the event. I wasn't sure how well this was going to work. Our men were, of course, very much of the old school, and our little stag party was supposed to be sans women — save for the entertainment. I wanted them to feel free to enjoy the show, even hoot and holler if they wanted to.

The reporter was every inch the professional and understood my concerns. She agreed to not intrude upon the show itself, but only to take pictures of Cassie in her outfit and ask the men what they thought about the show after it was all over. With this hurdle cleared, there was nothing left except to round up the men and get the party started.

And it was quite a party. The men relaxed over their glasses of near beer and joked with one another, as well as joking with me... at my expense. Harry, one of my favorite residents, made the usual comments about my receding hairline. I loved seeing the residents laugh and have a good time. "Your hair reminds me of the enemy during World War II — it's in full retreat!" The laughs and knee-slapping were worth a little ribbing, and I thoroughly enjoyed it all. These guys had long ago won my heart.

With a flourish of tiny, tinkling finger cymbals, Cassie swept into the dining room. We had closed off the dining room to give the guys privacy, and the scattered men lined the walls, leaving plenty of space in the middle of the room for the main entertainment. As she set up her cassette player, all conversation stopped. There was dead silence as everyone beheld our dancer, ample belly proudly displayed in an outfit straight out of the *Arabian Nights*.

Cassie was bejeweled and swathed in filmy layers of sheen, and as the music started, she came to life. Never had I expected this from her! She danced and twirled as several layers of silk flew from her quivering, heavy arms. The pale belly, with an appropriate rhinestone in the navel, undulated with precision, and she flirted up a storm, sitting on laps as her tinkling fingers played about the faces of the men. She gave it her all, and with abandon.

The men started to really get into it, and as Cassie's dancing was greeted with encouraging whistles and catcalls, she reveled in their enjoyment. But then came the supreme moment: Cassie arched her back and lowered on her bent knees completely to the floor. From that position, she advanced a penny down her abdomen and back up again. The room exploded in applause at that!

But it all finally came to an end, and the men didn't seem to mind at all when the reporter entered to take pictures and ask a few questions. I was giving Harry a refill on the near beer when she asked him how he had liked the show. Good ol' Harry, charming rascal that he was, replied with apparent gruffness, "I've seen better." He paused for a moment and smiled broadly before adding, "But not around here!"

We all collapsed into fits of laughter.

These precious men are now long gone, but I will always remember them and treasure the fun we shared. It was a Father's Day stag party to remember, without a doubt. And no one could have summed it up better than Harry did in answering the reporter's question.

Apparently, she thought so too because that became the title of the article in the next week's edition of the paper.

—Jack Byron—

64

The 103-Year-Old Man with a Plan

A little bit of beer is divine medicine.
~Paracelsus

The first day I met my husband's grandfather, he gave me a clock shaped like a frying pan. It was one of many clocks he created or repaired that hung on the walls of his small Newark, Ohio home. The shape made me smile. That smile earned me the clock.

It was a proper introduction to the man I know as Grandpa Mel.

Describing Mel requires one to be comfortable with opposites. He is both loyal and independent, shy and friendly, frugal and generous, stubborn and adaptable, anxious and calm. He enjoys bean soup as much as he enjoys cheese puffs.

And cookies. Man, does he love cookies.

He will be 103 years old this August. His memory, like the rest of his mind, is sharp, able to recall small details throughout his history — people, places, political climates, the price of gas. He is a man of science and of art, interested in what makes things tick and then trying his hand at them. He appreciates the past but isn't stuck in it. Everything he has survived is part of who he is now, from major events like the Depression to personal ones like losing his wife of fifty-six years.

Mel moved to a senior home at the age of 101. It wasn't an easy decision for this independent man, but, as with everything else, he adapted. When the COVID-19 pandemic hit, the home's management locked down the facility fast. The virus has made these safe places some of the most vulnerable in the world.

Recently, Mel called while I was grading papers. His voice was clear, and he could hear me just fine. He wanted to thank us for the card we sent, but mostly he wanted to know what life was like for us during this pandemic. I shared about online school, at-home work, and in-house squabbles, wandering away from my desk and into the kitchen.

After I satisfied his curiosity, he shared what life was like for him.

He told me he's not allowed to leave his room except during lunch, which is fine as he isn't big into joining things anyway. If he gets lonely, he yells through the wall to his neighbor, whom he likes well enough. He appreciates his son waving to him through the window, especially if the visit includes dropping off his "groceries" — cookies and cheese puffs — with the front desk. Basically, he is doing fine. And if that should change, he has a plan.

"I have one beer in my fridge. If things get really bad, I'll drink it."

I couldn't help but look at my fridge when he said that. Next to the fridge, over the stove, was the frying-pan clock, ticking away as it has been for the last twenty-five years.

I thought of all the moves, upheavals, heartaches, and joys that kitchen clock has witnessed, quietly serving its purpose in whatever place we've called home. I thought of my adult children living through this global pandemic along with their great-grandfather, the consummate survivor.

I'm glad the resilient blood that flows through his veins flows through their veins, too. May they face whatever challenges life brings with an open mind, a steadfast spirit, a sense of history, and one beer in the fridge in case things get really bad.

— Nicole L.V. Mullis —

Chapter 7

Lessons Learned

Behind the Things

All my possessions for a moment of time.
~Queen Elizabeth I

The power went out as my proud, independent ninety-three-year-old father was preparing for bed in his bathroom. As he groped his way into the bedroom in the dark, he tripped and fell, hitting his head on a chair on the way down. Although the alert necklace he wore brought the EMTs, his neck was already broken.

One fall. That's all it took to propel him into a downward spiral of hospitals, rehabs, and multiple living facilities. Six months later, he was gone. But not his stuff.

My father had warned us a few years earlier. "You know, when I go, you're going to have a lot of work to do. You're going to have to get rid of everything. I won't be cleaning anything out myself." And as he aged more papers accumulated and more things were stashed all over his big house instead of being discarded.

While we managed his rehab and post-rehab care, my siblings and I also tackled his house, which was stuffed to the brim with his possessions and my mom's. She'd died years earlier. The four of us had two weeks to clear out everything but some furniture that would remain for staging the house for sale. And with that, we lifted the curtain on his life.

In the basement, we found boxes crammed with receipts and check registers annotating the lives of our parents from the day they got married and moved to Alaska in 1949. How do you dispose of seventy years of records? We went to a shredding company, taking ten free boxes a week, in three cars for three weeks. We found a box of DDT, banned back in 1972. There were mountains of ancient-looking tools, keepsakes, and recipes clipped painstakingly from magazines over dozens of years.

Every clothes closet on two floors was filled. We kept a few good sweaters, ties, a suit, and dress shirts. All the rest was so old and out of style that even Goodwill wouldn't accept most of it. We ended up filling eighty-six heavy-duty trash bags with the remnants of Dad's life.

And the kitchen? Did an old man know how many bottles of salad dressing he already had, or cans of soup, or jars of mustard or ketchup? A trip to the grocery store provided a bit of entertainment for him, so he kept on buying the items he loved. We discovered funky food items we'd given him for gifts, and those cupboards told the story of our father's secret bachelor life. Some of the food had expired ten years earlier.

Like most siblings, my sister, brother and I are all very different. So cleaning out our father's house was an exercise in accepting our diverse personalities. My sister and her husband exhibited the "throw it out, get it done, haul it away, as fast as you can" style. Heck, they even took a saw to the old deacon's bench rather than deal with it. My brother was the curious explorer, talking non-stop, doing very little and asking endless questions while he pored over the computer for hours to "scrub" it safely.

There's one in every family: a sentimentalist. That was me. Everything I touched carried my parents' energy. I was reminded of my mother's love of entertaining when I went through her tablecloths. And my dad's love of clocks of all kinds, which decorated every room. What do you do with forty-four clocks at the end of a life? I created my own "wall of clocks" with some of them.

There were countless pieces of furniture, all polished and protected for years. My sister said no one would want them, and yet I was able to find new owners for everything. It wasn't about the money. It was about the living on. The joy in seeing a refugee family take my childhood desk, or a woman who loved traditional cherry furniture see its beauty all over again…. Those donations made me happy, and they validated the life of my parents. When my sister placed the grandchildren's Hitchcock highchair out in the rain, I wiped it off, took it home, and made a new grandmother happy, for now she had a special highchair for her granddaughter. I know my mom was smiling alongside me in that moment.

So where does this end? Possessions are only possessions. The things families collect over many years don't matter. And yet, as I spent many months breaking down and turning out into the world all my parents' possessions, they did matter to me. And over the past year, as I have assimilated some of their favorite pieces into my home, I continually feel their love and presence. I feel the values that they instilled in me, like "Take care of your things, and you can have them for a lifetime." I am immensely grateful for the year that allowed me to both grieve and celebrate life, death, and my own transformation.

And my beloved father? His fall that spring night of 2019 marked the beginning of his end. I've told you about his "things." As a man, my dad will be remembered in our hearts for so much more. Three special words among many… caring, charitable, and steadfast.

If only there'd been a flashlight in every room… I want to leave you with that.

— Pattie Craumer —

A Line Crossed

Every problem has a gift for you in its hands.
~Richard Bach

He irritated me the second he pulled up right next to me. Yes, I had parked right down the center white line of two parking spaces. I usually don't do that, but the parking lot had plenty of open spaces, and I needed the extra room to load and unload the wheelchair while I escorted my ninety-four-year-old mother-in-law from store to store in her quest to "look around and see what I might want."

Okay, maybe my irritation had begun before the man pulled up. Don't get me wrong, I adore my mother-in-law; she is one of the real treasures of my marriage to Steven, more of a mother than mother-in-law. Over the decades of my marriage, she and I became best friends and comfortable companions.

But I had two daughters-in-need at home, a million things to do, and a small business to run. She'd been calling me several times a day, day after day, to take her shopping because she "needed to get out."

We'd been out more than four hours and had accomplished little as forgetfulness, indecision, and backtracking appeared to be the hallmarks of my mother-in-law's old age. In fact, I had just helped her into the car, strapped her into her seatbelt, found her water bottle, adjusted the rug under her feet, and hefted her wheelchair into the back of my car when she announced that she needed to use the restroom and would need to return to the store.

My face remained serene, but I'm ashamed to admit that my temper did rise in my chest.

So, when the guy in the stinky, dilapidated truck pulled up too close to my car and dragged his trailer into the space needed to maneuver my mother-in-law's wheelchair, I seethed inside.

Then to add to the affront, he came my way.

His face was contorted as he wrung his hands and limped toward me. Days, no, probably weeks of dried-on dirt and grease caked his clothes and beneath his nails. His hair was disheveled, his beard was several days old, and his odor was distinct even at a distance.

As he approached, I took a step back.

"I saw you and just had to talk to you," he said, breathing the sweet-and-sour smell of alcohol, both old and new, into my face.

Something in his eyes made me stop and wait.

"I saw the gentle care you were taking of your mother, and I had to stop and tell you that you touched my heart. You really touched my heart," he began as he beat his grease-smeared hand against the chest of his tattered overalls.

"You take such care of this good woman, and it fills my heart because my mama is gone now these five years, and I can never take care of her again. And I pray every day that she will forgive me. You see, I loved my mama, but I didn't always show it as much as I should have. I wanted to be a good son, but I know I failed her sometimes."

As he spoke, the man's eyes filled with tears. The cynical side of me wanted to brush it off as the alcohol talking, but the man would not be silenced.

"Oh, how I wish I could do the things for my mama that you are doing now for yours! Because, you know, I tried. I tried, but I failed. Too often, I failed. How I wish I could show her how much I love her and ask for her forgiveness!"

His pain was so present, so intense, it was clear he was experiencing her loss as if it were the first day. His remorse was so raw and his pain so deep that I could only open my arms and let him fall into my embrace.

There he stood, crying on my shoulder, lamenting, over and over, his faults as a son.

"It's okay," I said, patting his shoulder. "Your mama knows how much you love her, and I'm sure she forgives you any faults you might feel. Mamas know their children's love. They know the good souls of their babies."

As I spoke, his crying ceased. He lifted his head and looked up at me, blinking rapidly.

"Really?" he asked. "Do you think she knows? Do you think she forgives me?"

"With all my heart. I think she knows," I said with a knowledge, certain in my heart that I spoke his mama's truth.

And he felt it, too.

"My mama forgives me," he said quietly.

In the next moment, the man looked in my car and blessed my mother-in-law. Then he hugged me again and walked over to his truck. But this time, his limp seemed less pronounced and his step lighter.

I watched him as he left and wondered if had I crossed a line. Was it my place to offer forgiveness to a stranger on behalf of a woman I had never met? But even as I asked myself, the answer felt sure and right. I don't think it was my absolution that was offered. I think I merely gave voice to a loving spirit from the other side.

And with that, I closed my car door, hauled out the wheelchair again and helped my mother-in-law into the seat and back to the restroom.

Only this time, I was no longer irritated at the imposition. We all get old. What does it matter if I have work and chores? I have this mama of mine now and the opportunity for as many loving interactions as we can squeeze in before it's too late.

— Susan Traugh —

Not About Me

Love recognizes no barriers. It jumps hurdles,
leaps fences, penetrates walls to arrive at its
destination full of hope.
~Maya Angelou

"Why can't the two of you just live together?" I inquired over the phone from my home in Pennsylvania. "There are so many things to consider."

"I'm lonely," my father said from his two-bedroom apartment in the Florida retirement home.

"I understand, Dad. Remember, I was widowed twenty-two years ago," I countered. "Are you prepared to possibly say goodbye to another wife?"

Dad was eighty-eight and his new love interest, Grace, was ninety-one. Mom had died less than two years earlier after a sixty-four-year marriage, and I felt he had not totally completed his grief journey.

"Just move in together," I sighed.

"We don't do that here. This is a nice community."

I could not see his face, but I could feel the reprimand in his voice.

"Fine. But you need a pre-nup."

This would be the retirement home's first wedding and reception. Everyone was excited. Wedding-day tasks were assigned to each of his four daughters. My youngest sister informed me of my job shortly after I arrived in Florida.

"Ken will help you with the place cards. Just don't annoy him. He has post-traumatic stress disorder."

It took about thirty minutes for all the guests to be seated. A parade of walkers and canes slowed the pace. A motorized scooter brought up the rear. After all the white table cards had been handed out, Ken, twenty years younger than the average guest, stood at attention next to the empty circular table in his tuxedo. He complimented me on my assistance, although I had not touched one card, and told me to take my seat.

I sat down at table number two.

Moments later, dwarfed by tall double doors, Dad entered wearing a tuxedo. He shuffled toward the flower-decorated wooden trellis guarding the stage area at the far end of the cavernous multi-purpose room.

A black cloth banner spread across two folding chairs on the raised platform announced the evening's musical entertainment, The Velvet Touch. An electric keyboard, a tarnished saxophone tilted on a stand, and tall microphone awaited the trio.

Dad looked just like his father now. Gone were the dyed sections of hair on the top of his head that my mother insisted on perpetuating with Lady Clairol. My father's compromised hearing prevented him from accurately repeating all the vows as his betrothed stood next to him in a long, platinum-colored gown. She nudged his side twice. "Say it," she urged.

The minister prompted him again. "…In sickness and in health…"

Dad's words never fully came out of his mouth as the couple faced each other and held hands to steady one another.

Dad and his new bride kissed. Vigorous applause erupted. Forks clinked on water glasses prompting another kiss. Then the happy couple waltzed to a 1940s love ballad for their first dance as husband and wife. The Velvet Touch's lead female singer swayed back and forth and sometimes just hummed the tune in her red sequined top and black pants. The former Miss Pennsylvania 1976 did her best to keep up with the keyboard and saxophone accompaniment. I felt like I was front row at *The Lawrence Welk Show*, except there were no bubbles circling around the stage.

The smell of roast beef and mushroom gravy wafted out of the opened metal warmers. Ken commandeered the microphone and called the forty-five guests to the buffet by table number. Again, under Ken's watchful eyes, walkers, canes and the motorized scooter headed toward the food tables.

My gravy congealed before I got back to my seat. The mushrooms peeked out of the sauce like seashells in wet sand. A guest on my right explained her family history as I sculpted my cold mashed potatoes.

Steady music from the trio encouraged audience participation. Settled in for the evening in their banquet chairs, few guests were able to get out of their seats. Feeling a need to fill the empty dance floor, I jumped up to lead the Alley Cat. My shoes clicked on the parquet floor as I hopped around doing the familiar dance.

"Thank you for coming," Dad whispered in my ear as we waltzed together on the dance floor. Moisture built up under his glasses.

"You are welcome, Dad. I love you."

Following wedding-ceremony tradition, the elderly couple cut a fancy, three-tiered wedding cake and posed for pictures. A similar image of Mom and Dad's 1949 wedding photo flashed through my mind as I held up my cellphone to capture the moment. I blinked to erase the black-and-white memory.

After three hours, the celebration ended. A few guests had already trickled out and were fast asleep in their apartments. Miss Pennsylvania and the two musicians packed up and left the stage. My sisters, my daughter, my ex-brother-in-law and I gathered up Mom's silver candelabras from the cake table. We returned them to what was our mother's last residence. Now, it would be the newlyweds' apartment.

"…Until death do you part." The vows replayed in my ears as I looked out the airplane window. I didn't want to be reminded.

The wedding was over. The evening was not about how I wanted things to be. It was not about me. It was simply about the unconditional love between a father and a daughter. And that was how it should be.

— Kim Kluxen Meredith —

68

The Dollhouse

*We can only be said to be alive in those moments when
our hearts are conscious of our treasures.*
~Thornton Wilder

He let me in the door. He looked afraid. I was a substitute professional caregiver, and no one had told him I was coming. Or he just couldn't remember. I followed him to the kitchen, sat down at the kitchen table and introduced myself again. But he had a difficult time and wondered where Sharon, his full-time caregiver, was.

I tried to create conversation by asking about his family, but he seemed confused. He knew he had a daughter who was responsible for his care. But he must have been having a bad day because he couldn't remember her. However, as time moved uncomfortably forward, he did remember. She lived in Colorado, or was it Chicago?

Sometimes I can find family photos or souvenirs on the refrigerator when I visit a home. A colorful "Happy Birthday Grandma" magnet caught my eye, but his wife, he explained, had left some years ago, although he wasn't specific on date, time, year, or even whether she had passed away.

I had been told to clean the bathroom upstairs in this tri-level home, so I attempted to do so, but not without his companionship. He was suspicious while I constantly tried to reassure him.

After the bathroom was cleaned, I looked inside a bedroom. A miniature dark blue Victorian two-story dollhouse with white trim dominated the room. It sat on a platform that extended pretty much the length and width of the bedroom. Workbenches surrounded it along with a few cabinets.

"My wife and I worked on this together," he said. "We worked on everything together up until the end."

Each room of the dollhouse was intricately decorated with furniture from the 1930s and '40s and was uniquely wallpapered, sometimes with wainscoting or borders. Clocks and artwork adorned the walls, along with bookcases, removable books, and ornate Oriental rugs that covered the floors. He still knew what switches worked as he lit each room. One room was adorned with a Christmas tree for the holidays. Rooms had even been designated for the grandchildren with dolls and toys.

The porch was somewhat empty compared to the rest of the home, and he said as he caught my eye, "That is where we had to stop… That is when she…" He did not finish but walked out of the room.

He sat back in his chair in the kitchen, lost in confusion for a moment. "Who are you?" he asked again, somewhat disturbed. At that point, we called his daughter to explain. She was able to get through to him. But during my brief time there, he was quiet, still not sure of the next moment.

Before leaving, I noticed that each room in the dollhouse was still glowing with soft light. Even the Christmas tree blinked with color.

"The lights in the dollhouse are still on," I reminded him.

At first, he looked at me with fear, and then his eyes finally relaxed.

"Maybe I will keep it that way," he said.

Finally, I got it… My own lights shimmered in realization. The collaboration on the Victorian dollhouse truly defined the magic of his marriage. And regardless of his Alzheimer's, he was able to remember the details of his love, which offered him peace during moments of uncertainty.

Now, he and his Victorian dollhouse inspire me as I build my own dreams of love, companionship and total commitment to the one I love.

— Karla Sullivan —

69

What Would You Choose?

Caring is the essence of nursing.
~Jean Watson

"Geez. That new resident, Mr. Bauman, just took my head off," Cory said. "All I did was forget those little salt-and-pepper packets when I took his lunch tray to his room. You'd have thought I committed a horrible crime."

Cory had just started to work for me as a dietary aide in the nursing home where I worked as the kitchen manager.

"He depends on you," I said. "Do you like it when they forget ketchup for your fries at the drive-thru?"

"Guess not," he said and shrugged his shoulders.

After the noon dishes were finished, I gathered my kitchen crew together. "Remember, everyone, we've got mandatory training for the entire facility in half an hour with Jackie, the regional administrator, on new government regulations."

We all filed into the crowded meeting room. Every department was represented.

"Glad to see you all," Jackie said, and flashed her familiar smile.

The employees echoed her greeting. She was their favorite from corporate.

"Before we start," Jackie said, "Carolyn, if you'll assist me, please hand out these packs of paper and a pen to each person.

"I'd like each of you to number your sheets from one to seven," Jackie said. "Take a few minutes to think about the most important things in your life. Then pick the seven that mean the most and write them down, one per sheet. Number one should have the greatest value."

"How do I choose between my husband and my kids for number one?" a nurse asked.

I couldn't imagine trying to make these choices. I watched as people hesitated to put pen to paper.

"This is hard" and "I don't ever want to have to choose who and what are most important" were common declarations.

A few minutes later, Jackie said, "Okay. Please finish. We have more updates to cover."

She lectured for a few minutes on regulation changes and stopped suddenly.

"Carolyn, take this trash can," she said, handing me the metal receptacle. "Each one of you wad up one of your papers and throw it in the trash."

I was puzzled. What was she doing?

Whispers of "She can't be serious" and "What kind of cruel training is this?" along with a few expletives passed among the staff.

Jackie returned to the topic at hand. "Quiet down, please. We have a lot of changes to cover," she said over the grumblings from the group.

Five minutes later, her unsettling exercise continued with another pass to collect the papers that now took on deeper meaning. Jackie, unmoved by the protests and anger from the attendees, stared out with a coldness I didn't recognize.

"Why are we doing this?" a secretary asked.

My thoughts exactly. What was she trying to accomplish?

"No time for questions," Jackie said. "There are additional requirements we need to learn to improve the quality of care for our residents. These will affect all of us in our jobs as caretakers," she explained as she projected the information onto a screen.

Again, another pause. I couldn't understand the purpose of this exercise she insisted on continuing. This was not the lady I had considered one of the best bosses I'd ever worked for. I'd learned a great deal from this lady.

This exercise played into my worst fears. I had three children, and I had nightmares of not being able to save them all if we had a housefire. How could I choose one over the other? As a single mom, my work would be in my top seven. I was terrified of ever losing my job. My palms were moist with sweat pondering those decisions, even though I hadn't written them down.

By the sixth round of impossible decisions, I couldn't look people in the eye. I felt like the grim reaper, taking pieces of their lives with each paper thrown in the trash.

"How could you be a part of this? Did you know what she had planned?" one of my cooks asked me. She crumbled up her paper, tossed it away, and wiped her eyes. "That was my dog. He and my husband are all I have left in this world."

"I'm quitting," a nursing aide shouted. "Only a cold-hearted person could do this to someone."

"Are they paying you to humiliate us? You can tell 'em it worked," a laundry person said. "I just threw away my health. Looks like I can't work here anymore."

Several stood up, about to walk out. I stood still, not daring to move.

"We're not done here. Please take your seats," Jackie said.

Her tone was flat, and I wondered if she'd had a medical issue. After she completed her presentation, she motioned me to make my rounds.

"Carolyn, collect their last piece of paper."

I hesitated, but Jackie gave me a sideways glare and waved me forward.

"You're inhuman, Jackie," another aide shouted. "I have nothing left. You've taken it all." She clutched the last piece in her hand, kissed it and surrendered it to the trash. The rest reluctantly gave up their last cherished treasure as well. The death stares on their faces had me concerned we were headed for a mutiny and walkout.

"Now that you've broken our hearts, do you mind telling us what you were trying to prove?" a nurse asked.

It was the very question I needed an answer to as well.

Jackie's voice softened, and she clasped her hands together in front of her chest. "Just for one moment," she hesitated, her eyes damp, "I wanted each of you to feel the losses our residents endured before they walked through our doors."

A collective sigh, like the air out of a balloon, filled the room. We sat in stunned silence for a few minutes.

"I'd never thought of it like that before," an aide said, breaking the quiet. Others nodded in agreement.

I closed my eyes and shook my head in relief. I should not have underestimated Jackie. Not only was she a great teacher, but a good actress, too.

Tears streamed down several faces. A number of people got up to hug Jackie and apologize.

I caught Cory's eye. He looked at me and nodded. As we filed out of the room, he caught up to me. "That's the last time I forget the salt and pepper."

— Carolyn Hall —

Moving Mom

The universe is made of stories, not atoms.
~Muriel Rukeyser

om's long road from the nursing-care center to a room of her own at the retirement home was almost at an end. Her new life would start as soon as we got her belongings moved.

Too quickly, I sifted through piles of carefully folded slips. Whole slips, half-slips and camisoles. Long slips and short slips. White ones and black ones. Each had a story.

But I was too busy packing to listen.

After the box was brimming with too many items to give away, I caught a glimpse of Mom's face.

She knew she had to pare down, but did we have to go so fast? Her expression said it all. All night long, my mind alternated between the vision of the overflowing box and the wistful expression on Mom's face when she looked at it.

The next morning, I went to see her, and we started over. I wanted to know the story of the long silver full slip and the black one with a flounce on the bottom. How could one arrive at the age of ninety-three with two dozen new pairs of stockings still in their wrappers?

Then there was the drawer full of jewelry in little boxes marked with the name of the person who had given them to her and the occasion. "From Patty and Sara on my 80th birthday," read the box containing the three-generation gold charm bracelet my daughter and

I had made for her.

When I opened her nightstand drawer and saw it overflowing with papers, I thought, *Oh, dear, it will take her hours to go through all this.* Looking more closely, I saw they were my newspaper columns, each folded carefully and in chronological order.

My mother's life was in these drawers, and I had almost walked away and missed it. So, I am going back again tomorrow, the next day and however many more days it takes. I am going to sit and listen and treat her stories as the treasures they are.

— Patricia Bunin —

Taking Turns

Embrace a caregiving perspective that looks forward
to the years ahead with excitement
rather than disenchantment.
~Author Unknown

In 2007, my father moved in with me. He had been diagnosed with Alzheimer's several years before and had been taking some meds that had helped. But now the medicine was starting to fail, he was deteriorating, and my mother decided she didn't want to care for him anymore. She divorced him to marry someone else.

Three years before, I had found myself alone in a big house I loved. There was way too much space for just one, so I converted part of the house into a bed-and-breakfast. Repeat bookings and long-term stays made the business lucrative. But now the B&B had to close. I couldn't have paying guests with an Alzheimer's patient in the house.

He had signed over power of attorney to me in 2000. Now his mind faltered, and I needed to step up with investment decisions, insurance claims and legal issues.

My son was in the army and deployed in a very dangerous part of Afghanistan. Stress pressed in on me until I began to have debilitating migraines and insomnia. There was a lot going on in my life, and I was feeling out of control.

One day, I talked to a supportive friend. He asked me how things were going, and I ranted and raved about how life was so unfair, how I had to carry the weight of the world, blah, blah, blah. After I finished,

I slumped back in my chair and sighed in frustration.

My friend waited (probably to make sure I was done!) and then said, "What do you call all that?"

I didn't hesitate. I sat up straight and took a deep breath. "Righteous indignation!"

He waited again, expressionless, with no supportive or understanding smile. So, I asked, "What do *you* call it?"

He smiled. "Piss and vinegar."

Surprised, I started to laugh. "Explain."

"Whose happiness is more important right now: yours or your father's?"

I thought about my father struggling to process emotions and events that seemed ordinary to me. I remembered his tears when he talked about his wife of sixty years and how he didn't understand why she had left him. He even lost the ability to process his pain, and my stress and frustration added to his confusion and hurt.

My heart broke for him. "His" was all I could say.

This moment changed my life. I turned my attention to my father and thought about all the love and support he freely gave me through the years. He had rescued me time and time again. Now I could give back. His life was coming to an end; mine was before me. Why hadn't I seen it before? I could put my life on hold for him. I threw this newfound compassion into our life together, determined to make his last few years happy.

Abuse suffered during his marriage began to emerge. One day, he was washing dishes and dropped a glass in the sink. The sound of broken glass urged me to run to him. I envisioned cut hands and blood everywhere. I raced up behind him and checked his hands. They were fine, but he sobbed uncontrollably. Through his tears, he apologized and told me his fear of punishment. He pleaded with me not to throw him out of the house.

I took his hands. "You can buy glasses anywhere. You are irreplaceable. I'm just glad you're alright."

We hugged until his tears subsided, and we settled in the living room to watch his favorite TV show. We talked about the show and laughed about life. By the time the show was over, he was fine. His memory of the trauma was gone.

My father was 5'11". The first time I took him to the doctor, he weighed 134 pounds. I was shocked. He didn't understand how to navigate all the steps to prepare himself food, and his wife had refused to help him. He had been slowly starving before he moved in with me. I became very attentive to his eating. After a few months, he was weighed again, but he still needed to gain more weight.

"Well, that's it!" I paused while he looked concerned at my reaction. "It's ice cream for you!"

His eyes sparkled, and a big smile filled his face while we shared a laugh together. I'll never forget it.

The quality-of-life talk with my friend changed our lives from stress and pain to love and patience. At the end of his life, he wandered through the house at night, and I would guide him back to bed. Those long nights were opportunities for caring and tenderness.

He was diagnosed with Parkinson's, and the medication made him hallucinate. I would sit with him while he talked to sisters and brothers who had predeceased him. I took their voices and gave him conversations of reconciliation.

I lived to make him smile. Even when he no longer remembered me and I became the nice lady who took care of him, I was grateful that he thought I was nice. This was about his quality of life, after all, and I wanted it to be good. He deserved that much from me.

Dad died in November 2010, but my friend's advice has stuck with me. Sometimes, things are about my quality of life; sometimes, it's about someone else's. Over the years, I've learned when to give and when to take.

—Joy Simons—

72

It's Good

Caring for our seniors is perhaps the greatest
responsibility we have. Those who walked
before us have given us so much and made
possible the life we all enjoy.
~Senator John Hoeven

"Stella, we're making fruit salad. Would you like to join us?" I asked. Stella regarded me with an eyebrow raised in suspicion. I was working as activity director at a residential-care facility for patients suffering from Alzheimer's disease, and Stella was a new resident with whom I was just getting acquainted.

"Okay, I'll make the fruit salad," she said with a slight edge in her voice, "but there's one thing I won't do."

I was half-distracted by another resident, Dolly, who was devouring the banana I had given her to slice with a butter knife. "What is it, Stella?" I asked, one eye on Dolly and the banana that I had decided was pretty much lost for the fruit salad.

"I won't love you up, mister!"

That got my attention fully back on Stella. "Stella! I wouldn't ever..."

But Stella wasn't finished speaking. "You're not as handsome as you think you are. I can do *much* better than you!"

I found myself speechless, feeling my skin burn lobster red and wondering how I could get her focused on the fruit-salad disaster happening at the table. Joe had seized the whipped topping and was spreading it on his face like shaving cream, and Dolly had been joined by Martha and Lily in eating the unassembled salad.

"Stella, can you help me with the fruit salad? It looks like it needs our help before it's all eaten up."

To my relief, Stella nodded and started accompanying me to the table. But she seized my arm and stopped me after a few steps, appraising me sternly with jaw set and brows knitted in serious authority. "Just don't beg me, mister! I can't stand it when a man makes a fool of himself trying to win my heart!"

I hastily replied, "You don't have to worry about me, Stella. Now let's see about our salad."

Dolly, Martha and Lily looked up at me, contentedly munching pieces of banana, grapes, and orange slices. Joe was patiently "shaving" the whipped cream off his face with the plastic butter knife that had been meant for the banana.

At my side, Stella said, "I'm not helping you clean this mess up, mister!" Turning and marching away, she looked back over her shoulder, adding, "And don't beg me!"

***

I had begun working with Alzheimer's patients for lack of a career — an art career. I had gone to art school and trained to be a commercial illustrator but found very little work. If I had moved someplace else, some big city like New York, things probably would have been much different, but I never strayed too far away from the Southern California desert communities that were my home.

Needing something to do, I began to work as an activity director. It was one of the jobs you were qualified for if you had a basic degree in absolutely anything, and my art background allowed me to add creativity to the routine.

And I found that I loved the residents. I loved them for their sweetness and the feisty side I saw when others saw only the anger and frustration that sometimes characterizes the Alzheimer's patient. I loved the silly moments and the touching moments of sadness that revealed the one thing that Alzheimer's disease never robs someone of... their heart.

I decided that the patient dealing with this disease was approaching a suddenly confusing world in which they could no longer trust their own judgment with no less than pure courage and dignity; they taught me a lot about both, lessons that I have never forgotten. Besides, there were many laughs, more often than not at my expense. Some residents had a wicked wit, which I truly appreciated.

One day, I was working on an art project with a group of ladies — there were far more women than male residents, something common to all care facilities — and found my rapidly retreating hairline a subject of discussion. Bobbie was having difficulty working with the sand we were using to make sand paintings. Looking up in frustration, she said, "I can't see this well enough!"

I was distracted, motioning over one of the nurse aides to help me keep Dolly from eating the brightly colored sand and glue, but asked, "Isn't there enough light? Maybe I should open the blinds."

Bobbie sat back, crossing her arms as she watched us try to get glue and sand out of Dolly's smiling mouth. "No, there's *too much* light! It's shining off that bald head of yours!"

I turned back, grinning sheepishly as I rubbed sand off my gluey fingers. "Do you think I should get one of those fancy hairpieces? Maybe it will improve my appearance!" A general note of sympathy issued from the ladies, with comments as to how I was fine without such a thing.

But no such sympathy came from Bobbie. "Oh, it *would* improve your appearance," she said with the mischievous grin that I loved plastered from cheek to cheek, "especially if you got one of those long ones and combed it down over your face."

Looking over my little group of laughing ladies, all glue and sand and cheerful mayhem, I felt my ever-present lobster blush burn as I joined in the laughter. Another lesson in courage and dignity from these teachers of mine.

***

Alzheimer's disease only ends one way, and there is no escaping it.

One by one, the laughing voices went silent. The tables of glue and sand and fruit and mayhem saw new hands replace the recently absent ones. And I mourned each passing as I would a member of my family — which they indeed became. It was hard every time, but there was always someone new — new laughs, new tears.

On the patio of the facility, Stella sat, shielding her eyes from the setting sun. "Stella," I said, "would you like to come in? It's pretty hot out here." Stella shook her head, eyes peeking out from under the outstretched hand above her brows. I started to leave, but she called me back.

"Mister, are you afraid of getting old?" I kneeled beside her chair and looked at the horizon too, all the pinks and purples of the cloud-flecked sky. "I don't think so, Stella. Why?" She didn't turn her fixed gaze one bit.

"Don't be. It's good to get old. I'm like that sunset, my day almost done. You take a sunset just the way it is, no matter *how* it is. But ain't a sunset pretty like nothin' else?" I had a lump in my throat, but Stella continued, "Even when things are rough, it's good. Life's full of rough things, whether you're old or young. Remember that and appreciate it. It's good."

We watched the sunset together. She reached over and patted my hand, wisdom imparted; another lesson, another gift. The sun lit her face, a faint smile appearing.

I miss the days of sand and mayhem, new laughter and new tears, and shared sunsets. I miss my gentle teachers, their courage and dignity. I miss them all but appreciate their lessons.

I remember. It's good.

— Jack Byron —

73

You'll Never Know, Dear

When you look into your mother's eyes, you know that
is the purest love you can find on this Earth.
~Mitch Albom

As chaplain in a senior-care facility, I dealt daily with patients suffering with various forms of dementia. Harriett was one of many. She had a vacant, glassy stare, and her speech was repetitive, often incoherent. My usual routine on Harriett's floor was to lead in worship with my guitar on Thursday mornings in the common room. Most of "worship" involved singing hymns and old favorites requested by the residents. Old, familiar songs tap into long-term memory banks, and words come easily for many when set to music. Even some who are generally nonverbal are able to sing some of the words.

Harriett always joined us for these gatherings. She would sit in her wheelchair and smile as I belted out all kinds of tunes from "The Old Rugged Cross" to "How Much Is That Doggie in the Window?" It was the oddest conglomerate of songs for a worship service ever compiled, but we sang whatever the residents wanted to sing. For Harriett, her song was "You Are My Sunshine." Often, she would sing the chorus. Some days, she would simply smile and nod her approval. On other days, despite my effusive introduction that we were now going to sing "Harriet's Song," she would stare blankly into space. That's when

I wondered if she comprehended anything that we were doing or if she was simply lost in the din of my guitar and the offbeat jangle of accompanying plastic instruments played by the residents.

Harriett's son Joe would often visit during these times of singing on Thursday mornings and stand around awkwardly on the outskirts of the circle of wheelchairs, watching his Mom and listening. He was a lawyer and worked nearby. Usually, Joe would check in with a "Hi, Mom" and then, not knowing quite what to do, would leave after about ten minutes. Once, when I introduced myself to him, he told me that Harriett had been a dancer in her younger years and loved music. He wanted his mom to be happy in this place, but she was becoming less verbal and frailer, and it was increasingly difficult to communicate with her. This slow loss of a loved one was a very familiar scene for me as a chaplain, and I was as supportive as I could be while I listened to him talk.

Joe kept visiting as Harriett declined. One day, I saw them sitting together just outside of the circle of wheelchairs when I arrived. Joe was holding her hand. I decided to start by playing "Harriett's Song," and I gave Harriett the heads-up. She didn't look like she responded at all. She stared at me blankly.

"Harriett," I said again. "We are singing your song, 'You Are My Sunshine'!"

Harriett seemed to stir a bit, and a tiny light glinted in her eyes. She had been unable to sing for a while, but I could see that something in her seemed to awaken. Then, as I began, she turned to Joe and looked intently at him.

The guitar strummed, the maracas shook, the tambourines jingled, and Harriett's gaze never wavered. Her message to Joe that day was sung by others and filled the room. Yet she wanted her son to know it was from her. She waited until exactly the point in the song where there would be no doubt about the message. Then the stanza…

You'll never know, dear, how much I love you…
Please don't take my sunshine away.

For each word, she pointed at Joe with her index finger in perfect time to the music, meeting his eyes with resolute candor, as if wanting him to know that the very deepest part of her heart was still functional, even though other faculties were fading fast. When it was over, she studied his face, the face she knew and still recognized. Joe wiped a tear from his cheek.

"Thank you, Mom," he said.

— Kim V. Engelmann —

74

Curtain of Memories

Compassion makes us pause, and for a moment
we become better people.
~Author Unknown

October 2015 brought huge changes to my family, especially to my eighty-seven-year-old grandfather. My grandmother, his wife of sixty-seven years, passed away suddenly from a stroke. We did not think he would recover from this loss, and he began to slip into a depression.

That's when I stepped in. As the only grandchild, I decided that it was time for me to consider moving back home. My sons were both headed to college, and I would be an empty nester in the coming fall. The timing would be perfect, and Granddaddy would not be alone anymore. I thought it might be the thing he needed to survive.

The moving-in process started by rearranging his house. He and my grandmother had shared a set of bedrooms with a Jack-and-Jill bathroom that was located at the rear of the house. There was also a master bedroom, which had been a guest room for years but never housed any guests. My mom and aunt agreed that switching his room to the master bedroom would be good for him since it would get him away from my grandmother's bedroom. My sons and I would take the bedrooms at the back and share the bath when they were home from college.

At first, Granddaddy did not want to do this. He wanted me to take the master bedroom, and he and the boys would share the bathroom at the back. When I explained that I might have friends visit, and he would have to share the bath with them, he decided the master bedroom would be better for him. Not that he would mind sharing, but sharing with his granddaughter's friends was not what he wanted to do! He grumbled at the beginning after making the move to his new room. Change was difficult for him, to say the least.

As we began to clean out cabinets and reorganize things around the house, he grumbled even more. We rearranged the furniture in the living room to better suit the angles in the room and to get the most out of the living-room space. As we did this, we noticed that his "newspaper sofa" (the one he sits on every day to read his newspaper) had ripped down the side. It was coming apart at the seams.

We asked if he wanted us to repair or re-cover it. Oh, no way! He liked it the way it was because my grandmother had picked out that sofa set. Memories were more important than a stylish living room.

In the room where the "newspaper sofa" sat, the sheer curtains on the windows were the same way — dry-rotted. They had big holes in them, and the holes grew if you touched them. Those sheers covered the wall of windows in the mid-century modern house and were so large that they had to be customized to fit. My grandmother had bought enough sheers back in the 1980s but had to sew them together to make them fit properly.

Thinking that I was helping because he did not want to spend money to replace them, I called a home-improvement store and had the wall of windows measured for new vertical blinds.

I did this all strategically while he was at his water-aerobics class. He went three times a week and was gone for several hours, so I knew that I would have enough time to get the installer scheduled and the blinds ordered. Operation Curtain Replacement commenced.

I planned the surprise perfectly. The installer showed up during the perfect time frame and was in and out lickety-split. He put up the new blinds, and they were beautiful. No more rotting curtains!

After lunch, Granddaddy came home and walked into the living room to read his newspaper on the "newspaper sofa."

"My God, what happened to my curtains!" he said.

"I bought you new blinds because the old curtains were rotting off the window," I said excitedly.

Granddaddy got very quiet and didn't say anything. The silence became like an elephant in the room.

"Granddaddy, don't you like them? The old ones had holes in them," I replied just to break the silence.

"They're different."

That was the only response he gave. I was disappointed. He was hurt. Neither of us understood the other's point of view. I was beginning to understand some of the things my grandmother had always told us about him.

The real issue with the new blinds came in many pieces. First, I had changed something that I didn't ask permission to change. Even though this was now my house in my mind, it wasn't that way in his. The house still belonged to him and my grandmother. I was just a guest. Of course, I didn't ask because he would have told me he didn't need new blinds. He didn't care about the rot or the holes in the curtains. Only I was bothered.

Second, I had committed the ultimate sin. I had removed my grandmother's handiwork and replaced it with something new. He was hurt because I had removed another piece of her. Once again, I had overstepped my boundaries as his new housemate. I thought his rotting drapes were caused by his frugalness. I failed to realize that they were reminders of my grandmother. He had watched her sew them together in this very room!

The lesson I learned was that new is not always best. Sometimes, a curtain of memories is more important.

— Amy Mewborn —

Chapter 8

Self-Care

Journaling
the Journey

Writing is medicine. It is an appropriate antidote to injury.
It is an appropriate companion for any difficult change.
~Julia Cameron

Countless books and articles describe dementia. Hospital support groups educate caregivers and families. The Internet offers an overload of information. But even with all these resources, when my husband had several little strokes and was diagnosed with vascular dementia, I felt overwhelmed and ill-equipped to handle my role in his recovery. I discovered one activity, however, that proved helpful to me and my husband's medical team — something many people may not have considered — and that's journaling.

I've kept a journal or diary, off and on, for much of my life, especially when facing difficult times. My journal isn't a fancy, leather-bound book filled with words of wisdom, written on parchment with a feathered pen. Instead, it's a Microsoft Word document where I note my observations, feelings, and uncertainties.

When I first noticed changes in my husband's behavior, I tried to make sense of what was happening. I started writing about what I observed, while also including my reactions. His "episodes" seemed puzzling and innocent at first. Most notably, after being our family's cook throughout our marriage, why was he suddenly messing up familiar

Self-Care | 241

recipes? The chicken breasts in one of our favorite dishes were raw when he served them, even though I'd suggested he thaw the frozen pieces before baking. He'd scoffed at my advice, said it wasn't necessary, and refused to adjust the baking time or temperature.

Why had he left the refrigerated dessert melting on the counter hours before dinner guests arrived? He'd successfully made the dish in the past and knew it needed to be kept cold. Why did he overcook the steaks until they were hard and dry and forget to add the sauce?

I acknowledged that everyone makes mistakes, and we were both getting older. Maybe this was a normal part of aging. But because of his love of cooking, these lapses were warning signals. I noted my concerns in my journal along with the dates the situations occurred.

As my husband's behavior became more worrisome, I wrote about those instances, too. He gave access to his computer to scammers more than once. He scraped the side of the car on the garage. Strange charges appeared on our credit-card bills. I discovered all these things accidentally (he began being secretive) and dealt with them as best I could.

As his condition progressed, I wrote more often. With no one having access to what I recorded (the file has a password), I was able to vent my confusion and fear without restraint. By organizing my thoughts in writing, I often found clarity and was sometimes able to come up with solutions to situations that at first seemed hopeless. Almost every day, I made an entry.

One afternoon while I was away from the house, my husband fell in our back yard. When I came home, he was disoriented and in pain. He couldn't tell me what had happened. I called the paramedics. He was taken to the hospital with a broken clavicle, and there he was diagnosed with vascular dementia. And that's when another benefit of my journal came to light. When the doctors asked me how long ago I'd noticed changes in his behavior, I couldn't think of a specific date. It had all happened so gradually. Then I mentioned I'd kept a journal. They were delighted that I had a record and asked me to share it with them.

I edited my raw journal to create a list of circumstances and dates (removing my personal comments) and provided a picture of events as they'd occurred. This gave the doctors a view of my husband's situation, a timeline for his behavioral changes, and insight into the progression of his disease.

After his hospital stay, my husband was transferred to a rehabilitation facility. From there, he went to memory care. In my journal, I explored the pros and cons of that move. I included countless to-do lists. I met with an attorney and a financial advisor. I talked to doctors and researched everything I could find online. I spent hours on the phone, took care of what had to be done, and reacted to unexpected challenges, all of which I wrote about. After being given medication to improve his cognition and help prevent future strokes, my husband is now in assisted living. He's slowly improving and regaining many of his abilities every day.

I still write in my journal. It helps me work through the decisions I need to make regarding my husband's care, and it gives me an outlet to admit my frustrations and a place to celebrate our occasional triumphs. I write about my own shortcomings, anger, sadness, fear, and other negative feelings in their rawest forms — expressing things I would feel embarrassed or ashamed to reveal to my friends or family. My journal is my safe space.

Writing in my journal has been a priceless tool for me and my husband. It has led to better care for him, and better self-care for me.

— Sandra White —

Care for the Caregiver

There are only four kinds of people in the world:
Those who have been caregivers. Those who are
currently caregivers. Those who will be caregivers,
and those who will need a caregiver.
~Rosalyn Carter

My first caregiving experience involved driving 180 miles round trip every day to see my grandmother who was terminally ill. It left me physically and emotionally exhausted, and I felt I was neglecting my two young daughters. I was certainly torn as the weeks turned into months, but the desire to comfort my grandmother in her last days was overwhelming.

Years later, my eighty-seven-year-old father required more nursing skills than my siblings or I could provide. He was admitted to a long-term veterans' facility. Living 700 miles away, I made the trip as often as I could for six long years. I deeply regretted not being his caregiver, but I did act as his health advocate. I'd like to think our nightly phone calls, filled with laughter and family news, provided him emotional support. When I visited, I brought old photos and DVDs of our home movies. They always brought a huge smile to his face. I also took tasty baked goods for all the staff who paid special attention to his wellbeing.

Then, ten years ago, I became a cancer patient. Now, I was the one who needed care. After having been the first one to offer comfort and support in times of misfortune, I found it humbling to be the recipient and accept help. Friends provided meals, house cleaning, and rides to appointments. The gratitude I felt for these wonderful acts of kindness was beyond words. Their thoughtfulness enabled me to find my inner strength and focus all my energy on healing my mind and body.

Now in my seventies, I'm long past the "sandwich generation" part of my life. In trying to find a meaningful purpose, I came upon the idea of offering my assistance to the next generation of caregivers. I knew both sides of the struggle, and these efforts allowed me to pay it forward for the incredible amount of support that I received in my own journey back to wellness.

A challenging opportunity arose when two dear friends were unable to travel to their winter home in Florida. My friend has multiple sclerosis and is wheelchair-bound. While recovering from surgery, her husband and sole caregiver was not allowed to drive. When they asked me to be their chauffeur, I didn't hesitate, so we headed south on an adventure.

I also engage in cooking marathons as I prepare chicken soup, quiche, and apple pie to help out the caregivers I know. I find joy in taking over this responsibility for those attending to a loved one.

I had to modify my schedule due to the pandemic, but I look forward to resuming my visits to the caregivers I know. Offering a listening ear, presenting a meal, and helping with household chores can be a great blessing. Having someone temporarily take over these duties was a godsend to me.

As I continue my ministry of caring for caregivers, I strive to bring peace to these compassionate souls and smiles to their faces. I welcome the chance to lift the burden off their shoulders, even if it's for just a minute.

— Terry Hans —

77

No More Superwoman

For fast-acting relief, try slowing down.
~Lily Tomlin

"**M**ommy, I'm hungry," my five-year-old son, Nathan, whined from the back seat. My other kids seconded his complaint. I'd just picked them up from school, and now we were headed to the hospital to see my father-in-law, Larry. The week before he'd suffered yet another stroke and had ended up in the intensive-care unit, where children were not allowed to visit. That morning, they'd moved him into a regular room. I thought my kids would be excited to finally see their grandpa, but they were all in sour moods.

I sighed, trying to shake off the feeling of being overwhelmed that had become a constant in my life. "I know you're hungry, guys. We'll get something in the cafeteria at the hospital."

More protests from the back seat.

"Why can't we stop on the way?" one asked.

"I hate the food at the hospital," another griped.

"Grandma has been at the hospital all day by herself, and I'm sure she hasn't eaten," I said. "It'll be nicer if we wait and eat with her, even if we don't like the food."

When we arrived at the hospital, the kids and I headed through the now-familiar hallways, looking for Larry's new room. Nearly a year ago, Larry had suffered the first in a series of strokes, which had left him almost completely incapacitated. We were caring for him at home, and although my husband has a large family who were all pitching in, it still felt like a huge responsibility.

When we got to his room, my mother-in-law, Judy, was standing in the hallway. Immediately, I felt panicked. "Is he okay?" I asked.

"He's fine. The nurse is with him, so I stepped out for a breather. We can take the kids in when she's done with him." I understood without words that the nurse was changing him, and she didn't want the kids to see.

Judy hugged the kids and said, "I'm so glad Grandpa moved to a regular room so you can visit him now." My kids nodded, but none of them looked excited to be there.

"Have you eaten anything?" I asked. "The kids are hungry." That word restarted the barrage of complaints.

Judy smiled at the kids in that way only grandmas do. "Didn't you have lunch at school?" she asked.

Nathan scowled. "No, the lunch today was a burrito, and I don't like that. Mommy was supposed to pack my lunch, but she forgot."

"I didn't forget," I said. "I just couldn't remember what day it was. I thought they were serving pizza, and you like pizza."

The scowl grew. "But it wasn't pizza. It was a burrito, and I hate that."

My daughter, Julia, chimed in. "Yeah, and usually when Mom picks us up from school, she brings us a snack, but today, she forgot."

"I said I was sorry…" I started, but the kids weren't done.

"Mom has been forgetting a lot of stuff lately," my middle son, Jordan, said. "She was late to pick me up from practice yesterday. And last week, she said she checked my math homework, but I still got two problems wrong."

My face burned with embarrassment, but Judy seemed amused. "Take it easy on your mom, guys. She's been busy lately."

Jordan shook his head. "It's been like this for a long time."

"Yeah, like a year," Julia said.

"Your mom is doing the best she can," Judy said quietly.

I smiled at her, appreciating her efforts to defend me. It wasn't her fault that even my best wasn't very good.

Before my kids could point out any more of my shortcomings, a woman poked her head out of an office across the hall. "Can I talk to you for a second?" she asked me.

I moved quickly, thinking that she had news to share about Larry. But when I walked in, she was holding a package of graham crackers. "I couldn't help overhearing your kids say they were hungry," she said. "I know it's weird to take food from a stranger, but would you like to have these?"

She was a hospital employee, and the crackers weren't opened, so I thought it was all right. I glanced at her name tag. "Thank you, Amy," I said. "I appreciate this."

"I'm happy to help," she said. She invited the kids into her office to sit down and eat. When they were settled, she said, "I'll be in the hall with your mom and your grandma." Then she closed the door behind her, shutting my kids in her office by themselves.

At my surprised look, she laughed and said, "I had to rescue you from them. Kids can be brutal sometimes."

My heart dropped when I realized that this kind lady had overheard my kids complaining about my many recent parenting failures. Before I could say anything, she shook her head. "Nope. Don't do that. Don't you dare beat yourself up for not being Superwoman." She nodded at Judy. "Your mother-in-law and I had a long chat this morning. She told me that you all have been taking care of Larry at home for the past year. Caregiving can be overwhelming."

I shrugged. "We're a big family, and everyone is doing their part. I only help a few days each week."

"Don't minimize what you're doing," Amy said. "Caregiving is stressful, especially when you've still got young kids. They call it the sandwich generation because you always feel smashed in the middle."

I nodded. "I do feel overwhelmed. I've got a lot of balls in the air, and lately I've been dropping more of them than I've been juggling. I just can't keep up."

"Of course, you can't. You can't add a huge responsibility like caregiving into your life and expect to do everything else perfectly, too. It's impossible."

I nodded as I felt a lump in my throat. I was awfully close to crying.

"You need to give someone else a few of the balls you've been juggling."

"There's no one to give them to," I said. "My husband has a demanding job, and he helps with Larry every day."

"Your kids are old enough to help," Amy said. "Judy told me that your extended family is sharing the burden of Larry's care. But at your house, you're carrying everything on your own. It's time to stop juggling more than you were designed to handle."

"Thank you," I said quietly. "I think I just needed someone to set me free of my own expectations for myself."

Amy squeezed my hand. "None of us is Superwoman, and that's perfectly okay."

That night, we had a family meeting. "Grandma and Grandpa need my help, and that means I need your help," I told the kids. We brainstormed some ways to lighten my load and minimize the number of balls that dropped each day.

Life is always a balancing act, and caregiving is a huge responsibility. When we're overwhelmed by the juggling act, it's fine to hand off — or even set aside — a few of the balls we're juggling. Sometimes, we just need someone else to see our struggles and give us permission to slow down and take care of ourselves, too.

— Diane Stark —

78

Freeing Ruth

*It's not an easy journey, to get to a place where you
forgive people. But it is such a powerful place,
because it frees you.*

~Tyler Perry

I could hear her death rattle even before I entered her room in
the nursing home. My mother-in-law, Ruth, lay motionless in
the bed, struggling to breathe. Though I'd heard those sounds
before, I would never get used to them. I felt torn. This woman
made it apparent she had never liked me. Yet, because of the love I
have for my husband, I took care of her for years.

Ruth grew up one of eight children. Her mother died during
childbirth when Ruth was six. Her father, a farmer, couldn't handle
all the responsibilities and committed suicide when she was nine.
Afterward, the kids were split up. Ruth and her older sister were sent
to boarding school and spent the summers with different relatives. My
mother-in-law never got over the feeling of being abandoned.

Unfortunately, Ruth went on to marry men who were abusive in
many different ways. Her first husband was physically and emotionally abusive. The second left her for another woman. And the third
emotionally and verbally abused both Ruth and my husband, Tommy.

While I understood how she must have felt after all that, I never
could comprehend why she turned on Tommy and me. Nothing we
did was enough. All the while, we tried our best to care for her as she
went through two heart surgeries and cancer treatment and eventually

went blind. I took her to doctors' appointments and spent days on end sitting with her as she received chemo. Nevertheless, she told me daily I was not the woman she would have picked for her son.

Ruth demanded to stay in her own home as she grew more ill, and we did everything possible to follow her wishes. It started out with daily visits, cooking her meals for a week at a time, and monitoring her medications. When that wasn't enough, we hired caregivers to help her ten hours a day. She said she was capable of staying alone at night. However, we soon learned she was asking different friends to spend the night. She lured them in by saying that Tommy and I wouldn't help her at all.

At her doctor's request, we moved her to an assisted-living facility. The facility asked to have her removed. She constantly caused trouble. She would call her stepchildren and threaten to commit suicide with knives she had picked up during her meals. (The knives were plastic.) Another suicidal ploy involved a phone call—again to her stepchildren—saying she had tied a sheet around her neck and was going to jump out the window. (The facility only had one floor.) All of this caused angry phone calls to my husband and drove a deep wedge that divided us from the extended family.

We finally had to place Ruth in a skilled nursing facility. Tommy visited her after work every day, only to be met with more complaints. We both visited every weekend, but each time the verbal abuse heightened. Still, we tried our best to honor and care for her as effectively as possible.

Then one day, Ruth fell and had to be taken to the hospital. Her body was riddled with cancer. She deteriorated very quickly.

Now, here we were, just the two of us. I called my husband to come. He was an hour away, and I knew he wouldn't get there in time. I called hospice, my dad (who was also her pastor), and my best friend.

The years of abuse didn't matter to me, but I felt what she had done to my husband was unforgivable. He was the best son anyone could ask for. He took care of her despite the mistreatment. He loved her. But I saw the pain and scars she had created.

It is harder to forgive pain inflicted on the one you love the most.

I had a huge decision to make. Should I forgive her? She had given birth to the man I loved, and I did love her for that. She had also been a victim most of her life, and abuse was a lifestyle for her. But forgive her? I didn't know if I could.

At the same time, I could hardly stand to see her suffering, so I stroked her hair and talked quietly to her. I had heard that a person's hearing was the last to go. Finally, my heart couldn't stand it any longer.

I got as close to her as I could and said, "I love you and forgive you." Her body relaxed. Just as this happened, my dad and my friend arrived. We all held hands, and my dad prayed. She drew her last breath, and I watched as her spirit left her used-up body. It was a beautiful sight. She had finally found peace. I don't know if she was waiting to hear my words, but they seemed to set her free. A huge weight had been lifted from both of us. She was finally free, and I was no longer angry.

Anger bound us together in unhealthy ways and wounded my heart, but my unforgiveness hurt me more than it did my mother-in-law. By forgiving her, healing took place.

In freeing Ruth, I also freed myself.

— Jennifer Clark Davidson —

79

Kleenex Capers

The only real mistake is the one from which
we learn nothing.
~John Powell

One, two, three, four. My head nods to the annoying rhythm of the sounds. They're worse than nails on a chalkboard! I feel the muscles in my shoulders tighten and realize I'm holding my breath. Who would have thought that the sound of Kleenex being pulled from the box could be so incredibly nerve-wracking!

At first, I thought she was using the tissues to wipe her nose, until I took a moment to sit and watch closely as she pulled out one at a time, unfolded it, and carefully added it to the growing stack on her lap. When the stack finally reached the correct height, she took the top one into her hands, meticulously folded it into a perfect square and gently placed it in the small wicker wastebasket on the floor next to her recliner. She continued until the pile on her lap was gone and then began the process all over again. One, two, three, four.

Repetitive actions are the most frustrating part of Mom's cognitive-behavior issues and make my job as her caregiver more stressful than all her physical needs combined. I've tried a variety of methods to wean her from the tissue routine without success. It's possible to distract her for a while, but she goes right back to it.

My one attempt to talk with her about it didn't go over well. Thinking I was upset because she was using too many tissues, Mom reached for her purse and tried to give me money to pay for them. It made me feel so sad that I've never been able to broach the subject again.

Probably the only real harm in this repetitive activity is that it causes me anxiety. However, going through a large box of tissues every day is also a waste of money and resources.

I don't mean to sound so self-centered, especially with everything my mother is having to endure, but I do believe there is truth in what I've read about the importance of relieving caregiver stress and fatigue. Our doctor also cautions me that if I don't stay healthy, my mother's health suffers as well.

So, I hatched a plan to reduce my stress caused by this particular behavior. I decided to salvage the unused tissues from Mom's waste-basket. Perhaps, if I could recycle them, my anxiety level would drop.

I squatted down behind Mom's chair, reached around and grabbed a handful of the neatly folded tissues from the basket. I ran to the laundry room with my booty and opened each tissue, laid it flat on top of the previous one, forming a nice little pile on the ironing board.

I did this several times a day. Watching my stack grow over the weeks was extremely gratifying. I felt so much better until the day my daughter came to visit and went to look for something in the laundry room.

"Mom!" she shrieked. "What is this huge stack of tissues doing on the ironing board?"

Grasping at the chance for a little humor to soften the situation, I yelled back, "Isn't it nice that I've finally found a use for the ironing board?"

When I walked in to explain what I was doing with a nearly two-feet-high pile of tissues, I wasn't prepared for her response. "Mom, don't you see you're doing exactly the same thing Granny does? I'm afraid that I'm going to be caring for both of you before long!"

That jolted me right back to reality. Jacqui was right! I decided it was time to bite the bullet — forget about Granny's tissues and find something that works to safely relieve my anxiety.

In my search for a solution, it came to mind that I hadn't been going on long walks like I used to. Perhaps that was one reason I had been feeling more anxious and fatigued. I didn't like leaving Mom alone these days while I walked several miles from the house, but we had the perfect place to walk on our own acreage.

With camera in hand, I ventured to the pond one sunny fall afternoon. It was much more peaceful than I had remembered—a nature reserve, a sanctuary for my troubled spirit. The birds were chirping in unison from their perches on tree limbs, while the geese and ducks floated together on the pond. Heart-shaped, mating dragonflies fluttered among the reeds of pond grass and cattails. I got lost in the sounds of nature as I snapped beautiful photos of the natural habitat.

I strolled back across the field to the house feeling refreshed with the warm sunshine on my face. I hadn't felt this peaceful in a long time. I vowed that I would walk to the pond at least once and maybe twice each day.

I have managed to keep that promise to myself, and I have gotten much better at dealing with Mom's repetitive behaviors. I no longer collect the tissues she discards. I have come to the conclusion that the excessive tissue use is her way of coping with anxiety. Perhaps it is both mentally and physically therapeutic for her. I have also made an attempt to get her outside every day. There is nothing more rewarding than sharing Mother Nature's therapeutic beauty with those I love.

— Connie Kaseweter Pullen —

80

Treading Water

Caregiving often calls us to lean into love
we didn't know possible.
~Tia Walker

I'm swimming with my mom. We dive deep into the clear water. Resurface. Float. "You are now swimming with the jellyfish," a man whispers.

I can feel Mom tense up ever so slightly. "Farah, doesn't he know jellyfish are dangerous?" she asks — too loudly.

I snap out of the sea.

My mother and I are sitting side by side in her bedroom. Mom, eighty-three, is on her new plastic shower chair, which I dragged from the bathroom. I'm perched on a desk chair. I check to see if the laptop is muted. Phew, it is. John, our virtual chair-yoga instructor, raises his arms. We breathe in and shake out.

This is Mom's second online exercise class. I'm not sure she knows how to use Zoom, so I'm sitting in on the first few classes. I also want to make sure she completes the class — and does it safely. Other than infrequent neighborhood walks and short sessions on our stationary bike (aka "the clothes rack"), this is the only movement option for her during this COVID winter.

Eight years ago, in my mid-thirties, I returned to my hometown of Toronto and moved back in with Mom. It wasn't by choice. I tried for three years to seize my American dream in Los Angeles, but through a series of visa issues, I got deported. Banned for five years.

I felt defeated, deflated, and depressed. When I reached Mom's front door, she offered open arms and a shoulder to cry on. I was so grateful to be home, to have my mother — and her help.

The plan was for me to live there for a while until I got my life back on track, found a new job and an apartment. Until then, we'd be two grown women bunking together — *The Golden Girls* meets *Sex and the City* — who hadn't lived together for two decades.

I'm a bit of a control freak and immediately took charge of managing the house — repairs, cleaning, bills, groceries, appointments, everything. That was good because I discovered something: Mom had fallen behind in all these areas, which wasn't like her meticulous self.

Her age was showing. One of our first battles was about her new hearing aids, which she'd "forget" to put in. I wasted half my days repeating myself. I became a loud talker.

"Turn down the volume!" my friends begged when we chatted on the phone or in person.

A few years ago, Mom's motor skills began declining. We were driving to IKEA, and she almost sideswiped a car and then drove over a grass island. I'm sure I left fingernail dents in the dashboard. Her memory, too, was failing. She was asking the same questions and making the same comments over and over. I enrolled her in a geriatric daycare program at a nearby hospital. After weeks of tests, the doctors diagnosed Mom with mild dementia and said it would get worse.

I fought back tears in the doctor's office. That night (and many nights after), I screamed into pillows and punched air. I drank too much wine. I was angry with her. My twin sister Julia (who lived in Manhattan) and I felt that her complacency toward health, exercise, and social activities after she retired a decade earlier might have contributed to her dementia.

And where did this leave me? I was still living with her, still at a crossroads. Career? Partner? Unknown. Forty was looming, and my biological clock was ticking. But how could I even think about leaving her now?

Dementia was hereditary on Mom's side. "Senility" is how they diagnosed my grandfather in the early 1980s. Uncle Billy had Lewy body dementia. In a way, there's been family preparation for this disease for generations. Still, no one is ever ready for it.

After the driving mishap, Mom forfeited her driver's license, and we sold the car. Boy, was she mad! Humiliated, I think — and sad. But safety was top priority. One night as I sneaked in late from a party, tiptoeing like a naughty teenager, Mom heard me and came down the stairs — missing the last step because of her slippery, slip-on mules.

She fell to the floor. I ran to her and scolded her. She went pale. Her ankle blew up to the size of an orange. She soiled herself and felt nauseous. I helped her to the bathroom in time for her to vomit. As she did, I held her head, and I bawled.

I'd returned home because I needed her, and now she needed me. This time, it was her world that was shifting under her feet, status and future unknown.

Fortunately, a friend got us to the hospital. Her ankle was broken, and she'd need major surgery involving screws, metal plates, wires, and pins. Our first night home afterward was hell. She had to pee frequently but couldn't manage the crutches, and I couldn't carry her. So, I spread a big beach towel on the floor. She lay on it, and I dragged her back and forth between the bedroom and bathroom throughout the night. At one point, she looked up, wincing in pain. "One day, we'll laugh about this," she predicted.

As Mom's dementia progressed, I signed her up for a memory study.

"If this research can help our family and others in the future," she said, "I'm on board."

I was really proud of her for that.

I sought help for myself, too. The Toronto Alzheimer's Society offered support and educational groups. I hadn't heard the term "self-care" before. Other caregivers told stories and made suggestions. One woman described her different methods for changing her mom's diaper in bed. (If only I'd known this during the broken-ankle phase!) One man hid a jar of peanut butter in his shoes in the closet because his wife searched for it in the middle of the night. Another man's wife wanted sex all the time (poor guy!). I told them about the beach towel. They told me yoga was good for stress.

I returned home from these meetings relieved that Mom wasn't that bad yet. And then she'd clear her throat like a cat heaving a hairball, and my blood pressure would rise.

"ARE YOU BREATHING?" I'd yell.

Yes, she was breathing. Yes, I'm still yelling. (On the plus side, I'm now in a relationship with a hearing-impaired fella, and it doesn't bother him one bit.)

This year, I'll be turning forty-five. My theme for 2021 is "healthy"—for both my mother and me. Every morning, I say "Namaste" to the day. I was never the yoga type, but damn, it is calming. I laugh at myself trying to become a human pretzel.

And I laugh with my mother, too, like she predicted. And we deep dive together into uncharted waters, resurface, and float.

I'm still home with Mom. We have rough waters ahead.

But at least we're treading them together.

— Farah Menassa —

81

Growing Through Dementia

*Self-care is never a selfish act — it is simply good
stewardship of the only gift I have, the gift I was
put on earth to offer to others.*
~Parker Palmer

It was a rainy Saturday morning in June. The yellow roses in the garden were blooming. I had just finished giving my mom a shower. She smelled so clean and fresh as I coiffed her hair. Looking pretty in her light blue housedress, she sat at the kitchen table while I prepared pancakes for breakfast. She let out a sigh as she gazed at the sidewalk across the way. Her new thing was to sit by the window and watch for any sign of activity. She pointed and laughed as kids splashed their bicycles through a puddle and rode down the street.

I knew I was one of the lucky caregivers after reading stories of others who battled abusive or violent behavior from their loved ones with dementia. Their stories were heartbreaking and often brought me to tears. As I flipped a pancake, I ruminated on the many changes since my mom had moved in with me a year ago. I had grown to accept the odd behaviors such as finding her in the shower at 3:00 a.m., and discovering food hidden in drawers and under her bathroom sink. I adapted to her following me around the house because she didn't know what to do with herself.

And then came the day I realized that she no longer recognized me as her daughter. We had been looking through a family photo album, and she stopped at a picture of my dad. She commented on his handsome appearance and asked, "Who is he?" I felt as though someone had kicked me in the stomach. All I could think to ask her was, "Who am I?" She couldn't answer me and had a blank look on her face.

I was numb for days as I tried to process emotions I couldn't even describe. It's almost like a rite of passage that becomes a badge of courage on this journey we walk together. Still, I counted my blessings because my mom was physically fit and agreeable. So far, there were no medications to monitor or hallucinations to worry about. She was easy to maneuver when we went shopping or dined at a restaurant.

As I placed her food on the table, she looked up and thanked me with appreciative eyes. From the outside, it looked like a manageable situation. My kids were grown and on their own. I was financially stable and had the ability to care for my mom at this time in my life. As I gave her my warmest, loving smile, I couldn't understand why I felt so stressed out. I had overcome difficult situations before and found my way through them. During law school, I got married and had my first child just weeks before final exams. I went through a divorce and raised two children while running my law practice. I made it through the untimely death of my father and orchestrated two cross-country moves. Yet, dealing with dementia was like nothing I had ever known.

Identifying as a caregiver imposed a responsibility to know and do more. I read every book and researched all the information I could find on dementia and caregiving. And while it was important for me to cherish this time with my mom, I was beginning to feel isolated and alone. My life, which used to feel so big and full, had shrunk to the four walls of my living space. My social connections dropped off over time. Even though people cared, they couldn't really understand what I was living and didn't know how to help. I felt guilty for wanting to live my life and I felt grief because I was losing my mom. Eventually, I became worn down and noticed that my identity was fading. My life was morphing into the world of dementia, and it scared me. I felt helpless, exhausted, and overwhelmed.

I realized I wasn't taking care of myself. But I also worried I was being selfish for thinking that. Then I faced the fact that my caregiving years were far from over, and this unbalanced lifestyle would never sustain me. I needed to treat myself at least as well as I treated my mom. That wasn't selfish. It just made good sense. I wouldn't be any good to her anyway if I collapsed.

I promised myself a thirty-minute walk at the lake, alone, every morning to breathe fresh air and clear my mind. There were walks when I laughed and many when I cried, but I would always try to focus on loving myself and grounding myself in the present.

Within a few weeks, I added a fifteen-minute nightly meditation to wash away the stress of the day. Eventually, I had clarity and felt more in touch with myself. I was afraid to stop there, so I set more goals to nourish my body with water and healthy food. What amazed me was that the same fear that took me to my lowest depths was now fueling me to rise above it all. I stopped judging myself for things that were left undone and rewarded myself for all that was done right.

It is said that when you choose to improve one area of your life, it will spill over into other areas, and I found this to be true. I decided to invest further in myself and became a certified integrative nutrition coach to expand my knowledge of health and wellness. During that year, I recognized that the energy of my mood directly affected my mom's attitude and behavior. She was excited when I was excited. She focused on trying to express herself instead of criticizing herself for not remembering something. She wanted to color mandalas and help me in the kitchen instead of sitting in front of the television. Her dementia would never go away, but it wasn't robbing me of creating new memories for us going forward as long as I continued to "meet her where she was."

There are days when this disease drops us to a new low. It's easy to fall into the victim mode as we continually grieve the loss of our loved one's relationship, memory, or ability to perform certain tasks. Ignoring our emotions is never the right answer because they will only manifest into problems later. But everything in life carries the meaning we assign to it. Dementia prevents my mom from regretting the past or becoming anxious about the future. She continues to teach me the power of patience and enjoying the moment because that is all we really have. She still has a sparkle in her eyes and always wears a smile on her face. I've learned that when the mind goes, the heart grows.

My experience of caregiving led me to create a new business, Caregiver Wellness, to support the health and wellbeing of carers everywhere. I teach the skill of resilience because, without it, most of us wouldn't finish the journey. We know that when we fall, we'll almost always get back up. And we're not alone.

—Denise Schaub—

82

Lightsharing

*Service to others is the rent you pay
for your room here on Earth.*
~Muhammad Ali

A while ago, my dad was in the hospital because his blood sugar dropped dangerously low. For most people, this is manageable in a few days, but not so for my sweet dad, who has not been the same since his stroke eight years ago. These days, walking to the kitchen is doable with a helper, but getting to the mailbox is off the list. The fall risk is too high. Actually, remembering to check the mail is now a big challenge.

So, on the occasion when my dad needs a hospital stay, he understandably gets confused and disoriented. In response, my heartrate goes up thinking about how he will react to being in an unfamiliar room that smells like alcohol and is filled with beeping machines. I'd been pushing that angst aside for many years, and that day I needed to do it again. So, the plan for my day was to go to church and then head straight to the hospital, which is an eighty-mile round trip. I've put on at least 150,000 miles and worn out several sets of tires by driving eighty miles through Detroit traffic for eight years to manage the care of my post-stroke dad.

While in church, my mind was divided. I was half-listening to the pastor and half-worried about the traffic and what I might find when I got to my dad's hospital room. I couldn't bring myself to ask my husband yet again to go with me. It was the weekend, and he works hard. I just can't ask him every single time I need help with my parents. That day, I was on my own.

But, as sometimes happens, I heard the perfect message that morning. Fortunately, it came during the 50 percent of the time I was actually checking into the sermon. Pastor Chris was preaching about the reasons we help others — a generic topic, or so I thought. Yeah, yeah, I get it. Helping others is very important. But what if you are so burnt out from eldercare phone calls, appointments, and drugstore runs that doing one more thing feels like lifting ten bags of potatoes at one time? I have so many days when my muscles can't get me off the couch, and my heart just doesn't have it to be empathetic one more time. And that Sunday was no different.

But, after listening to Pastor Chris, I realized that driving across town had nothing to do with managing my dad's hospitalization; it had everything to do with doing God's work. Doing humane work. Call it what you will. In the end, easing a burden is just that. And when I reframed my day that way, the nervousness about the traffic and potentially seeing my dad in an unhealthy, unsettling way all dissolved like sugar in water. It actually happened that fast.

Nope, no longer did I need a partner to help me handle the day. I wasn't scared; I was focused. The purpose of my day was helping to ease another human's scary circumstances. The X factor was that the human happened to be my old dad. While driving through Detroit on I-94 after church that day, I kept waiting for my stomach to start churning. Nothing. All I kept thinking about was that I wasn't helping my dad for the umpteenth time; I was doing God's work. Everybody's work, actually.

When I got to the hospital, the nurses filled me in on my dad's status. I walked into his room with the same ease as I did in stopping at CVS on the way home from work. It didn't even bother me to hold my dad's thin-skinned and bruised hand while I explained his admission and got the TV on so he could watch the Detroit Tigers game. Before I left, I told him that I loved him, and he asked me again why he was in the hospital. No problem, Dad. I get confused, too.

As a veteran on the worldwide eldercare team, I deeply know

it can feel impossible to extend yourself one more time, especially if you've been doing it for years. It's not that I don't want to help. The truth is that I'm out of gas and my patience is spent, but I'm forced to move forward. But when I changed that Sunday from doing more "parent stuff" to doing God's work, doing humane work, my tank suddenly filled.

I had woken up that morning feeling like I was facing another impossible day. I couldn't believe when I started to feel brave, determined even — feelings that are rarely found in the haze of eldercare. It saved me to fully understand that I wasn't just easing a burden. I was giving some of my light. It just happened to be for my dad in a lonely hospital room.

I walked out of the hospital and easily cruised all the way back across Detroit. I even arrived home with a spring in my step. I didn't immediately collapse on the couch like I did after every other demanding parent day. Instead, I had a few cookies and noticed my shoulders weren't touching my ears. I was warmed by the confidence that my dad felt at ease and cared for enough that he got lost watching the Tigers game.

All that from a little light. Eldercare, maybe. Lightsharing, definitely.

— Patricia Cosner Kubic —

83

Determined, Distraught, and Demented

Caring for myself is not self-indulgence, it is self-preservation,
and that is an act of political warfare.
~Audre Lorde

As soon as I got home from the hospital I ran down to the basement and disconnected our home phone line. Then I blocked my father on my iPhone.

I'd already experienced his frenzied calls during the wee hours of the morning during the vacations my mother took, and I knew, because she was now in the hospital, the onslaught would only get worse. My mother had tried to be compassionate about my father's dementia, but after sixty-five years of marriage she didn't have much left to give. She'd been sneaking off on trips without telling her three children, leaving us to learn "Betty's in Mexico" from our anxious father. I'd finally persuaded her to disclose the trips ahead of time so I could hire someone to stay in their house to keep my father calmer.

Over the six days my mother was in the hospital my father became more and more frantic, calling anyone he could think of to somehow cure my mother and bring her home. When my mother passed, we rushed to tell my father in person before he found out some other way and had a heart attack.

Thus began one of the most stressful periods in my life. We could barely process the loss of our mother as we dove headlong into caring for a determined, distraught, and demented man. Dad was already quite feeble, and had to crawl up the stairs in the house, but he insisted on remaining in charge. He'd driven his tractor into a ditch while trying to plow the driveway; he'd recently driven an hour into New York City, undoubtedly going 40 miles per hour on the highway; and he was still trying to climb ladders and fix things. He was also visiting the bank almost every day, withdrawing large sums of money and then hiding the cash, forgetting where, and calling the police.

I quickly cobbled together a team of caregivers so that my father was never alone. That was a struggle, as he refused to have a new person come to the house. He knew two of the three women already, and the way I finally got him to agree to interview and hire the third one was to tell him that she was afraid of the steep driveway and he needed to help her by turning on the outdoor lights and greeting her reassuringly at the front door. Once I turned him into the person *giving* the care, he was okay with "interviewing" the caregiver I had already hired.

At the funeral, my mother's aide told me that in the ambulance my mother had said, "Allan killed me. Don't let him kill anyone else." I knew it was true. The stress of living with my father in his demented state had made my mother so unhappy that she'd deliberately disobeyed doctor's orders about her own health. In the hospital, she kept saying, "Just let me die." She didn't *want* to go home. When I went through her desk, I discovered that she'd known she was in renal failure and had done nothing about it.

Over the next couple of months, my brother and I pulled off a miracle. We got my father to "pick" the assisted living facility we had already chosen for him. But then the stress continued. It turned out that our father was not well suited to communal living. He refused to be alone in his apartment, so we had to continue the 24/7 care, now with four aides who I had to manage. He was often rude to the staff and other residents, unwilling to wait to be served in the large dining room.

After someone mistakenly programmed all the speed-dial buttons on his new landline phone, we continued to have a terrible problem with his calls. In addition to his three children, he had several elderly friends he'd call repeatedly to complain about his situation.

Eventually, I was able to change the speed-dial settings on his wired phone and his cell phone so that he only had everyone's cell phone numbers. That way, all of us lucky phone pals could block him. It took five months, but I was finally able to reconnect our home phone in the basement.

That day when I'd unplugged the phone was the beginning of my self-care. It wasn't selfish; it was mandatory. When you're trying to handle a cantankerous old man with dementia, you have to protect yourself. If you don't, you turn into my mother, fleeing to Mexico and neglecting her own health.

When I would review my "Blocked Voicemail" I would find dozens of messages from my father, spaced two minutes apart. He would leave the exact same message twenty times in a row, having no memory that he had just called.

I would call my father back for one phone conversation on the days I didn't visit in person. That was my rule. Two or three visits a week and one long phone call on my days off.

I tried to have fun with it. If my father had been perseverating too long on one topic, I would deliberately switch him to a new one. I'd even text my brother ahead of time: *I'm tired of talking about downloading Kindle samples because we've been on that topic for two weeks. So tonight I'm going to switch him to discussing where he bought his furniture.* That evening, I'd ask him about one of the pieces we'd moved with him to the assisted living, and we'd discuss his furniture for the next two weeks.

Texting my brother and sister helped, too. When the dementia got bad enough, I could text them without my father realizing I was doing it. I'd provide a running commentary on our conversations. We all deserve some comic relief when we are caring for someone with dementia.

My husband would comment on how patient I was when he heard my side of the phone conversations. They were endless loops, answering the same question or discussing the same topic a dozen times in a matter of minutes. That wasn't difficult for me. I was going to spend twenty minutes on the phone with him anyway, or an hour or two visiting him, so it didn't really matter what we talked about. He owned that time. If we covered the same ground twenty times in a row, fine.

If everything we talked about was utter nonsense, no problem. I entered my father's new reality. His ninety years pancaked into one flat continuum. He was still living with his parents… and he'd just come back from a business trip to Europe… and his mom who'd died in 1996 had just called… and my mother was away on one of her trips. I called his recliner "the magic chair." That chair took him all over the world. He told me he'd never traveled to Paris as much as he had during the past year.

Sometimes, it was even entertaining to hear how he would rewrite history. I learned that my grandfather, who ran a commercial real estate firm in Manhattan, had coined the term "the garment district" and invented the concept of designer showrooms. Probably not true at all, but I think I learned that my grandfather at least managed some commercial buildings in the garment district.

We started this caregiving journey more than four years ago and I have to say it is way easier now. Over time, the dementia worsened and it was like a hard shell cracked and fell off my difficult father, revealing a very sweet guy underneath. We moved him to an incredibly well-run memory care unit a year and a half ago. We'd been told that the move would be easy, and it was. The moment he got there he forgot about the two and half years he'd been at the assisted living. He thought he'd moved directly from his original house!

Now my father's in hospice and we don't talk about anything. When my husband and I saw him the other day for the first time in four months due to the COVID visiting restrictions, he was asleep in his chair and I couldn't wake him. I left him an old photo album from the 1930s and 1940s to look at with his aide. I retrieved the envelope of fake money I'd given him a year ago so he'd have some "cash" and feel secure. He doesn't feel the need for cash anymore, so I gave it to the front desk to pass on to another dementia patient coming up behind him.

The stress is over now. Dad's but a shadow of that determined distraught man from four years ago. I feel like we did a great job for him, and a good part of our ability to do that came from strategically protecting our sanity and our own health. We took my mother's warning to heart.

— Amy Newmark —

All You Need Is Love... and Patience

84

Beauty Doesn't Have to Come with Pain

And it is still true, no matter how old you are,
when you go out into the world it is best
to hold hands and stick together.
~Robert Fulghum

I had to cut her nails today. She hates having her fingernails cut. She fusses and squirms. Actually, her behaviour is often unpredictable and embarrassing.

I take those dear old hands in mine, calmly look deep into that mischievous face, and kiss each one of those old, gnarly fingers. I search inside myself for a little bit of the wisdom and lessons that this woman, my mother, so gently gave me.

I clearly remember the lessons about fingernails. Nails were very important to my mom. She was an "Avon Lady." Her nails were part of her sales pitch. "Your nails must always match your lips," she'd say.

My mom changed the colour of her nails every Friday, a ritual that my sister and I were thrilled to share with her. For Mom, manicures meant a two, maybe three, Manhattan night. For my sister and me, it was one small bottle of ginger ale each, chosen from the cardboard six-pack with the carrying handle on top. We always drank from the bottle with two white paper straws. We felt so grown up, so special, sitting in our flannel nighties. Mom would get out the wooden box with all the mysterious manicure supplies: the cotton batting, the "dangerous" nail-polish remover, the black leather pouch with a silver zipper. Unzipped, it opened up like butterfly wings. On one side, there were little nail clippers and files. On the other side, there were tiny pearl-handled tools to dig out the dirt and push down the cuticles. I can still hear her saying, "Beauty always comes with a little bit of pain, my dears." Mom would then take an oval bowl, fill it with warm water, and put her fingers in to soak. And the stories would begin.

The family stories. The generational stories. There were stories about her life, her mother's life, and her mother's mother's life. We listened to their adventures and heard about their strengths, hopes and dreams. Mom always used her quiet voice, which was only used when talking about "the family secrets." With each new layer of polish, the stories would get deeper and richer. As her stories ended, we gently blew on her nails — but not too close so we wouldn't smudge them.

Then it was our turn to tell stories. We shared stories about our strengths, troubles at school, what we had done and hoped to do. Yes, there was a little sisterly tattling, trying desperately to outdo each other. While we were telling stories, Mom would get out the pearl-handled tools and dig all the muck and dirt out from under our little nails and push down our little cuticles. And it hurt, not a lot, but it hurt. Despite the pain, I cherished those moments and stories. The night always ended with Mom taking our hands in hers and kissing the tips of each of our little fingers.

As I kissed each of her old, gnarly fingers today, my heart softened. I said, "I have a bottle of the newest colour." She grinned. I felt that grin in my belly — that childhood excitement, the anticipation. Would I hear one of her old stories? But there were no stories today. Finishing her nails, I said, "You know, I do believe I have a lipstick in my purse that matches this polish." She gasped. Applying her lipstick, I looked into her joyful, pale blue eyes, puckered my lips, and said, "Go like this." She did, and we giggled and laughed like we were a couple of kids. I said gently, "You know, beauty doesn't always have to come with a little bit of pain."

When I was little, Mom put on fresh lipstick at 4:15 p.m. every weekday. Then she went outside and called, "Girls, it's time to come in. Your father will be home shortly. Go and brush your hair." I was so grateful when I was old enough to brush my own hair, because it had hurt when she did it. I would wrap my arms around her waist and press my head into her stomach, and she would start to count: one, two, three… one hundred strokes. It didn't matter how many knots and tangles I had. "One hundred strokes make your hair shiny and strong. You know, the Avon customers are not just looking at my hair. They are looking at your hair, too." I felt like we were some kind of poster family for Avon!

Mom was always the businesswoman. "Count your pennies, and the dollars will look after themselves." "Waste not, want not." And she counted each and every penny. Mom would gratefully spend a few of them every Friday for a fashionable coiffure at the corner beauty parlor. That hairdo would last her all week. She would put little clips on her curls at night and sleep on a smooth purple satin pillowcase so her hairdo would not get messed. But every morning she would have this flat spot where she had slept. "Oh, Peter!" she would say to my dad. "Can you see that flat spot in my hair? Can you get that flat spot?" Dad, who knew she was beautiful, would find the pick with the long prongs, fluff out the flat spot, and finish it off with a quick kiss on her lips.

Today, I was so grateful I watched Mom and listened to her stories. I intuitively know what brings her joy.

It was time for us to go down to the Lodge dining room. I went to her drawer and got out the old pick with the long prongs, and I started to fluff her thin grey hair the way she likes it. She started fussing and squirming, saying some inappropriate phrases. Yes, sometimes her behaviour can be unpredictable and embarrassing. I said, "I'm just getting the flat spot." She stopped fussing and looked at me. My heart skipped a beat. A fleeting smile came across her face. Then her eyes became blank as she retreated into her muddled mind, and our moment was over.

Holding hands, we walked together to the dining room. Before I sat with Mom and her friends at her table, I gently gave her hand our secret family signal: two quick, little squeezes. It means, "I am going to let go of your hand now — never you, just your hand." It's the secret signal she taught me.

Alzheimer's has given me the gift and the opportunity to "mother" my mother. But, sometimes, I simply miss the mom she was.

— Sandra Cole —

85

Saying Hello Again

I love her, and that's the beginning
and end of everything.
~F. Scott Fitzgerald

My father wanted to do what? This was a man known for being logical, but nothing about this idea was. He wanted to celebrate his fiftieth wedding anniversary with my mother. Who had dementia. And he'd never planned a social event in his life, and I wasn't positioned to provide much help.

He even expected the original bridal party to travel from Ohio to South Carolina. And Mom was more fragile than ever, following a bout with the flu. She'd regressed more and could no longer walk. Or talk. She was twelve years into her Alzheimer's and she wouldn't recognize anyone. She probably didn't even know she was married.

But Dad had always been persistent — possibly to a fault. So, when almost all the bridesmaids, groomsmen, and their spouses accepted his e-mail invitation, he reserved the nursing-home conference room, booked hotel rooms, and ordered party trays and a cake. He even hired a professional photographer.

Because Dad chose to stay by Mom's side at the nursing home for twelve hours a day, for years Dad's home had been little more than the place where he slept. A few days before Dad's longtime friends arrived, I began decluttering the kitchen countertops and saw where time in his world had stopped. The cream-colored Formica was littered with

Post-it Notes written by Mom. With magazine articles she'd cut out. With recipes she'd wanted to try. I attempted to organize the dreams and plans Mom had been forced to leave undone — the real-time moments that had metamorphosed into memories.

Next, I moved to the dining room. A pile of photos Dad had selected to display lay on the table. They spoke a beautiful story, minus the fairytale ending. As I mounted them on the presentation boards, I remembered.

One non-picture item sat in the stack. With a glance, I knew what it was. My hands shook as I slipped it into a folder to be placed at the board's base. Even though I knew the words by heart, my eyes scanned the brief essay penned three years earlier by my thirteen-year-old daughter before her too-early death:

> *The beautiful tale of my grandpa's "in sickness or in health, till death do us part" devotion inspires me. My maternal grandmother and I used to spend time together feeding the birds, baking sugar cookies, and drawing with stencils. Until something happened. An intruder, a dreadful disease called Alzheimer's, wormed its way into her mind. It slowly took over all that used to be hers — her demeanor, her speech, her capabilities — leaving nothing except a dry shell. Afraid of the unknown, angry woman she'd become, I tried to weather the storm of her spontaneous outrages until the fury subsided. When my grandpa and my mom checked Grandma into a hospital so she could be medicated, I gave her up as gone for good.*
>
> *But there was someone who didn't give up. Someone who never gave up, no matter what. My grandpa. I'd caught glimpses of his tenacity when he refused to quit the Sudoku puzzle he was working on or kept searching the dictionary for clues to the crossword in the newspaper. Although I had heard stories of Grandpa's iron will and resolve, I never witnessed it so fully until Grandma went to live at a nursing home. Grandma could hardly form coherent sentences anymore, but Grandpa treated her like she was still his princess.*

Finally, the day of the celebration arrived. Dressed in black pants and a flower-print shirt, Mom sat in her wheelchair. Dad leaned in close on her left, with the immediate family and bridal party gathered around her. As the photographer snapped pictures, Dad smiled big even though Mom had forgotten how.

Then Dad began to talk. With a memory that holds details and refuses to let go, he told the story about the first time he met Mom, about their brief time dating, about their years parenting, working, and looking forward to growing old together. Mom sat stone-faced.

A filet-mignon meal that made me forget I was in a nursing home followed. Soon, my brother Tom and his family rose from their chairs. Accompanied by a keyboard and strings, they began to sing. A few songs later, Tom spoke.

"My mom was a big fan of Neil Diamond. So, for this last song, I arranged one of her favorite songs, 'Hello Again,' for my family to share with you."

"Hello, my friend, hello," Tom began. His baritone voice blended with violins, a cello, and piano keys. I lifted my Nikon to snag a quick photo of Dad's friends and then stopped. Everyone sat brushing away tears. Everyone except Dad, who didn't seem to notice.

There he was, turned toward Mom, singing the song to her. She rotated to face him, tapped in time to the melody, and mouthed the words back. In that moment, I knew Dad had been right, and I had been wrong.

It's said that in order to grieve what's lost, we have to say hello before we can say goodbye. With a press of my finger, I took the picture of a true knight who grasped that truth — a man who, by choosing to celebrate the little time still left, had turned what should have been bitter into something precious and sweet.

— Beth Saadati —

86

Lessons of Life, Love, and Alzheimer's

Being deeply loved by someone gives you strength,
while loving someone deeply gives you courage.
~Lao Tzu

The mall was ridiculously crowded that day, the way it usually is around Christmastime. We navigated our way through the food court, and my mom saved us a table in front of Saladworks. I could see her sitting there as I stood in line, waiting impatiently and feeling annoyed by all the people.

Finally, I got our salads and drinks and walked back to my mom. As I approached the table and began putting down my stuff, a woman looked up at me and politely said, "I'm sorry, but someone is sitting here." I stared back at this woman, completely stunned by what she had said. I replied, "Yeah, I know. I'm sitting here." The woman looked confused and laughed nervously for a second. She said again, "Oh, I'm sorry. Someone is sitting here."

My heart raced as I quickly tried to process this encounter and figure out what exactly was happening. The chatter and buzz all around me continued, but for me the whole world had stopped moving. I was solely focused on this one woman sitting in front of me. Eventually, I could formulate a response. I said, "Yeah, Mom, I know. I'm sitting here. Mom, it's me. Lauren."

The woman, my mom, looked even more confused, and her cheeks reddened with embarrassment. She quickly realized her mistake and tried to play it off as she continued laughing nervously. But I knew that she knew what had just happened. I knew she also felt the significance of that moment.

For a split second, I had lost her. She was gone. But how could that be? She was still sitting right in front of me. Well, someone was still sitting in front of me. She looked like my mom, but she felt like a stranger.

I introduced myself to my mom that day. It may have been the first time, but it definitely wasn't the last. There were many more "first times" in the years that followed.

There was the first time she forgot how to get dressed. The first time she got completely lost in her own house. The first time I had to help her use the bathroom. The first time she forgot how to answer the phone. The first time I said, "I love you," and she didn't say it back. The first time I held her hand as we walked down the street. The first time I helped her up after she fell down. The first time I pushed her in a wheelchair. The first time I fed her with a spoon.

In many ways, that day at the mall was just the beginning of a long, heartbreaking journey. I lost so much more of my mom as the years went on. The thing about Alzheimer's disease is that you lose so much of the person along the way that, by the end, you are practically begging for them to die. But for all that is lost, even more love is gained. Sometimes, people say something is a blessing and a curse. I will never say my mom having Alzheimer's has been a blessing, but I will say that it has taught me a lot.

Strength.

Courage.

Patience.

Compassion.

Empathy.

Purpose.

I already had a little bit of each of these things, but now I have a whole lot — more than I probably would have ever had if my mom had never gotten Alzheimer's. Watching her struggle has taught me lessons I might not have ever really learned.

My mom has taught me the true meaning of unconditional love—not only by giving it to me, but by allowing me to give it back to her. She may have forgotten many things, but I know she will never forget my love for her. She no longer knows who I am, but she knows me. Her soul knows me. Her heart knows me. She knows she loves me, and I love her. Love is the gift that knows no boundaries, disabilities, or illnesses. It is not something the brain remembers. It's something the heart and soul feel. Not even Alzheimer's can take that away from us.

— Lauren Dykovitz —

87

Saving Mom

Mother is a verb, not a noun.
~Author Unknown

I was lying on the snow, calling for help. I'd slipped on the ice and dislocated my knee. Soon, there was an ambulance ride, pain-killers, the surprise of being "relocated," the great relief from the pain, and hobbling home on crutches. A week later, I enjoyed the challenge of learning to drive with my right knee wrapped up. I took a tentative ride to the corner store, bought some milk and bread, and counted on resting the balance of the day. Which I did… until the phone rang.

"My leukemia's back," my mother said quietly. I didn't say a word. I just packed my cane, braced my knee and got into my minivan for the eight-hour drive.

Breaking up the trip was the best idea. With the help of cruise control, I drove south on I-87 without incident and stayed overnight in my in-laws' chilly spare bedroom. Early the next day, as I entered the ramp for I-90 West to Niagara Falls, my nose began to drip, and my chest rattled. Undaunted, I stopped at the first rest area to get some cough drops and some sugar to fire me up.

In retrospect, caramels were not a good choice. No sooner had I popped one into my mouth than it took off about two-thirds of a rear molar. What was left behind had razor-sharp edges. As I drove, it scraped my tongue, which started bleeding. But I had a mother to save, so I pressed forward.

At 4:00 in the afternoon, I leaned forward on my cane to press her doorbell. She answered, looking bright and, as always, well-dressed.

"I'm here to rescue you!" I lisped cheerfully with my swollen tongue, looking every bit the disaster that I was. She took one look at me and did what any mother would do: She put me down for a nap and started cooking some soup.

Later, I sat like a wreck at her table, which was laid with all her favorite china cups and plates. Being elegant was her stock in trade, but I felt more like a destitute Charles Dickens character.

As we sat over dainty cookies and sorbet, she told me something I never expected to hear. "When does the doctor want you to go in?" I asked.

"Well," she wavered, "I dunno. Maybe by Tuesday or Thursday."

"But last time, he ordered you to get there right away," I urged.

She sighed. "Well, I'm not sure." My decisive mother waffled, checking her nails. "I'm not sure I want to do that again." We both knew that the doctors couldn't believe she'd made it this long and had no clue if another round of chemo would do any good. She was coming up on seventy-nine. Without the treatment, though, they knew the results: It would take about a month for her to die.

"It's your decision, I guess," I said softly.

We spent the next morning at the ER because she insisted on knowing what was going on with my wheezing. We dropped off my prescription at her pharmacy, and then I hobbled in after her to eat breakfast at her favorite coffee shop. As I tried to negotiate my eggs with my torn-up tongue, she shook her head.

"We gotta get you to a dentist." We spent the next morning calling around. Who was going to take an out-of-town patient? Finally, her own dentist decided to take me. As she drove me downtown, I broached the subject again.

"Do you know if you, um, want to go yet?" I asked tentatively.

"Maybe," she said softly as she shifted into Park. I didn't know then what made her change her mind, but eight years later, I do.

My mother, widowed for the second time in 1981, had been alone for a long while. I visited twice a year, and she came for Christmas; I called every Sunday. She volunteered a bit, shopped, kept an immaculate house, had lunch with girlfriends, did crosswords, or read the Bible. She stared out the picture window at the bunnies that ate her petunias, voted, picked up sticks in the spring, raked leaves in the fall and, I suspect, felt a loneliness I could never bear. It was a life easy to say farewell to.

But then, on that afternoon when I showed up tottering on her doormat, she changed her mind. She'd been ready to hand in her car keys for good, but her youngest child needed her. And, because of that, we had nearly a whole year more together.

— Kathy L. Baumgarten —

88

Dancing in the Dark

*I see dance being used as communication between body
and soul, to express what is too deep to find for words.*
~Ruth St. Denis

I look at the clock and groan. It's 3:16 in the morning. As my body creaks in protest, I crawl from my bed and limp across the hall to check on Mom. My daily routine has begun. Every day, I reluctantly awaken her about this time to take her to the bathroom. It seems so cruel, but this is the time that works best to avoid her waking up soiled and cold. It's a quick trip to the bathroom, and she's usually grateful to go. But this time, a narrow strip of light shows beneath her door, and I think to myself, *Uh-oh.*

When I find the door locked, that's clue number two that all is not well. Sighing, I shuffle off to the kitchen to get a screwdriver, and then return and unlock the door. I am in mid-yawn when I focus on Mom, wearing only a pair of incontinence pants, completely soaked judging by the rivulets trickling down her legs, pushing her walker around her bedroom.

It's something I don't see every day, but well, I guess I do now. Mom has dementia, and every day is a new adventure.

"Hey, there, beautiful. I'll bet you're cold, aren't you?" I say softly, careful not to startle her.

"Someone took my clothes," she snaps, clearly agitated.

"No one took your clothes, Mom," I reassure her. "I'll bet I just put them into the wrong drawers again." It's a lie but one of love and mercy. Almost visibly, she relaxes and then looks at me expectantly.

Pulling fresh pajamas from her dresser, I help her to the bathroom. When she is clean, warm and dry, I dust her lightly with her favorite powder. She almost purrs, enjoying the soft, floral scent.

Seating her upon her walker, I smile as she begins to stroke the velvety softness of her pajamas. She looks up at me in happy anticipation. She loves being wheeled about on her walker. I do it when necessary, but occasionally I'll push her about on it just because she enjoys it so much. When she looks up at me so expectantly, I can't resist. Pushing her along, she "helps" by clutching and pulling at the woodwork. It hinders rather than helps our progress, but I grin at her look of concentration. Even now, at eighty-five, she needs a sense of purpose. Mom worked hard her entire life, and she still takes pride in being productive, whether it's dusting, peeling potatoes or yanking on the woodwork while riding on her walker.

I park her next to the dresser where she can watch while I strip her bed. Dropping the soaked sheets into a garbage bag, I toss the bag onto the landing to be washed later in the morning. Sleepily, she watches me from her perch upon the walker. I put a fresh blanket and sheets in her lap to hold for me as I remake her bed. Immediately, her fingers seek out the satiny binding of the blanket. Mom has become very tactile and glories in the softness of clothing, blankets, or anything soft. She is convinced it is the same blanket that we children called "Snowy" during our childhoods. She begins to explain how this blanket came from her grandmother and how she wrapped every one of her babies in it. As she tells me the familiar story, she sits caressing this impostor, queen-size Snowy, finding comfort in her memories of when she was young and cradling her now grown babies within its folds.

With her eyes closed, she raises the satiny binding to her cheek and smiles softly. At that moment, I believe she is once again holding her babies. To interrupt this moment feels cruel, but it's now 4:30 in the morning, and I'd like to snatch a nap in my chair before I have to get the housework done. She loathes the sound of the vacuum cleaner, so I avoid running it when she is up. I think the noise reverberates painfully in her ears. I try to remain mindful of her new discomforts.

Because of her dementia, she no longer has the capacity to use her words to communicate properly. She can't always tell me when something bothers her, but if I watch carefully, her body language speaks volumes.

Gently, I break the moment of her reverie and help her stand up. She rests her weight within my arms as she awakens from her memories. Briefly, she looks dismayed as she stares around the room, her brow furrowed with confusion. Mom doesn't recognize her room anymore, despite having lived with me for twelve years. When she looks up at me, she no longer recognizes me as her child. Hopefully, I at least look familiar.

On the days when she insists that she wants to go home, when I tell her that she is home and that I am her daughter, she looks at me in confusion and with some fear. I can almost read her thoughts. *If you really are my daughter, why don't I know you?*

So, I begin to softly sing the old familiar "Tennessee Waltz." Music and dancing were her passions, and this brings a degree of comfort and familiarity to her almost every time. Softly, she begins to sing along. Together, in the glow of the room's nightlight, we sway lightly in rhythm. Somehow, it doesn't feel odd. It feels perfectly normal. Mom taught us to dance as children, but now I must take the lead.

In the dim nightlight's glow, she looks up at me and smiles her beautiful, sweet smile, and I find comfort in the familiar scent of her powder. Mom always smelled softly of perfume. As children, we would burrow into her arms when we were tired, frightened or just for the comfort of her embrace. I cherish this brief moment and close my eyes against sudden tears. I miss my mom so much.

We "dance" a little longer. I'm tired but don't want this moment to end. For this brief moment, she's Mom again, her eyes sparkling, doing what she loves, and I don't want to let her go. But soon she tires, so I tuck her into the warmth of her freshly made bed, kiss her good night once more, and say, "I love you, Mom."

She smiles back and sleepily says, "I love you, too."

That makes it all worthwhile.

— Laurel L. Shannon —

89

A Year of Goodbye

*There are some who bring a light so great to the world
that even after they have gone the light remains.*
~Author Unknown

I stood on the wide porch of the hospital and stared out into the vast parking lot, not even seeing the hundreds of cars. I felt numb. It was happening again: a death sentence for a beloved parent. With my mother, it had been complications from breast cancer. The disease had spread into her lungs, spine, and finally the brain. I remembered her courage as she faced the inevitable and how we had quoted the Twenty-Third Psalm as her spirit faded before our eyes. Don Edwards, my daddy, had been devastated, but in the intervening twenty years, he had made a life for himself.

Now, it was his turn. Leukemia. His bone marrow, which had lasted for ninety-three years, was just plain worn out. The kind oncologist had called us into his office and told Daddy in his warm East Indian accent, "Sir, at your age, you are not a candidate for a bone-marrow transplant. However, we could try to treat the disease."

Daddy interrupted, "No. I saw what my wife went through. I don't want that."

The doctor nodded. "I understand." He smiled at Daddy. "Then, sir, my prescription is that you enjoy your friends and family, play your music, and live to the fullest during the year ahead."

And my father did. He continued to play piano, enjoyed spending time with his lady friend at his retirement center, and went out to eat with us every Sunday. By Christmas, though, his condition became apparent. He found it harder to laugh with us and had no energy at all. Even the beneficial effects of a blood transfusion at the oncology center lasted less than a week. The day finally came when an ambulance carried him to the hospital.

He only had a few weeks left, the doctor explained. I was sure Daddy heard, but he didn't embrace the news, didn't pay attention to it. It was his way of coping. A hospital social worker told me, "I'll call around for a bed in one of the skilled nursing facilities." I told her I needed to think.

So, there I was, pacing back and forth outside the hospital, praying, "Lord, what shall I do? He's been in those facilities before. He gets so lonesome. I can't put him there." I paced some more.

You have that extra bedroom on the ground floor, said a voice inside my head. He could come home to be with you. Your mother was at her home when she died. It was a great comfort to her.

Tears filled my eyes. "He would need round-the-clock nursing. Is it possible, Lord? Can we do it?" All the reasons why we couldn't whirled in my head: finances, meal preparation, medicines…

It's less than a month.

The realization hit me hard.

"Less than a month," I repeated through a sob. "Oh, Daddy! We'll only have you for a month more… Yes, yes, you'll come to our house to be with us!"

I pulled my phone from my pocket, called my husband and outlined the plan. "Yes, of course, we'll do it." He loved my Daddy, too.

It wasn't an easy few weeks, but we'll always treasure that time we had with my father. Right up to the end, he remained my kind, loving dad, always a gentleman, though he was suffering. He was so patient with the variety of practical nurses; they soon came to love him. One or two of the ladies sang hymns for him, little realizing that he had perfect pitch, and some of their renditions were painful to his ears. He always thanked them for the song.

One by one, family members came to see him — my brother and sister, our cousins, all his grandchildren. His appetite was low, so we called ahead for takeout of his favorite meal: a sampler platter from Red Lobster. When the feast arrived, he couldn't handle a single bite. That was another clue that he was failing.

On his last day, although we didn't realize it was the last, he said, "I'd like to go outside for a little bit and see the sunshine." We eased him into his wheelchair and wheeled him to the screened back porch, where he sat looking at the birds on the lawn for about five minutes before saying, "I'm ready to go back in now." As we wheeled him back to the bedroom, he asked to stop at the electric keyboard standing just outside his door. Once again, he laid his hands tenderly on the keys and played a random snatch of a song that I recognized: "As Long as He Needs Me." Then he said, "I'm tired. I'd like to get back to bed."

That night, the nurse on duty came and woke me up. "He's going, ma'am. I thought you'd want to know."

I roused my brother and sister who were spending the night, and we all gathered at his bedside, holding his hands and saying the Twenty-Third Psalm to him, just as we had with my mother. Gradually, his breathing slowed, and he drifted away from us.

A few weeks later, at his retirement community, we had a memorial gathering of his friends. After telling them how much their friendship had meant to him, I then asked if anybody had anything to add. From the back of the room, an elderly lady stood and, with tears in her eyes, declared, "I just wanted to say this: Every woman in this place was in love with Don Edwards!"

It was a tribute that would have tickled him no end!

— E.E. Kennedy —

All Dressed Up and No Place to Go

*To keep the heart unwrinkled — to be hopeful, kindly,
cheerful, reverent — that is to triumph over old age.*
~Thomas Bailey Aldrich

"The bride was stiff as a board until she had a few drinks. Then she loosened up and enjoyed herself," my mother said. She proceeded to tell me about her grandson's wedding and reception, a simple, elegant affair held on the front porch of her house.

The only thing is, my 100-year-old mother didn't host a wedding at her house. She was already living with me.

My siblings and I had realized that dementia and age had caught up with our independent mom. I'd talked her into visiting for the Christmas holidays, persuaded her to stay longer than planned, and finally convinced her to move in. In her most lucid moments, she knew she couldn't take care of herself, and it was in those moments that she agreed to stay.

Then coronavirus broadsided our world, and the decision to move her in seemed like perfect timing. Elderly people in her hometown were dying, and she was safely quarantined with me.

But because of the pandemic, there would be no traveling back for her grandson's wedding, the event she had anticipated for over a year.

Dementia is a curious thing. My mother forgets what time of day it is and whether she has had breakfast, but she remembers the time and date of her grandson's wedding. She knows the wedding has been reduced to a handful of people — the bride and groom, their parents and siblings — but she wants to buy the perfect dress to wear anyway.

I kept telling her she didn't need a dress since she wasn't going. I thought she would give up, forget about it. Who needs a dress when you're sheltering in place and slouching around in pajamas or sweats?

But my mother didn't give up. Instead, she grew sly and hatched a plot.

"I know I'm not going to the wedding, but I need a new dress," she said day after day until I succumbed to the relentless pressure and pleading.

As soon as Macy's announced they were reopening, we put on masks and drove to the mall. We weren't supposed to be there. Even with the loosening of quarantine guidelines and the reopening of businesses, people over sixty-five were to continue sheltering in place.

But I took comfort in the nearly empty mall and our masks. No need to social distance when only a few intrepid souls were venturing out. We didn't stay long, either. My mother spotted the dress she wanted right away.

I was surprised by her choice. She had always liked plain, practical clothes — Alfred Dunner brands with elastic waists and solid, matching jackets. But the dress she spotted was flowing and frilly, all soft swirls, chiffon and pastels. It was the kind of dress that makes you feel like you're floating rather than walking into a room.

"Are you sure…?" I began.

"Yes, that's the one I want. Isn't it beautiful?" She fingered the soft material. "Do they have a 16?"

They did, so I bought it.

"Where are you going to wear your dress?" I asked her later that evening.

"Oh, I don't know. Maybe I never will. Maybe I'll just look at it in my closet," she said.

But a few days before the wedding, my brother (the groom's father) let us know the wedding would be streamed live on Facebook, and we could watch. This was my mother's cue to spring into action. At 6:00 a.m. on the day of the wedding, she slipped on her dress. "I'm going to wear it to watch the wedding," she announced. She sent me on a frantic search for shoes because "you don't wear a dress like this with tennis shoes."

I found her a pair of my sandals, and then curled her hair and fetched her lipstick, which she hadn't worn since moving in with me. She outlined her lips in bright red, smacked them together and said, "How does it look?"

"Perfect, Mama. You look beautiful," I told her.

At wedding time, we had one heart-stopping moment when we thought the Facebook feed wasn't going to work. But somebody got the technology figured out, and with a sigh of relief, we watched as a beautiful bride glided toward my mother's precious grandson.

It wasn't the wedding the bride and groom had envisioned, this Facebook-streamed event, but they looked so young, happy and in love that I blinked back the tears threatening to spill down my cheeks. I didn't want Mama to catch me crying.

My mother complained that the preacher talked too long (he did), admired the decorations (two rows of potted ferns), and smiled as the groom kissed the bride. She wore her dress the rest of the day, and after lunch she fell into a deep sleep.

Afternoon lengthened into evening, and I felt a prickle of alarm. I couldn't wake her for dinner. I rang her cellphone, which usually startles her from sleep. Then I shook her gently, offered ice cream, and caressed her face, but she didn't stir from a slumber that verged on unconsciousness.

I couldn't get her into pajamas or into the bedroom. Sprawled in the recliner, with the dress flowing around her, she slept.

Finally, I went to bed but got up around 3:00 to see if she was breathing. She was, barely. I crawled back in bed, and the tears I had held back during the wedding flowed freely, threatening to turn into a flood.

I didn't pray that she wake up. She's 100, after all. So, I just prayed, "Lord, your will."

At 6:30, I emerged from a restless, troubled sleep. Slipping out of bed, I tiptoed nervously toward the recliner. My mother's eyes flickered open. The sunlight of another day streamed in, lighting the room.

She said, "I'm ready to get out of this dress."

— Bebe Nicholson —

91

Miracles Happen

Don't believe in miracles — depend on them.
~Laurence J. Peter

When my father was diagnosed with Alzheimer's, I braced myself for what was coming. "Forewarned is fore-armed," I told myself. But, of course, it wasn't. There were times Dad knew my name but wasn't sure who I was. There were times he knew who I was but didn't know my name. There were times he thought I was my mother and eyed me suspiciously. (They were divorced.) And there were times he didn't care who I was. I was just someone in his way.

I wanted to grieve, but that felt wrong. I wanted closure, but that time had passed. So, I lived with regret. Regret that I'd never sat down and talked to my dad about what was happening and what was going to happen. I'd never said, "How are you feeling about this, and how can I help you?" I couldn't forget the many times I'd wanted to say, "Hey, I want you to know that I'm sorry for..." or "I want to thank you for..." but hadn't. After two years of home care, I moved my father to a small memory-care unit located a few blocks from my home. Run by the sisters of St. Francis, I loved its tranquil environment. I saw it as a place where he could get the care he needed and the love and respect he deserved.

I visited my dad daily. For the most part, our visits consisted of walks down the hallway, with occasional stops so he could work on the exit door, which wouldn't open and needed "fixing." Then I'd sit with him at dinner. One night as I watched him push the food around on his plate, I felt an overwhelming sadness. Trying not to cry, I focused on the light fixture above our table. After a few minutes of staring at the light, I heard my dad say, "Well, hi, Crys. I didn't know you were here. How are you?"

I looked at him and said, "I'm fine. How are you?"

Taking a bite of his mashed potatoes, he replied, "I'm good."

After several minutes of continued "normal" conversation, I excused myself from the table, telephoned my sisters and my daughters, and said, "I don't know why, but Dad is very lucid right now. I don't know how long it will last, but if you want to be part of it, you should come down right away." My sisters couldn't come, but my daughters came immediately.

Even with my back to the entrance, I knew the exact moment my daughters arrived. It was the moment my dad's face lit up. "Look who's here!" he cried, standing to give them each a kiss and big hug. As everyone settled into chairs at the table, Dad gave the girls his undivided attention and asked what they had been up to. They told him and then, just as he had done so many times before, he smiled and said, "I'm proud of you both." After that came a lot of laughing as we took turns dishing up our favorite family memories. My dad joked right along with us.

As we all paused to take a breath, Dad said, "I haven't been to my place in Florida in a long time. When can we all go again?"

"Soon," we said.

"Good," he replied. "I want to hurry and get down there."

As our evening drew to a close, I realized that this was the moment I never thought I'd get. My moment of closure. Leaning into my dad, I gave him a big hug and whispered, "I love you, Dad. I'm sorry I wasn't a better daughter." Swallowing the large lump in my throat, I added, "Thank you for being such a wonderful dad and grandpa. We all love and miss you so much."

He said, "I love you, too. I wish you didn't have to leave yet. Are you coming back tomorrow?"

"Yes," I answered. "I'll be back bright and early tomorrow morning."

All You Need Is Love... and Patience |

As my daughters and I turned to walk away, he yelled, "It was good seeing you! Thanks for coming!" Then he added, "Don't forget I love you."

That night, with tears streaming down my face, I thanked the Universe for the gift of one more "family night" and for the closure it brought.

— Crystal Hodge —

92

A Good Day

*Cherish every moment with those you love
at every stage of your journey.*
~Jack Layton

"Georgia, I want to go home, and I mean it!"

I look into my beautiful mother's watery blue eyes. "I know you do, Mother, and I plan on taking you. It's not a good time now. Let's wait until you get better, and the weather is warmer. Then you can go home."

It isn't a complete lie. I truly intend to take her home if she improves. It looks doubtful at this point, but I am a strong believer in miracles. For now, Mom is residing in a long-term care facility where I work as office manager. I never wanted to place her here, but her health at eighty-eight years old is deteriorating, and her mind is weaker. I have been told by her home health therapist, her best friend, the doctor and the fire department that she is not safe at home. Still, my heart breaks when I walk in the door and see her just sitting here. She is miserable, and so am I.

She has ventured into my office today and is speaking her mind. "Give me one good reason I need to stay here," she declares. Now her blue eyes are blazing a bit.

"You might fall, Mother, and no one would find you until late in the evening. Also, what if someone breaks in on you? What if you choke and no one is there to help you?" I continue to go through the endless list of reasons why she cannot live alone.

"Well," she retorts, "I might fall out the door and lie there. I might choke and die. And so what if someone breaks in on me? I don't have anything. They would just leave. That being said, I would rather all that happen than to have to live here where I can't do anything I want to."

"What do you want to do, Mother?" I know my reply is sharp because I am almost at a breaking point. I am running out of solutions and ideas.

Her reply practically brings me to my knees.

"I want to sit on my couch in my favorite spot and look out of that big picture window at the mountains across the way and see the sky. I want to hear that mockingbird sing every morning while I eat breakfast in my favorite chair facing the sunrise. I want to smell the fresh-cut hay and see it in bales scattered across my twenty-acre farm and sleep in my own bed, in my own room, as I listen to music that your daddy and I used to dance to. I just want to be who I am and know where I am all the time."

She has no idea of the sleepless nights I spend just trying to figure out a way to take her home, keep my son in college, keep my job, and help my young daughter and her small son. I recycle my plan over and over in my head, but it just comes out the same. At this point, there is no way.

"I can't take you home to stay, Mom," I tell her, "but I can take you home for a visit." She looks at me doubtfully but says okay for now. I make arrangements with my boss to check her out for a road trip. Her place is about ten miles out of town. As we ride, we talk and laugh. For a little while, things feel sort of normal. It feels good to be with her away from medicine and orders.

We travel up her long dirt road to the front door of her little farmhouse. It looks quite shabby to most, but not to her. It's a mansion to her. We don't go in. It's too hard to get her up the steps and then back down. She agrees with that. She stares at her front door. "Maybe we can come back soon. Maybe I will get better."

Eventually, we back out, and I turn around to leave.

"Wait a minute," she says suddenly. "Stop for just one minute." I stop, and she opens her door and leans her head out.

"What are you doing, Mother?" I ask.

She closes her eyes and just breathes deeply, three or four times. "I just want to smell it again. I want to take the memory of the smell back with me to that place where I am safe."

We venture back into the city and stop for a small hamburger and a milkshake. It has always been her favorite combo. While sitting in the parking lot at the facility, she takes another breath and says, "I dread it. I know it has to be this way, but I dread it." Dear God in Heaven, if she only knew how much I dread it, too. Still, we walk slowly to the entrance and up to her room. She sits down on her little bed and tells me how tired she is. I tell her I love her and that I will see her tomorrow.

She looks at me once again with those now sleepy blue eyes. "Thank you. I appreciate you taking me home for a visit," she says. I tell her how the trip did as much for me as it did for her. We smile at one another in agreement. I leave wiping tears from my face and taking those long breaths as she did. This stage of life is hard, but this day was good. I am thankful for a good day.

— Georgia Hendrix Shockley —

Chapter 10

It Takes a Village

Tequila at Ten

We do not know the true value of our moments until
they have undergone the test of memory.
~Georges Duhamel

I sat in the rental car with my feet on the dashboard enjoying the view of the road and trees ahead. My mom and I sang along to the radio, enjoying the crisp morning breeze through the open windows. The rising sun illuminated this little Michigan town, a place I could slow down and relax versus the quick pace back home in Denver.

My husband called. "Hi, babe!" I exclaimed enthusiastically as I reached to turn down the radio.

"Good morning, beautiful! What adventures do you two have planned today?

"We are on our way to visit my great-aunt at the memory-care facility," I replied.

"Was she the one we had tequila shots with early in the morning when we visited with your grandparents a few years back?"

"Yep, that's the one."

"She's one of my favorites," he said. "Give her a big hug for me and enjoy your time. Stay strong. I know it's difficult, but she will appreciate you two visiting her. Love you. Call me later and let me know how your visit goes."

"Will do. Love you, too."

I needed his emotional support and strength more than he realized in that moment. I took a deep breath as we neared the parking lot of the memory-care facility. The memory my husband had mentioned brought a smile to my face, along with a vivid image of that morning years ago. We had come out the same time as my grandparents that year and went over for a morning visit. My grandparents had just gotten back from Mexico and had brought back some tequila for my great-aunt and uncle. My great-aunt Shirley was sitting in her rocking chair, and as she received the bottle from my grandfather, she twisted off the cap, took a sniff, and then a swig. She swirled the tequila in the bottle around once more, took one more swig, and then handed the bottle to me.

"It's never too early for tequila when family is in town!" she exclaimed, and we all erupted in laughter. We passed the bottle around, and enjoyed some breakfast and the best conversation, catching up and talking about family.

My mom saw my smile, and she must have been reading my mind because she spoke up about her memory of that morning as well. "I remember I was teaching that morning and had just taken my students to specials when I texted you to see what you were up to," she began to giggle. "All I remember is getting a text from you saying you were having shots of tequila with Aunt Shirley, and I had to take a double glance at the clock to check the time! My teammate happened to pop her head in, and it was all I could do to stop laughing when I told her my daughter was having shots of tequila at 10:00 a.m. with her grandparents and great-aunt and uncle!" I laughed and laughed with my mom until we had tears rolling down our cheeks.

When we went in to visit, we didn't know what to expect. Aunt Shirley was asleep when we first arrived, so we wandered around the facility and checked in with her later. When she woke up, there were brief moments of recognition and smiles, and a few attempts at conversation. Most of it was incoherent due to her dementia, and it made me so sad.

At one point, a nurse came in to see if we wanted to take Shirley to breakfast, as she had slept late. My great-aunt was okay with this plan, and we got her situated in her wheelchair.

"Aunt Shirley, you must be starving! It's already 10:00 a.m.," I told her as I sat down next to her at the table.

She turned and looked at me with a grin on her face and a sparkle in her eyes. She smiled for a minute and then reached out to gently hold my cheek within her hand. "That just means it's time for some tequila," she said, and she threw her hands up the air, slapped them down on the table and laughed. We laughed along with her. For a moment, time stood still.

It was a rough goodbye when we had to leave, but I focused on that laughter and joy. It was a silly memory, but it tied our souls together. The fact that Aunt Shirley still found joy in that memory allowed us to connect and know she was still there, even if just for a moment.

— Gwen Cooper —

94

The Benefits of a Sandwich Family

In the family sandwich, the older people and the
younger ones can recognize one another as the bread.
Those in the middle are, for a time, the meat.
~Anna Quindlen

Fifty-two is too young to find out you have Alzheimer's, but my dad did. When he moved in with us, he was fifty-five, and our kids were one, three, five and seven. The journey over the next twelve years was wonderful and harsh, rewarding and stressful, happy and sad. It's tough, but there are blessings when three generations live together. The kids learned many life lessons.

The first thing they learned was patience. When Papa first moved in, his signature symptom was asking the same questions over and over. He could ask the same question thirty times a day. It was frustrating to have to repeatedly explain things. The older kids understood and would politely answer his repeated questions. But Ben, the baby, had just recently learned to talk himself. He would say, "Papa! I told you that already!" So, each time, I would take him aside and explain that Papa couldn't remember things the way that he could. It only took Ben a little while before he started to say things like, "Oh, you must have forgotten. I'll tell you again…"

The second thing the kids learned was what it means to help family members. By being immersed in the reality of Papa's disability and need, the kids were able to see firsthand that helping one another is a top priority for us. One Saturday morning, we were all bustling around getting ready for a busy day. Papa called me downstairs to help him "fix" his TV. There was nothing wrong with it. He had just forgotten which button to press in order to get it to turn on. The same thing happened fifteen minutes later as we were trying to get ourselves out to the car. Nine-year-old Jon piped up, "Yeah, I helped him three times with that already this morning." I was awestruck. Here, this little guy was helping Papa without my even being aware of it. He just naturally did it without complaining or taking issue.

Another thing the kids learned was to honor their grandfather, no matter his dementia. It was always my intention that we would help Papa, but that we were also going to do every "normal" thing that families with young children do. We were going to go to soccer games and have birthday parties and go on vacations. We were just going to have to be creative. Fourteen-year-old Sarah had a sleepover birthday party, where a bunch of girls were watching a movie late at night. I knew that Papa wasn't "settled" yet, so I was lurking around the house keeping tabs on things.

That night, Papa interrupted the girls multiple times asking who they were and why they were in his house. Sarah very kindly responded each time, "Papa, you're my grandpa, and I'm just having a birthday party. We're watching a movie." He was satisfied with that answer and went back to his room for a few minutes. At one point, I heard Sarah explaining the situation to her friends, very matter-of-factly. "He has memory loss, and we just have to keep reminding him. But he's okay."

The fourth lesson was about perseverance. As time went on, we needed to lock our cupboards and refrigerator. There wasn't any real danger, but Papa would forget that he had eaten and then proceed to devour an entire loaf of bread, pan of brownies or gallon of milk. We knew we wouldn't have to live "locked up" forever, but for about a year, we were all struggling a bit with our own kitchen.

At one point, thirteen-year-old Daniel went into the kitchen, and I heard him sigh and then leave. I followed him and asked what the problem was. He said, "Oh, I was going to get a snack, but it's just so much work. I'll just wait until I'm hungrier." But they all understood why. When Papa would question why everything was locked up, they would tell him, "It's so we don't eat too many snacks."

Here's something that most kids could do better. My kids learned to speak clearly and explain things carefully. Papa and Ben would have long conversations about cars and monkeys and vastly interesting "boy stuff." Ben learned early on that he needed to speak very clearly in order for Papa to understand. Because of this understanding, Ben was able to read to and with Papa and play games like hide-and-seek successfully as the years progressed.

We all learned to live in the present. Papa loved a good story. He would pay attention and laugh even if he didn't fully understand it. The story was all that he experienced. It was now. There was no recalling a story from earlier the same day. There was no feeling bad about something that happened yesterday. It was all about living in the now.

The kids also learned not to hold grudges — a seventh lesson. There were times when Papa would get frustrated or angry. Once, he was mad at a family friend who was visiting, and he locked her out of the back door. She walked around the front and rang the doorbell. He welcomed her in graciously, having already forgotten his anger. There isn't a lot of positive to find in this horrible disease, but if we could all learn to shed negative emotions as fast as Papa could, we'd all be better off.

Lesson eight was not to blame Papa. It wasn't his fault that he couldn't do a lot of things. We cut his food for him and helped him with personal grooming. The kids would help him zip his coat and put on his hat. In the car, they helped him buckle and unbuckle his seatbelt. They all understood that it wasn't his fault. He couldn't help it.

My kids learned to see through disabilities to the real person inside. Often a child (or even an adult) will feel awkward around a person who is physically or mentally disabled. They don't know what to say or how to act. Our kids know that they are just regular people. Ben and his middle-school class went to the local nursing home to visit with the residents. Ben and his classmate were assigned to be friends with a man who had memory loss. When the man started "talking" to the boys in a garbled language, Ben's friend was wide-eyed and didn't know what to do. Ben jumped right in and "conversed" with the man, saying, "Really? Oh, tell me more." The other boy watched and took Ben's lead. The three of them weren't speaking the same language, but they were communicating in a language of friendship and caring.

Lesson ten was gratitude. As his vocabulary diminished and even disappeared, Papa always remembered to say, "Thank you." Every meal, every hug, every time we helped him with anything, he was thankful. He was a great example for the kids to witness. Even when we said, "I love you, Papa," he responded, "You, too. Thank you."

Finally, lesson eleven was to show kindness. Papa demonstrated this to us well into his battle with Alzheimer's. One summer day, we were working on organizing the garage. Papa was "helping," but he didn't really understand what we were trying to accomplish. He wandered into the house for a while, and I took the opportunity of his absence to race around the garage and "fix" some of the things that he had organized. He was gone a long time. When he came back out, he was walking very carefully and holding a glass of water. He said, "You've been working a long time out here. You need a cool drink. I would have come back sooner, but I had to figure out the ice machine on the fridge." Indeed. Here he was, struggling day to day just to live normally, and still showing such kindness and love to me and to us.

Alzheimer's is a terrible disease, but the benefits of our family going through it together have made us stronger as a family, and the children have become better people because of it. When I asked fifteen-year-old Daniel what he learned from having Papa live with us, he said, "Never get tired of doing little things for others. Sometimes, those little things occupy the biggest part of their hearts."

— Jesse Neve —

95

Joint Effort Really Adds Up

*Sisters function as safety nets in a chaotic world
simply by being there for each other.*
~Carol Saline

There is a sort of sisterhood among daughters who care for their elderly parents. It's most obvious in the waiting rooms of doctors' offices where many a parent is accompanied by a daughter. While Mom or Dad complains about an ailment or the wait time, a knowing look will pass between the younger women in the room. Not that sons can't, or don't, care for their aging parents, but it seems that daughters are more likely to take on the lion's share.

In that regard, my mother, who loved a day at the casino, hit the jackpot with her four daughters. We weren't alike in many ways, each of us possessing a unique skillset, but that's what made it work out so well.

Our names were our parents' predictors for our differences. Dubbed Linda, meaning pretty or beautiful, the firstborn was delicate with blond hair and blue eyes. Next was Vicki for victorious. She was sturdy and, as she grew, likely to be out in the street playing ball with the neighborhood kids. Connie was constant, never deviating from a set goal, even when it led to a kitchen fire in the toaster oven where she'd hidden a bag of cookies from herself to stay on her diet. Finally, I arrived. Anointed Marsha, meaning "comes from Mars," I was awkward with a lazy eye and doomed to fail at the finer arts, like tap dancing and piano, which my sisters had adequately mastered before me.

After Dad died, Mom had a fall, dislocating a shoulder and spraining a wrist. She required our daily assistance for over a month. During this stint, we learned to schedule our help to avoid both overlaps and gaps in our care of Mom. We also discovered what each of us did best.

That dry run prepared us for the daily care required when her legs swelled up, and her lymphedema led to frequent infections. Her mobility was hindered, and her legs required daily bandage changes.

Linda, an excellent cook, brought wonderful meals to Mom or brought Mom to her house to join her husband and four grown boys for Sunday dinners. Mom loved those gatherings, which were frequently topped off by card and board games.

Vicki was Mom's buddy, and they would visit for hours. Vicki would regale my mom with stories about her elementary-school students and gossip about mutual friends. Vicki required Pepsi and chocolate-mint cookies to keep up her cheerful banter. I know because they were always on Mom's grocery list for me to fill.

Connie stood out as the financial genius and business tycoon of the family. Owning and managing a number of rentals, she took on all of Mom's legal and business headaches. Mom always kept a running list of calls for her to make and financial matters for her to clear up. Naturally, all Mom's banking matters were in Connie's capable hands as well.

Finally, I got my chance to shine. Up to this point, Mom only trusted me to go to the store, pick up prescriptions, do the laundry and bring takeout food. But I had a secret weapon, and it was time to use it.

Having taught a health component as part of my driver's training curriculum, I was a certified CPR and First Aid instructor. In addition to my high-school classes, I volunteered endless weeknights and Saturdays certifying adults at my local American Red Cross chapter. It also meant that I fancied myself a bit of a healer and longed for some real-life action. Once, I revived a German Shepherd that had collapsed from heat exhaustion in front of a CVS store. While others stood around gaping at the dog, I ran in the store and bought water and a bowl. Running out, I splashed water on the dog's face. When he responded, I allowed him slow sips from the now full bowl. He had a phone number on his collar, and I was able to return him to his owner several miles away. Inspired by this happy ending, I was poised to offer aid to one of my own species. That's where my mom's condition comes in.

Mom's swollen, seeping legs needed daily bandage changes, and I was more than ready. And this was not a task that any of my sisters wanted, not at all! I was proud that I could be of service to her every day. She looked so much better and said it felt good to be dry and clean.

As it turns out, I was no cook, storyteller or financial guru. I did, however, have a gift to offer my mom and my sisters, and it made up for my other shortcomings.

As a group, my sisters and I made my mom's life better. We couldn't provide the same things, but the sum of the parts we played was miraculously greater than the whole.

— Marsha Porter —

96

The SWWOOM Club

Call it a clan, call it a network, call it a tribe,
call it a family. Whatever you call it,
whoever you are, you need one.
~Jane Howard

SWWOOM was the acronym for our club: Seven Women Watching Over One Man. Who was the One Man? Dad. And the seven women? Dad's "gals" — three daughters and four granddaughters. There wasn't a male offspring until his two great-grandsons arrived!

Dad, a recovering alcoholic since 1982, became a widower in 2003. Before Mom died after a long illness, she scolded him, "I'll ask God if I can come and haunt you if you go back to drinking."

"I won't, honey," Dad promised.

Dad was never a jobless drunk living on skid row, but I detested his drinking. I realized Dad turned to booze when my mother and sisters were diagnosed with polycystic kidney/liver disease, a genetic disease without a cure. Mom asked him to stop drinking when she collapsed in renal failure.

When asked how he stopped drinking, he replied, "AA (Alcoholics Anonymous) and the grace of God."

A proud Irish-Catholic, Dad dressed as a leprechaun on St. Patrick's Day and toasted with his favorite beverage: ginger ale.

Ironically yet miraculously, on St. Patrick's Day in 1988, Mom was blessed to receive a kidney transplant. Then my sisters suffered renal failure, and both received kidney transplants. Mom and Dad devoted themselves to promoting organ donation.

After Mom's death, Dad remained sober and lived alone until… well, that's part of this story.

His daughters and granddaughters live in four different states. We gathered to celebrate Dad's eighty-fifth birthday together at an Irish pub. We noticed, though, that his memory was slipping. His health was sliding. The man who ran 5Ks at age eighty to promote organ donation was on the slip-and-slide of old age.

Although Dad served in the Army during World War II, he was known to cuss like a sailor. He cussed when we voiced our concern about him living alone, driving, and traveling.

"I do just fine," he harrumphed. "I can live alone."

That's when the SWWOOM club was formed.

Each of his seven "gals" chose a day of the week to telephone him in the morning, and again at night. That person sent an e-mail informing the others how/what he was doing.

Little red flags and telltale signs cause alarm. Our discussions included:

"Should he be driving?" "Good heavens, no, and not at night!"

"Should he be traveling alone? His car broke down because he didn't maintain it."

"Do you know that he called me from the bank? He didn't know his account number."

"He didn't know if he'd even eaten lunch today."

Then Dad suffered a mild stroke.

It was time to stop living alone.

When we approached him about it, what a ruckus. He viewed himself as Head of the Family and, by golly, he called the shots.

A conference call among the SWWOOM Club members brought the suggestion from my sister, Janice, "Let's ask Mom up in heaven to ask God to help us."

Exactly two days later, Dad called me. He said softly, "Honey, I've been thinking… maybe I better not live alone anymore."

Goosebumps. The power of prayer.

I notified the Club members. Everyone rejoiced.

Rejoicing is fun; executing a plan is difficult. Each of the seven women brought her skill set to the table.

We vowed to do everything it took to retain his dignity, and not to let any of what was ahead come between the seven of us. Easier said than done, we learned.

Where would he live if he didn't live alone anymore? For seven years, he answered with a twinkle in his eye, "They bounce me back and forth between houses like a red rubber ball. I have a room of my own in each place." Then, he explained, "I do what they say. It's easier that way. I call my three daughters The Board of Directors."

It was what he'd asked of us, to spend four months with each of his three daughters. It worked out well until… it didn't.

Dad was ninety-two years old and needed twenty-four-hour care. Plus, we, his daughters, were working and also aging. Dad, though, surprised us by saying, "I trust all of you; you know best."

We chose an assisted living residence in North Carolina with a small patio and garden. It was near me and my sister, JoAnn. Dad joined activities and starred in a few plays. His love of dancing initiated a new dance class. He made friends and blossomed.

When Dad turned ninety-five, he began to fail. Our sister Janice was also in very poor health. We worried we might lose them both. She mustered the strength to travel from Chicago to see him.

Dad recognized Janice's frailness and made the absurd yet love-filled comment, "What kind of a father am I not to take care of my daughter?" When she left, he was morose and worried.

Dad, too, was failing. Although he danced three dances in a row on Big Band Night, he didn't get out of bed the next day. "If I died on the dance floor, I'd die happy," he grumbled.

He never fully recovered. We brought him home. Hospice, an organization that can never be praised enough, taught us to care for Dad.

On a Friday morning, Dad became unresponsive. All weekend, his breathing was labored, and he never regained consciousness. On Monday, his favorite hospice nurse rubbed his head soothingly and said, "John, what is keeping you here? Hmmm?"

Then she asked Janice to call from Chicago. We put the phone on speaker.

"Hi, Dad," Janice's voice cracked, "it's me, Janice. I know you're worried about me, but I'll be okay."

Standing next to him, JoAnn and I vowed, "Dad, we promise we will take care of Janice."

That night, JoAnn and I dozed outside his room. I was startled awake. "JoAnn, his breathing has changed." We flew into the room. JoAnn sat on one side and me on the other as Dad peacefully took his last breath.

Dad donated his body to science. With all the transplants in our family, he wanted to pay back.

Everyone commented on how frail Janice was at his memorial service.

Three months later, we received a call that Janice was in the ICU and not expected to live. The next twenty-four to forty-eight hours were critical. She needed a liver transplant. We cried. There are never enough donors.

At midnight, a call: A liver was available, and it was a match. Today, Janice is enjoying life.

I don't understand the mystery of God, but I wonder: Did Dad plead for his daughter? I imagine Mom and Dad greeting the organ donors in heaven and thanking them for their selfless gifts that helped families like mine.

The SWWOOM Club is proud to have delivered one special man to the gates of heaven... and we did it "by the grace of God."

— Suzanne F. Ruff —

97

Culinary Travels

Creativity is intelligence having fun.
~Albert Einstein

My mother-in-law Camilla's spirits were flagging. She wanted to know where everyone was and when we were going to visit her friends and relatives. This eighty-nine-year-old stroke survivor was living with us before COVID-19 so we were lucky that she was already with us prior to the lockdown. But for Camilla, a former cosmetics saleswoman, child-care worker at a ski resort, and part of a tight-knit doll-making community, the extremely reduced social contact was close to torture.

She stared out the window, expressionless, one day. "I need to know how old I am," she said. I tried to catch her gaze, but it remained distant and unfocused.

"You're eighty-nine. You'll be ninety in May," I told her.

She gasped a little. "What?! How did that happen?!" She lapsed back into an unfocused stare for a while and then wandered into the living room to watch television.

There were phone calls. There was FaceTime. But we had to try something to help her feel like she was experiencing the world beyond a television or computer screen.

Her son and I made quesadillas while we brainstormed. "Why don't we play some kind of Mexican music?" I suggested.

"Sounds good," he replied while stirring the filling in the pan. He grinned. "You know, we still have a sombrero hanging on the shop door. Maybe we could have her wear it!" The dinner became a playful trip to Mexico, and we all had great fun with accents, décor, food, and music. It was such a success that we later "visited" Germany, Italy, France, and Denmark. We even took a special journey to Africa.

Sometimes, we stayed in America and had hoe-downs or visited the beach. Sometimes, it was just a trip to a 5-star city restaurant where we dressed to the nines, listened to classical music, and spoke in exaggerated, "refined" tones. Her son or I occasionally posed as fine-dining waiters, complete with a white towel over one arm. "The Chef" would come into the dining room to make sure that Camilla was satisfied with the meal. One time, her son played the waiter, a violinist, and himself all in one evening.

The faux travels didn't cure everything, but they helped bring the sparkle back into Camilla's eyes, and they were great fun for us, too. I picked up some grape leaves recently and I'm pondering how to best suit us up in togas. After all, when visiting historical Greece, one needs to fit in....

— Tanya Sousa —

98

I Think You Need a Treat

Happiness is life served up with a scoop of acceptance,
a topping of tolerance and sprinkles of hope…
~Robert Brault

"I think you need a treat," my father-in-law announced with a big smile. That signaled he was ready for one of his favorite things in the entire world — ice cream. I helped him to the car and off we went.

We had brought him to our home shortly after the death of his beloved Betty Jo, his wife of fifty-four years, because his dementia and Parkinson's required medical tests that could be performed at a facility near our home. Our daily routine included a medical procedure followed by a trip for ice cream.

Betty Jo had been his caretaker for the last seven years. As my father-in-law's dementia worsened, he believed there were two Betty Jos — the loving one and the one who was always chiding him about his medication. He loved the nice Betty Jo and suggested the other one might be better suited for somewhere besides his home.

When she was alive, we made the three-hour trip every possible weekend in order to give Betty Jo some much-needed rest. She did an incredible job of caring for her husband, but we could see the exhaustion on her face every time we visited.

My husband is one of three remarkable brothers. Each contributed to the care of their father. We daughters-in-law found our niche in what that meant as well. Ron, the oldest, who worked the night shift, tended their physical property; Larry, my husband's twin, took care of the financial oversight. I cannot recall ever hearing complaints as to who was doing what. Every family member grew in flexibility and patience... and in expanded waistlines as we participated in the daily ice cream ritual.

We acquired new talents we never expected, such as surveillance at night when my father-in-law thought it was morning and he needed to go to work, even though he had been retired for a number of years. Sometimes, he just wanted to get into the car he no longer could drive, turn on the radio and listen to a favorite country-western song. My husband would get in the car and gently refocus his dad's thoughts from work to the song on the radio. Content when the song ended, my father would be coaxed back to bed. Then we all went back to sleep.

The most significant thing we learned in the journey with dementia was to treat my father-in-law with the same respect as we had before he became diminished. Maintaining his dignity as father, husband, and grandfather was easy from our hearts' standpoint. The physical and mental challenges required much more determined constraints and artful maneuvering. This dear man was highly respected in every venue in life. The community, his neighborhood, and St. Luke's United Methodist Church produced constant accolades, no matter my father-in-law's fading mental faculties.

How painful to watch the man who was a jack-of-all-trades suddenly forget how to perform the simplest of tasks. When we first moved from Arlington to Austin thirty years ago, my father-in-law spent an entire week with us doing many projects, from putting in cup hooks to installing ceiling fans.

As his dementia progressed, he developed new habits we did not always understand, but they were projects to him. He began to secure his valuables, such as his wallet, with rubber bands. We still chuckle when we see any object wrapped with a multitude of rubber bands.

Humor helped us in our arduous journey with his dementia. Respect guided us in all things, and patience was the umbrella over all our dealings. As the patriarch of the devoted Patterson clan, my father-in-law modeled each of these traits to family, co-workers, and friends—even those who were neither kind nor fair to him. Our family chest always held these significant tools to use when needed… which was often.

Despite my engineer brother-in-law's precise medicine chart, it was necessary to repeat directions again and again when we came for the weekend. Patience was mandatory, not optional. It was not easy for us, but how much more so for my mother-in-law. Seeing her sweetheart, her strong husband, become more and more forgetful and childlike simply broke her heart.

Although saddened at her unexpected death two years before my father-in-law's, we saw God's mercy. We knew it would have totally devastated her to move him from the home they had shared for more than fifty years into the home that would ultimately take care of him when we no longer could.

What she would have found almost impossible to decide took three sons, their wives and eight grandchildren to do. We moved past our sadness over his condition to enjoy every lucid moment we could. Often, while he was still physically able, we took him out for his favorite treat. It turned out to be a sweet time for all of us.

—Sharon L. Patterson—

Fully Present
as Daughters

To love and be loved is to feel the sun from both sides.
~David Viscott

My mother's oncologist had a heavy Middle Eastern accent. It was difficult for her to understand him. The doctor's words were ones that I didn't want to hear, let alone repeat to her. "What did he say, Debbie?" Mama asked.

After her third surgery, one for breast cancer and two for the angiosarcoma that followed, the cancer had returned, and further surgery was not an option. I had to tell her. "He reminded you that this type of cancer doesn't respond well to chemotherapy. You could try it if you want, but your hair will fall out, and you will be very sick. It would only buy you a few extra weeks at most. Mama, he asked if you are ready to die."

The three of us sat quietly while she absorbed the words and weighed her options, neither of which were good. She was eight-two years old.

She looked at the doctor. "I don't want the chemo."

Then she looked at me. "Betty has to come home."

My sister, Betty, spent several months each winter in Florida. We called her as soon as we got to my mother's apartment. Betty came home the next day.

My mother loved her apartment. She called her house key the

key to heaven. She wanted to die at home. When her condition warranted full-time care, my sister and I took turns staying with her. Betty and I navigated the constantly changing ways that our mother's body functioned and needed support. I stayed during the week. Betty took the weekends.

Changing bandages, preparing meals, learning from the hospice nurse, and occasional visits from family kept us focused on the present moment. Those moments, however, were infused with the knowledge that my mother's life could no longer be calculated in years and perhaps not even months.

When "future" gets pulled out of the equation of life, it is not unlike water getting extracted from fruit in the dehydration process. There's a concentrated, intensified sweetness to the apples, cherries and grapes. In the same way, my days with my mother intensified in their sweetness.

For the first four weeks, our routine was reminiscent of other times together, except that it was me who was "doing." I made the breakfast and coffee, and we made our plans for the day while we ate. What would she like me to accomplish that day? Was there a food that she hankered for?

Mama was an early riser, which meant that mealtimes arrived earlier in the day than for most people. By 11:00 a.m., she would be sitting on the sofa or in her favorite wingback chair with a TV table and her lunch in front of her. It was time for *All My Children*, an hour that carried her away from the cancer and all its implications.

It was also my hour to get out of the house. She had her phone by her side if she needed anything, and I was free to run to the grocery store, go for a walk or take a bike ride.

When I cycled, I often went to the cemetery where my father was buried. I never liked the fact that my mother's name, LaBelle, and the year of her birth were already etched next to his on the tombstone. All that remained was to fill in the year of her death.

Now that the question was soon to be answered, visiting the cemetery helped me adjust to the truth while I could still cycle home again, hear her voice, play another game of 500 Rummy and share another meal.

I also recognized that I would soon be closing her door for the last time. Forty-two years of my life were spent growing up in and then visiting her first-floor flat. It was home despite the other places that I had lived during college and adulthood.

I wasn't focused on those things in a macabre way or starting to grieve early. I was planting the seed of acceptance. That seed would grow and give support to the loss and grieving that was to come.

The new normalcy of the initial month and a half of hospice was shattered one night during the third week of June. I heard my mother stirring in her bed and went to her. She was sitting up and needed to use the bathroom.

Her legs, for the first time, would not support her. I managed to get a basin for her to use and together we negotiated her onto it.

After tending to things, I returned to her room and knelt on the floor in front of her. She looked beyond me to the door and asked, "What is she doing here. Christmas dinner isn't ready yet."

As we were alone in the apartment, it was an eerie question to hear. I turned my head slowly while asking, "Who, Mama?"

"Marty."

My Aunt Marty had passed the year before.

That night was a turning point and a signal that the cancer had metastasized to her brain. She was having little strokes that diminished her functions even more. My cousin Chris, a hospice nurse, came the next day. A hospital bed and wheelchair were ordered. A catheter replaced the bedpan.

For the next two weeks, my sister and I both had to stay. Then Mama's pain and the physical demands of caring for her became more than we could handle. At first, we felt guilty that we couldn't honor her wish to die at home, but the expert care at the hospice assured us that it was the right choice.

The hospice center allowed for my sister and me to take off our caregiver hats and be fully present as daughters. We basked in every lucid moment that we could, holding her hand and telling her about her grandchildren, the birds and weather outside of her window or sitting quietly.

We were with Mama when she passed. Despite the sad and sometimes difficult moments during those last months, it was an incredible gift to spend them together.

— Deb Biechler —

Between Two Phone Calls

Many people will walk in and out of your life, but only
true friends will leave footprints in your heart.
~Eleanor Roosevelt

My elderly dad had been using a walker for a while, but he was able to get around. Then suddenly, without warning, he was unable to get out of bed. His legs had failed him completely.

We didn't want to put him in a nursing home because COVID-19 was raging, and we wouldn't be able to visit if he went. My mom didn't want to hire a caretaker to help her during the day, and I was busy raising three kids forty-five minutes away from their home.

So, I called hospice.

I was hesitant to do this as I'd heard mixed reviews from others about their services, but we needed help. The provider I called came highly recommended by a family member and, within twenty-four hours, they came to my parents' home to do an analysis of my dad. He definitely qualified for hospice, and they would provide medical supplies, nurses' visits, and nurse-tech visits several times a week.

So, we began a new journey with a new crew of strangers who would become friends.

The hospice nurses and technicians provided everything possible to keep my dad comfortable during the last three months of his life.

They had access to medical equipment that we didn't know existed! The nurses monitored his health and spoke to the doctor about new medication needs as they arose. The technician bathed dad three times a week and cut his hair and nails. She would make sure his brittle skin was thoroughly covered in lotion. She listened to his stories and gave him the comfort of friendship.

As time went by, we came to be on a first-name basis, and I wondered why I'd ever feared signing up for their services.

The last week of my dad's life, the nurses and tech began to come daily. I saw a sheen of tears in their eyes as they left, knowing they might never see him again.

Very early one Friday morning, I made the hardest call I ever made in my life — the call to let hospice know that my dad had drawn his last breath, peacefully thanks to them. The nurse on call came immediately to my parents' home and provided us with services that I never would have thought we needed. I can't imagine that night without their help.

Even in the days following Dad's death, I was able to call the hospice social workers for advice on how to handle certain matters. After all, I'd never done this before, and there really isn't a how-to book on what to do with certain business matters after the death of your parent.

I can never say enough about the kind women and men who helped my family during this time — the time between those two phone calls that I never wanted to make.

— Shonda Holt —

Even During the Most Trying of Times

*We can all make a difference in the lives of others
in need because it is the most simple of gestures
that make the most significant of differences.*
~Miya Yamanouchi

My dad spent eight months of 2020 in hospice battling congestive heart failure complicated by endocarditis. I was sitting beside him when the strict pandemic-related visitation restrictions went into effect in Ohio. Though the nurses did not ask me to leave that morning, I gave my dad a kiss on the forehead and headed home to shelter in place.

For the next two months, we visited my dad through his window. I'd call from the parking lot to let his nurses know we had arrived. Someone would raise the blinds and position his phone within reach. I'd then switch to speakerphone, and we'd talk about the adjustments required for our girls, their classmates, and their teachers so they could finish the school year online. We'd talk about the shortages of toilet paper, the barren grocery-store shelves, and the almost-empty meat cases. We'd talk about baseball and how the pandemic would affect our favorite pastime.

On Opening Day, my husband, our two daughters, and I stood in the mulch outside his window, ducking beneath the various bird feeders that provided entertainment for many patients. We recorded the five of us singing "Take Me Out to the Ballgame" together, cherishing the delay between our voices and his and knowing that I would treasure that video in the months to come.

To celebrate his seventy-ninth birthday, we decorated signs and baked the lemon cake with chocolate buttercream he requested. Around lunchtime that day, we paraded along the sidewalk outside his room before returning to the window to watch him open gifts. To make the room feel more like home, his granddaughters sewed a pillowcase along with a fleece blanket with a knotted fringe for him.

My dad's room was located at the back of the building. We cut through the grass behind the kitchen and then followed the sidewalk, passing windows on which hospice staff had posted room numbers so family members could more easily locate their loved ones. Every other day, I passed Room 108, which was situated on the corner near the playground. The nurses had swiveled the patient's bed to face the window, I later learned, so the man could watch the birds.

On many occasions, this patient would be awake when I passed his window. I'd pause and make eye contact with him before waving. He always waved back. Sometimes, he would smile. Several weeks into this routine, he would most often be asleep when we visited my dad. I'd see his loved ones' personal belongings in the window — an overnight bag, a purse, a quilt presumably stitched with love. This led me to assume his condition was declining. On subsequent visits, I approached the corner with hesitation, praying his bed would not be empty.

One afternoon, I followed an instinct and called the front desk, explaining the connection I had made with this patient. If I were to write him a note, would they deliver it to him? Hospice was more than delighted to grant my request, and I delivered the envelope on my next visit. In the card, I introduced the four of us, providing names for the faces who often stopped at his window to wave. I told him our high-school freshman loved participating on swim team and that our eighth grader loved to play the drums. I let him know my dad was in a room down the hall and assured him we knew they were both receiving the best care from a loving team who wanted to ensure their comfort and safety.

Not long thereafter, I received a call from one of the hospice social workers. The man's family had asked her to reach out to let us know he had passed away peacefully. They said my card had come at just the right time. They appreciated the gesture, and they were grateful that we had made a connection with their father.

I later learned this World War II veteran was a teacher and coach, referred to by many as "Coach." He and his wife of fifty-six years had managed a local swim club and ran a summer swim program in their hometown in West Virginia, not far from where my dad was raised. Our older daughter is a competitive swimmer. And many years ago, I worked alongside coaches as a certified athletic trainer. We would have had so much to talk about if we had ever been able to meet. On the other hand, if it weren't for the pandemic that caused me to pass by his window regularly, we wouldn't have formed the connection that we had. It was just one of those blessings that comes about even during the most trying of times.

— Laurie Stroup Smith —

Meet Our Contributors

Marc Alderdice has a Ph.D. in pharmacology and has managed clinical trials for Alzheimer's disease. But he also has had to deal with Alzheimer's on a personal level since his wife was diagnosed. You can follow the progress of his memoir *Don't Forget to Dance: A Unique Alzheimer's Journey from Bizarre to Blissful* on www.marcalderdice.com.

London Alexander is a graduate of Cal State Los Angeles and the New York Film Academy. He is a creative nonfiction author who focuses on the complexities of the human experience. He is currently driving around the United States working on his second book and filming for his travel vlog.

Donna Anderson is a wife, mom and grandmother who lives in Texas with her husband and dogs: a Border Collie who wants to rule the world, and a tennis ball-obsessed Golden Retriever. Her hobbies include genealogy, photography, antiquing, and writing. She recently completed the first draft of a novel set in the late 1880s.

Carole Harris Barton, a freelance writer, retired after a career in government service. Her stories have appeared in other *Chicken Soup for the Soul* books, in Tim Russert's *Wisdom of our Fathers*, and in *Mysterious Ways* magazine. A wife, mother, and grandmother, Carole lives with her husband Paul in Clearwater, FL.

Kathy Baumgarten began writing while earning her B.A. in social and cultural perspectives on the family (Empire State College, 2005). The author of *Strictly a Loner: My Life and Times with Plattsburgh's Poorest Millionaire*, her essays address the essential joys, sorrows, and conflicts at the heart of the human condition.

Marina Bee and her family live in Toronto, Canada. As a member of the sandwich generation, Marina writes a blog called "Living the Jam Gen," a light-hearted take on the topics of parenting, caregiving and life on the home front. To read more amusing tales, visit www.jam-gen.com/recent-posts or www.facebook.com/JamGenLife.

Deb Biechler is a freelance writer, mindfulness instructor and retired kindergarten teacher. She enjoys being in nature with her partner Randy Hestekin and their dog, Mocha. Deb is grateful to her sister, Betty, for her lifelong love and support. They made a great team of caregivers for their mother.

Lori Kempf Bosko is a freelance writer living in Edmonton, Canada. She graduated, with honors, from the journalism program at Grant McEwan College in 1990. Lori enjoys writing, reading, photography, and especially spending time with family and friends.

D.E. Brigham lives and writes in Tellico Village in eastern Tennessee. He enjoys pickleball, kayaking, bridge, hiking, bicycling, gardening, cooking, and traveling. E-mail David at davidebrigham@gmail.com.

Author **Monica M. Brinkman** believes in stories that touch the heart and have meaning, be they fiction or nonfiction. Check out her published books and weekly podcasts. She adores her readers and would love to hear from them, so e-mail her at mmariebr@gmail.com.

Cheri Bunch grew up on a small farm in Elma, WA. She moved to Salem, OR and received her Associate of Science degree in 1990. She is a master gardener, artist, and freelance writer who has written a couple of children's books and hopes to publish them in the near future.

Patricia Bunin is a freelance writer who has written extensively about family relations, aging parents, grief and becoming a widow. E-mail her at patriciabunin@sbcglobal.net.

Now retired, **Jack Byron** previously pursued a career as a freelance illustrator, as well as working for more than a decade with patients dealing with dementia. In addition to his stories that have appeared in the *Chicken Soup for the Soul* series, he has published several essays of art criticism.

Lizzy Carney's mother's diagnosis of Alzheimer's changed her life. The experience provided blessings and lessons in the roles of daughter and caregiver. She facilitates an Alzheimer's caregivers' support group and is on The Longest Day committee. On the first day of summer, the longest day of the year, teams gather to raise awareness and funds for research and services.

Christine Carter enjoys writing her on blog, "TheMomCafe. com," and for several online publications. She is the author of *Help and Hope While You're Healing: A Woman's Guide Toward Wellness While Recovering from Injury, Surgery, or Illness* and *Follow Jesus: A Christian Teens Guide to Navigating the Online World*.

Linda S. Clare is the author of seven books, including *Prayers for Parents of Prodigals* (Harvest House Publishers 2020). She has published dozens of stories for *Guideposts*, the *Chicken Soup for the Soul* series and others. She writes from Oregon and coaches other writers while caring for her family. Learn more at Lindasclare.com.

Capi Cloud Cohen is a Penn State grad who writes, sews, bakes, FaceTimes with grandchildren, and gratefully eats her hubby's cooking in southeastern Tennessee. She dedicates this, her second *Chicken Soup for the Soul* story, to her wise mom, hoping it will encourage family, friends, and strangers to follow Mom's example and save lives. Visit her on Twitter @sewcloudy.

Sandra Cole is a first-time *Chicken Soup for the Soul* contributor and gifted oral storyteller who writes and tells personal stories. Sandra married her high school sweetheart and has a daughter and a granddaughter who fill their lives with joy. Having sold their B&B now gives Sandra more time to write, garden, travel, and have fun.

Gwen Cooper received her B.A. in English and Secondary Education in 2007 and completed the University of Denver Publishing Institute in 2009. In her free time, she enjoys krav maga, traveling, and backpacking with her husband and Bloodhounds in the beautiful Rocky Mountains. Follow her on Twitter @Gwen_Cooper10.

Sheri Cragin is a short story inspirational writer. She has three grown daughters and five grandsons. She lives in the Pacific Northwest and enjoys writing, hiking, kayaking and traveling.

Pattie Craumer has worked for more than twenty-five years in education, coaching, and as an entrepreneur. Energetic, caring, and curious, she loves to explore the world through common and uncommon journeys — with people, food, books, places, hobbies and new ideas. Pattie and her two adult children live in Pennsylvania.

Brenda Creel received her Bachelor of Science and Master of Education degrees from the University of Southern Mississippi. She has two daughters and eight grandchildren. She enjoys spending time with family, traveling, hiking, reading and writing. She is actively involved in her local church and loves serving others.

Cindy Cremeans is a Midwesterner, a public-school teacher, and an emerging writer. She is a founding member of the writing group the Plot Sisters. Cindy explores self and place in her writing. She challenges readers to bridge the gap of differences to find the similarities in humanity.

A journalist for twenty years, **Kristen Cusato** switched careers when her mother and best friend was diagnosed with Lewy body dementia. Through the four years her mother was ill, Kristen learned a tremendous amount about caregiving. She now works for the Alzheimer's Association Connecticut Chapter helping others along this journey.

Susan Cushman is the author of three books — one novel, one memoir and one short story collection — and the editor of three anthologies of essays by other authors. Her seventh book and second novel, *John and Mary Margaret* releases June 2021. A native of Mississippi, Susan lives in Memphis, TN.

Darla Czeropski lives in Oklahoma and is a wife and mother of six grown children. She has almost completed her first nonfiction book with plans to publish in the near future. She loves leading a women's Bible-study group and mentoring young women to become their best version of who God created them to be.

Priscilla Dann-Courtney is a writer and clinical psychologist living in Boulder, CO where she and her husband have raised their three children. Her columns have appeared nationally and her book, *Room to Grow,* is a collection of her stories.

A yoga enthusiast, **Barbara Davey** is an adjunct professor at Caldwell University where she teaches the process of writing to undergraduate students. She holds a bachelor's and master's degrees from Seton Hall University where she majored in English. She and her husband live in

Verona, NJ, where she tries her best to avoid the kitchen. E-mail her at BarbaraADavey@aol.com.

Jennifer Clark Davidson has been freelance writing off and on for the last thirty-plus years. During thirty of those years, she was involved in different aspects of eldercare for several family members. She is trying her hand at writing a book on the experiences. She and her husband enjoy time with their kids and grandkids.

Lauren Dykovitz lives in New Jersey with her husband and two black Labs. Lauren writes about her experience on her blog, "Life, Love, and Alzheimer's." She self-published her first book, *Learning to Weather the Storm: A Story of Life, Love, and Alzheimer's*, on Amazon. Visit lifeloveandalzheimers.com for more of Lauren's work.

Cheryl Edwards-Cannon is the CEO of Clear Path Choices, a firm that provides support for caregivers. She is the author of *Taking Care of Miss Bee Bee*, a collection of heart-warming stories about her mother's journey with dementia. This is her third story published in the *Chicken Soup for the Soul* series. Learn more at www.clearpathchoices.com.

Dr. Kim V. Engelmann has authored numerous books and articles and is an ordained Presbyterian minister. Currently she works at the Palo Alto VA as a full-time clinical chaplain. She lives with her husband Tim who is a clinical psychologist in the California Bay Area. They have three grown children, Chris, Julie, and Jonathan, and three dogs.

A teacher's unexpected whisper, "You've got writing talent," ignited **Sara Etgen-Baker's** writing desire. Sara ignored that whisper and pursued a different career, eventually rediscovering her inner writer. Since then, her stories have been published in numerous magazines and anthologies. E-mail her at sab_1529@yahoo.com.

Sue A. Fairchild started out as a writer, but now also claims the titles of editor and writing coach. She has written and self-published three books as well as helped a variety of authors get their manuscripts into readers' hands. This is her third story published in the *Chicken Soup for the Soul* series.

Marianne Fosnow lives in South Carolina. She enjoys writing and loves to read heartfelt or humorous stories written by others. She also loves to photograph nature and her grandchildren.

Sheryl L. Fuller is a writer, singer, songwriter, and performing artist from Chicago, IL. She draws inspiration from her many life experiences.

Hannah F. Garson taught special needs children in New York City for thirty-five years. She is the coordinator of a writers' group in Queens, NY.

Catherine Graham is an intuitive energy healer, author and mother. She resides in Ontario, Canada with her husband and children. Catherine is passionate about helping people step into their truths as they navigate challenges.

Carolyn Gray was born and raised in rural west Georgia during the Jim Crow era. After completing high school, she moved to Southern California where she earned her Bachelor of Arts degree in mass communications and began her thirty-year career in marketing communications.

Julie Gwinn is a literary agent and vice president with The Seymour Agency working with both fiction and nonfiction authors. Prior to agenting, she worked as Fiction Publisher for B&H Publishing Group and before that spent several years working in marketing, and public relations for several nonprofits in Nashville, TN.

Carolyn Hall worked as a dietitian for nursing homes. She is the author of *Prairie Meals and Memories*, which was selected as one of the best books on Kansas. Her stories have appeared in previous *Chicken Soup for the Soul* books, as well as several magazines and anthologies. E-mail her at cbschreiber2626@gmail.com.

Terry Hans, a retired dental hygienist, is compiling a collection of hilarious stories as told to her by patients in the exam room. A previous contributor to the *Chicken Soup for the Soul* series, Terry enjoys spending time with her family, writing, scrapbooking and being at grandsons' sporting events. She and her husband are enjoying retirement.

Renée Brown Harmon, MD is a retired physician in Alabama. She and her husband shared responsibilities at their medical practice, and at their home with two daughters, until Alzheimer's disease forced his retirement. She now enjoys traveling and hiking. Her teaching memoir and blog are available at www.reneeharmon.com.

Crystal Hodge is a multiple contributor to the *Chicken Soup for the Soul* series. Her motivation for this edition's story was to honor her father.

Butch Holcombe lives the dream job of publishing a magazine he founded as well as releasing several books. His latest *No... I Won't Shut Up* is a compilation of humorous columns he has written for *American Digger* magazine and is available on Amazon. E-mail him at publisher@americandigger.com.

Shonda Holt lives in rural Oklahoma with her husband of twenty-two years and three teenage children. She works for her local public school. She loves Jesus, time with friends, and homemade cookies.

Meadoe Hora is the author of several books for children and teens. She loves stories and is usually reading multiple books at a time, often in the middle of the night. She lives in Wisconsin with her husband, kids and two spoiled rescue dogs.

Michelle L. Jones received her Master of Arts in Leadership from Augsburg College, Minneapolis, MN and her Bachelor's in Theatre from Brigham Young University, Provo, UT. She is listed in Who's Who of American Colleges and Universities 1998. She loves traveling, movies, forests, her condo and her cat, Princess Oreo.

Sharon Carraway Jones is a retired teacher living in coastal North Carolina. She is the mother of three daughters and has four granddaughters. In her spare time, she enjoys the beach, gardening, writing, and volunteering as a chaplain.

E.E. Kennedy is the author of the *Miss Prentice Cozy Mysteries*. She and her husband live in North Carolina.

Patricia Cosner Kubic earned her B.A. from Madonna University. Her monthly columns have appeared in multiple newspapers since 2016. She lives with her husband and at least two kitties in Michigan where she gardens, does paper crafting and cheers on the Detroit Tigers.

Pamela Lear received her B.A. from UC Santa Barbara. She is currently working on her MFA in creative nonfiction, with an emphasis on narrative medicine, at Bay Path University. She has two adorable granddaughters, and lives near them in Miami, FL. She is working on a memoir.

Brenda Leppington lives in Saskatchewan, Canada and recently retired from a career in health information. Brenda enjoys writing, travelling and the newfound freedom that comes with retirement. She has been a previous contributor to the *Chicken Soup for the Soul* series.

Barbara LoMonaco is the Senior Editor for the *Chicken Soup for the Soul* series. She graduated from USC and has a teaching credential. She lives in Southern California where she is surrounded by boys: her husband, her three grown sons and her two grandsons. Thankfully, her three lovely daughters-in-law have diluted the mix somewhat, but the boys are still in the majority.

L.B. Marshall shares the Alzheimer's journey she and her husband navigate in an effort to create awareness and provide support for other caregivers. Lisa's husband Peter was diagnosed April 30, 2018 when he was just fifty-three. She plans to one day write a book chronicling his progression of the disease. E-mail her at lisamarshall9@comcast.net.

Mary McGrath is a freelance writer based in Naples, FL. Her work has appeared in a number of publications, including *Chicken Soup for the Soul: Messages from Heaven and Other Miracles*, which came out in 2019. Beyond writing, she loves photography, travel, jazz and improv. E-mail her at grathy@aol.com.

Farah Menassa's career includes TV, event planning, film festivals (where she met that other iconic Farrah) and celeb stalking for *People* magazine. A former West Hollywooder with a degree in broadcasting and film, she's now based in Toronto where she writes, cares for her eighty-three-year-old mom, Evelyn, and keeps busy "Treading Water."

Kim Kluxen Meredith is a retired Spanish teacher. She resides in central Pennsylvania and enjoys traveling and inspirational speaking. Kim has three published books in various genres and numerous other published stories and articles. All of her works, along with her blog, can be found at www.kimkluxenmeredith.com.

Amy Mewborn received her Bachelor of Science in elementary education from East Carolina University in 1992. She teaches ninth grade English in North Carolina. Writing, blogging as The Pecan Seeker, reading, and gardening are some of her favorite pastimes. She hones her writing skills by writing a variety of pieces.

Ronald Milburn received his Bachelor of Arts from Eastern Illinois University. He is married with four children and ten grandchildren. While Ron cares for his elderly mother, he writes fiction and nonfiction books, movies, and plays. Samples of his writing can be found at RonaldCMilburn.com.

Cynthia B. Morningstar is choir director of the First Presbyterian Church in Shelbyville, IN, where her husband Mark is pastor. She has spent many years teaching piano, directing choirs, and accompanying. She has three grown daughters and two precious grandsons.

Nicole L.V. Mullis loves storytelling, whether on the stage, through the page, or over coffee. She is a produced playwright, a *Battle Creek Enquirer* columnist, a Mosaic storyteller, and the author of *A Teacher Named Faith*. She lives with her family in Michigan, where she is earning her MFA in playwriting.

Jesse Neve is a wife and mother of four from Minnetrista, Minnesota. She enjoys traveling with her big crowd and writing about her family's adventures and what she has learned from them. Jesse's life goal is to bring a little smile to everyone she passes. E-mail her at Jessedavidneve@frontiernet.net.

Bebe Nicholson received a Bachelor of Science in journalism from the University of North Carolina and later worked as a newspaper editor and book publisher. She and her husband enjoy spending time with their three children and twelve grandchildren. In addition to writing, she enjoys hiking and kayaking.

Linda O'Connell is an accomplished writer and teacher from St. Louis, MO. She is a frequent contributor to the *Chicken Soup for the Soul* series. A positive thinker, Linda holds her life together with humor, duct tape and dark chocolate.

Tammy Parker has worked as a telecom analyst, trade journalist, marketing executive, radio disc-jockey, swimming pool cleaner, janitor and cashier. One of her first jobs was mailroom clerk for her father's optical company. She's been trying to learn to golf for half a century (so far). Learn more at tammyparker.com.

Sharon L. Patterson, retired educator, women's ministry leader and author, is an avid fan at the sporting events of her five grandchildren.

She enjoys calligraphy, traveling, and fellowship over a favorite cappuccino with friends and family. She resides in Round Rock, TX with her husband.

Christina Peters lives in Southern California with her husband and two sons. She started her career as an elementary school teacher and has run a home daycare for the last nine years. She loves hosting meals with friends and being outside in the California sunshine! She loves to visit her Uncle Nelson whenever she can!

Amanda Pillow received her Associate of Arts in 2020 and is on track to graduate Arkansas State University with a Bachelor of Arts in English in 2022. Amanda loves traveling, playing games, writing, drawing, and spending time with her family. She plans to write books of poetry and stories in the future.

Co-author of a movie review guide and author of hundreds of articles, **Marsha Porter** got her writing start in grade school when the 500-word essay was the punishment *du jour*.

Connie Kaseweter Pullen lives in rural Sandy, OR, near her five children and several grandchildren. She earned a B.A. degree, with honors, at the University of Portland in 2006, with a double major in psychology and sociology. Connie enjoys writing, photography and exploring nature. E-mail her at MyGrandmaPullen@aol.com.

Cindy Richardson seeks to encourage, challenge, and inspire others through her blog at cindyrichardson.org. An award-winning kindergarten teacher, she resides in Missouri with her husband and dog Maggie. She enjoys the friendship of three daughters and loves being Nana to six grandchildren.

Suzanne F. Ruff is the author of the award-winning, non-fiction book *The Reluctant Donor*. A freelance writer for *The Charlotte Observer* and *Renal-Life* magazine, Suzanne has also been published in *National Kidney Foundation Journal of Nephrology Social Work* and the *Chicken Soup for the Soul* series. Learn more at www.suzanneruff.com.

Suzy Ryan is an author, ironman, and teacher. Named Valley Middle School's teacher of the year, she leverages her troubled past to inspire struggling students to see they are victors, not victims. Suzy lives in Carlsbad, CA. Be on the lookout for her debut novel, *Invincible*

Summer, on her website Suzyryan.com.

Beth Saadati is a high-school English teacher with an MFA in creative writing. She shares stories at bethsaadati.com that offer insight, understanding, and hope to those who weather the storms of suicidal thoughts and suicide loss… and to those who simply know how bittersweet life can sometimes be.

Morgan St. James is the author of nineteen books including *Silver Sisters Mysteries* series and *Revenge is Fun* series. She has also co-authored award-winning memoirs for two abuse survivors. St. James lives in Las Vegas, NV with her two dogs, Dylan and Cucumber.

Denise Schaub is a retired attorney, certified integrative nutrition coach, and founder of Caregiver Wellness, LLC. She conducts online programs to teach caregivers the skills and strategies to create a healthy and resilient lifestyle. She has two grown children and enjoys traveling, swimming and cooking healthy recipes.

Regina Schneider holds a master's degree in counseling and special education. She has experience writing both fiction and nonfiction.

Jonney Scoggin lives in a forty-acre forest in southern Mississippi with his two Collies. His interests include cooking, traveling and capturing the world around him with photography.

Laurel L. Shannon is the pseudonym of a northwest Ohio–based author. She has been previously published in the *Chicken Soup for the Soul* series, *All Creatures* magazine and other publications.

Susan K. Shetler grew up surrounded by thirty-seven acres of woods and thick walls of parental restrictions. Though intensely shy, her curious mind led her off the family map to college. Fears, low self-esteem and anger followed her until writing became a tool for self-exploration. Sue's story can be found at www.SusanKShetler.com.

Georgia Hendrix Shockley is from a small rural area in Alabama. She has two adult children and is blessed with greats and grands. Georgia enjoys all music, singing and playing guitar. Her career has been in healthcare administration, but her long-term goal has always been to be a well-loved author.

Joy Simons lives in rural Arizona with her dog and cat. She retired from a career in music and now enjoys writing, singing and blogging. Author of *Isaiah and Me*, she has also penned several Bible book commentaries and has now turned her attention to fantasy fiction.

Billie Holladay Skelley received her bachelor's and master's degrees from the University of Wisconsin–Madison. A retired clinical nurse specialist, she is the mother of four and grandmother of two. Billie enjoys writing, and her work crosses several genres. She spends her non-writing time reading, gardening, and traveling.

Caleb Smith is the teen CEO and visionary behind Peacebunny Island, where youth guardians train rescued and rare rabbits who share hope and hoppiness during stress, trauma, loneliness and grief. His memoir shares lessons from comfort rabbits, purchasing river islands, and a 100-mile boat journey. Learn more at www.PeacebunnyIsland.com.

While writing Amish and contemporary romance, **Laurie Stroup Smith** strives to inspire her audience to serve others. This former certified athletic trainer is the author of *The Pocket Quilt* series. She lives with her husband and two daughters in Cincinnati, OH. Learn more at Lauriestroupsmith.com.

Tanya Sousa's writing credits include the award-winning picture book, *Life Is a Bowl of Cherry Pits*. Her novel, *The Starling God*, was on the 2015 shortlist for the Green Earth Book Awards. She also writes for magazines and anthologies.

Diane Stark is a wife, mother, and writer. She is a frequent contributor to the *Chicken Soup for the Soul* series. She loves to write about the important things in life: her family and her faith.

Deborah Starling is a graduate of Carlow University with a master's in creative writing and a bachelor's in social work. She utilizes her education, experience and skills to help students achieve academic excellence. Debbie gives all honor and glory to the Lord and dedicates her story to her mother, father and Aunt Ruby.

Kim Stokely is an author, speaker and actor who survived 2020 by the grace of God and the love of her husband of thirty-two years. While she waits to perform again, she is busy editing her eighth novel and entertaining her two crazy dogs. You can find information about her performances and books at www.kimstokely.com and online.

Karla Sullivan graduated with a Bachelor of Arts in education and a master's in leadership. She has worked in education most of her life as a teacher or administrator, her favorite position being special education assistant. Writing has been a lifetime passion. Karla has raised two adult children and lives in Illinois.

Margaret Toman graduated from UNC's Senior Leadership Enhancement Initiative. She advocates for the elderly and the incarcerated and serves as liaison to a congressional office for Citizens Climate Lobby. E-mail her at margaret.tmn@gmail.com.

Joanna Montagna Torreano hopes her story helps others who are struggling with the care of an elderly parent. Joanna's latest book, *Written from the Heart*, chronicles her journey from hospital to healing. Each chapter ends with a lesson learned.

Susan Traugh lives in Oregon with her mother-in-law, husband, and two disabled daughters. Their challenges inspired Susan to write how-to books for teens with disabilities while her passions lead her to essays and short stories. Susan is also the author of her teen novel, *The Edge of Brilliance*. Learn more at susantraugh.com.

Samantha Ducloux Waltz is an award-winning freelance writer in Portland, OR. Her personal stories appear in the *Chicken Soup for the Soul* series, numerous other anthologies, *The Christian Science Monitor* and *Redbook*. She enjoys hiking, gardening, travel, and time with friends and family. Learn more at www.pathsofthought.com.

Sandra White enjoys sewing, quilting, writing, reading, playing with her granddaughter, and hiking in the Pacific Northwest. Author of two novels, her writing has been featured in *Woman's World*, *Northwest PrimeTime*, and *Chicken Soup for the Soul: Age Is Just a Number*.

Deborah Young has enjoyed writing all her life and authored articles on daily life, her spiritual journey, gardening, grief and one book, *Hanging On: A Painful Pilgrimage*. She plans to continue to write about her life experiences and the lessons and laughter they have provided. E-mail her at debyoung90@gmail.com.

Meet Amy Newmark

Amy Newmark is the bestselling author, editor-in-chief, and publisher of the *Chicken Soup for the Soul* book series. Since 2008, she has published 175 new books, most of them national bestsellers in the U.S. and Canada, more than doubling the number of Chicken Soup for the Soul titles in print today. She is also the author of *Simply Happy*, a crash course in Chicken Soup for the Soul advice and wisdom that is filled with easy-to-implement, practical tips for enjoying a better life.

Amy is credited with revitalizing the Chicken Soup for the Soul brand, which has been a publishing industry phenomenon since the first book came out in 1993. By compiling inspirational and aspirational true stories curated from ordinary people who have had extraordinary experiences, Amy has kept the twenty-eight-year-old Chicken Soup for the Soul brand fresh and relevant.

Amy graduated *magna cum laude* from Harvard University where she majored in Portuguese and minored in French. She then embarked on a three-decade career as a Wall Street analyst, a hedge fund manager, and a corporate executive in the technology field. She is a Chartered Financial Analyst.

Her return to literary pursuits was inevitable, as her honors thesis in college involved traveling throughout Brazil's impoverished northeast region, collecting stories from regular people. She is delighted to have come full circle in her writing career — from collecting stories "from the people" in Brazil as a twenty-year-old to, three decades later, collecting stories "from the people" for Chicken Soup for the Soul.

When Amy and her husband Bill, the CEO of Chicken Soup for the Soul, are not working, they are visiting their four grown children and their three grandchildren.

Follow Amy on Twitter @amynewmark. Listen to her free podcast — Chicken Soup for the Soul with Amy Newmark — on Apple, Google, or by using your favorite podcast app on your phone.

Thank You

We owe huge thanks to all our contributors and fans. We received thousands of submissions for this popular topic, and we spent months reading all of them. Our editors Laura Dean, Jamie Cahill, Crescent LoMonaco, and Kristiana Pastir read all of them and narrowed down the selection for Associate Publisher D'ette Corona and Publisher and Editor-in-Chief Amy Newmark.

Susan Heim did the first round of editing, D'ette chose the perfect quotations to put at the beginning of each story, and Amy edited the stories and shaped the final manuscript.

As we finished our work, D'ette Corona continued to be Amy's right-hand woman in working with all our wonderful writers. Barbara LoMonaco, Kristiana Pastir, Mary Fisher, and Elaine Kimbler jumped in at the end to proof, proof, proof. And yes, there will always be typos anyway, so please feel free to let us know about them at webmaster@chickensoupforthesoul.com, and we will correct them in future printings.

The whole publishing team deserves a hand, including our Senior Director of Marketing Maureen Peltier, our Vice President of Production Victor Cataldo, and our graphic designer Daniel Zaccari, who turned our manuscript into this beautiful, inspirational book.

Sharing Happiness,
Inspiration, and Hope

Real people sharing real stories, every day, all over the world. In 2007, *USA Today* named *Chicken Soup for the Soul* one of the five most memorable books in the last quarter-century. With over 100 million books sold to date in the U.S. and Canada alone, more than 250 titles in print, and translations into nearly fifty languages, "chicken soup for the soul®" is one of the world's best-known phrases.

Today, twenty-eight years after we first began sharing happiness, inspiration and hope through our books, we continue to delight our readers with new titles, but have also evolved beyond the bookshelves with super premium pet food, television shows, a podcast, video journalism from aplus.com, licensed products, and free movies and TV shows on our Popcornflix and Crackle apps. We are busy "changing your world one story at a time®" Thanks for reading!

Share with Us

We all have had Chicken Soup for the Soul moments in our lives. If you would like to share your story or poem with millions of people around the world, go to chickensoup.com and click on Submit Your Story. You may be able to help another reader and become a published author at the same time. Some of our past contributors have launched writing and speaking careers from the publication of their stories in our books!

We only accept story submissions via our website. They are no longer accepted via mail or fax. Visit our website, www.chickensoup. com, and click on Submit Your Story for our writing guidelines and a list of topics we are working on.

To contact us regarding other matters, please send us an e-mail through webmaster@chickensoupforthesoul.com, or fax or write us at:

Chicken Soup for the Soul
P.O. Box 700
Cos Cob, CT 06807-0700
Fax: 203-861-7194

One more note from your friends at Chicken Soup for the Soul: Occasionally, we receive an unsolicited book manuscript from one of our readers, and we would like to respectfully inform you that we do not accept unsolicited manuscripts, and we must discard the ones that appear.

Turn the page for more stories of caregiving, coping, and compassion, from *Chicken Soup for the Soul: **Living with Alzheimer's** & Other Dementias*

My Mom
the Fighter Pilot

We can do no great things, only small things with great love.
~Mother Teresa

A few years after Mom was diagnosed with Alzheimer's she started to believe what her mind was telling her. A few Alzheimer's caregiver seminars had taught me not to question her imagination, so that made it easier for me to just listen and accept it when one summer day Mom said she was a fighter pilot in the Air Force.

We were at Mom's favorite diner. She was well liked there because she always kissed the manager and all the waiters, but I noticed Mom was not her happy self that day. She just wanted to go straight to our usual table and stare out the window, gazing up at the sky. It was a perfect blue-sky day, with cotton ball clouds.

"What are you thinking about, Mom?" I asked. That's when she told me she was once a fighter pilot in the Air Force and that one of her missions was to rescue all the children from the war. As Mom was saying this, tears rolled down her face and she told me she had jumped from the plane to rescue the children, but she was not able to rescue them all, because she could only take as many as she could carry. She cried when she said she had to leave some children behind.

I looked at her and said, "Mom, you did the best you could, it was better to save some than not saving any at all." I'm not sure she was listening; I could only hope it helped.

Then one day Mom told me she got a call from the military telling her she was going to receive the highest Medal of Honor for rescuing those children. For weeks Mom would tell me she got another call, and another.

I decided to buy her a medal, and tell her the military had contacted me and was sending me her Medal of Honor, to be presented to her on her upcoming birthday. My daughter said she wanted to make up a Certificate of Honor, so she could give it to her grandmother with the Medal of Honor.

Mom was getting worse by the month now, and I had a feeling this might be the last birthday where she would be able to communicate very well. I knew I needed to make this birthday extra special, and the one thing Mom loved to do was dance. I decided to take Mom, Dad, my daughter, her husband, and my partner to a Latin American restaurant that had a band.

When I told Mom where I was taking her for her birthday, she was so excited she told me she wanted to wear something red. My older sister, who is in the military and was away, sent her a beautiful red silk blouse, and I took Mom to the salon.

When we all got to the restaurant, Mom was so excited she was smiling from ear to ear. I ordered Mom her favorite drink, sangria, and as soon as the band began to play, my daughter took her to the dance floor for her first birthday dance. After that Mom danced with me, with my partner, and with anyone who wanted to dance with her. She was on a roll, having the time of her life.

Then it was time for the cake. We all stood up when it came, and my daughter read Mom the Certificate of Honor, and I presented her with the Medal of Honor. Everyone in the restaurant stood up and applauded, congratulating Mom. Mom was so surprised and so happy that she got up and kissed every single person in that restaurant.

It's been a year now and Mom is unable to talk or walk on her own, but I am so thankful we took her dancing for her birthday and presented her with her Medal of Honor.

~Doris Leddy

Join the Journey

When we are no longer able to change a situation,
we are challenged to change ourselves.
~Victor Frankl

I work in senior housing—a safe, friendly, comfortable community for seniors that provides them with an opportunity to live independently or with some assistance while still maintaining their sense of self-worth and independence. I have done this work for more than twenty years, and many times have heard family members say, "I don't know how you people do it! I can't deal with just one elderly parent, and here you all are having to work day in and day out with so many of them!"

Here's my answer: We join the journey. We love them and care for them just the way they are now. They are brand new to us. Because we have no history with Aunt Mae or Grandpa Joe, we aren't disappointed by their need to use incontinence products, or their inability to remember their address, or even their constant questions about what day it is.

We love and care for the people they have become. There's no past history for us. No memories of how they built their own company from the ground up, or helped raise funds for the Sunday school wing of their church, or organized the neighborhood carpools. We love them today—incontinent, feisty, forgetful.

We join their journey, and we know lots of ways to help them help themselves when family members get frustrated. Almost everyone grows up seeing their parent or grandparent as strong and capable, but when that former math professor can no longer remember how to write a check, families can get embarrassed—not for themselves, but for the parent who used to be. It's okay with us. It's our job, and more importantly, it's our calling to love and respect the person that math professor is today—not to try to steer him down a path he no longer sees or understands.

Once, one of our residents became agitated during an afternoon cloudburst. Daughter Carol was trying to reason with her mom, who was standing in the hallway, wearing her raincoat and looking for an umbrella so she could go outside. Miss Caroline, a normally gracious woman, but a woman with Alzheimer's, had not been outside of our building unaccompanied in quite some time. She had never, as far as I knew, become upset because of rainy weather and we were all—her daughter, her assigned caregiver, and I—at a loss as to how to calm her and encourage her to stay indoors. Finally, after about ten minutes of trying to talk her out of going outside, someone asked her a question she could grasp and answer:

"Miss Caroline, why do you need to go out in this awful rain?" This mother of eight sons and one daughter gave a deep sigh and looked each of us in the face as she answered: "The children will be coming home from school. I don't want them to get wet—I have to meet them at the bus stop."

This was a Join the Journey moment. A light dawned for us all—including the grown daughter who was standing right there. We quickly assured her that a neighbor was picking up the children and that she would bring them home. Satisfied that her children were safe and dry, Miss Caroline returned to her apartment, took off her raincoat, and settled in her room for the rest of the afternoon.

Join the Journey. It's hard. So very hard—especially for those who remember when their loved ones were titans of business, supervisors of factories, the go-to moms for bake sales and carpools.

But to live in their moment, to allow them to have the pleasure of the day without forcing a reality they no longer understand—now that is love at its finest.

It's not easy. And not everyone is a Miss Caroline, willing to hear your words and absorb them and accept them. But many are.

Join the Journey. Let go of their past, and your own, and spend whatever time is left to your loved one on their terms. Don't take their loss of memory personally. Those memories you shared from your childhood are still precious to them. They're just locked away. They aren't deliberately forgetting their keys… their glasses… their teeth. Those things just aren't important to them the way they are to you and me.

Join the Journey. Love them for who they are in this moment. Be old enough, wise enough, and caring enough to set yourself aside. Take heart that the parent who raised you, the grandmother who baked you cookies, the father who taught you to fish is still in there and still needs your care, your love, your patience. Though you may be a stranger to them, they can still recognize kindness.

It's not easy loving someone with Alzheimer's or other forms of dementia. But it's oh so important that you do, and it's a lot easier when you love the new person they've become and join them on their journey.

~Ginny Dubose